THE FAITH OF THE OUTSIDER

THE FAITH OF THE OUTSIDER

Exclusion and Inclusion in the Biblical Story

Frank Anthony Spina

May God richly bless you,

Frank Anthony Spina †

WILLIAM B. EERDMANS PUBLISHING COMPANY
GRAND RAPIDS, MICHIGAN / CAMBRIDGE, U.K.

Wm. B. Eerdmans Publishing Co.
255 Jefferson Ave. S.E., Grand Rapids, Michigan 49503 /
P.O. Box 163, Cambridge CB3 9PU U.K.

Printed in the United States of America

09 08 07 06 05   7 6 5 4 3 2 1

Library of Congress Cataloging-in-Publication Data

Spina, F. A. (Frank A.)
The faith of the outsider: exclusion and inclusion in the biblical story /
Frank Anthony Spina.
p.   cm.
ISBN 0-8028-2864-7 (pbk.: alk. paper)
1. Outsiders in the Bible.   2. Gentiles in the Bible.   I. Title.

BS579.O87S68   2005
220.6 — dc22

2004056406

www.eerdmans.com

To the two Stanleys:
Stanley T. Dubelle and Stanley D. Walters
Exemplary Teachers and Scholars Extraordinaire

Contents

Acknowledgments

This book is the culmination of over a decade of lecturing to university students and numerous lay or clergy groups. In countless ways, the people in these academic and ecclesial settings not only provided me with extraordinary stimulation, but confirmed for me the timeliness of this book's subject matter.

Those to whom I was privileged to speak on "The Faith of the Outsider" include: All Saints Episcopal Church (Bellevue, WA); Church of the Good Shepherd ([Episcopal]; Federal Way, WA); Church of the Resurrection ([Episcopal]; Bellevue, WA); Emmanuel Episcopal Church (Mercer Island, WA); Episcopal Diocese of Spokane Clergy Conference (Spokane, WA); First Baptist Church (Seattle, WA); First Congregational Church (Bellevue, WA); First Covenant Church (Seattle, WA); First Free Methodist Church (Seattle, WA); First Methodist Church (Seattle, WA); Glendale Evangelical Lutheran Church (Burien, WA); Lake Forest Park Presbyterian Church (Lake Forest Park, WA); Moreland Presbyterian Church ([Breakaway Week-End]; Portland, Oregon); Northminster Presbyterian Church (Seattle, WA); Roberts Wesleyan College (Rochester, NY [McCown Symposium]); Rolling Bay Presbyterian Church (Bainbridge Island, WA); St. James Episcopal Church (Kent, WA); St. John's Episcopal Church (Snohomish, WA): St. Margaret's Episcopal Church (Bellevue, WA); St. Mary's Episcopal Church (Lakewood, WA); St. Matthew Episcopal Church (Tacoma, WA); St. Paul's Episcopal Church (Bellingham, WA); St. Stephen's Episcopal Church (Seattle, WA); St. Thomas Episcopal Church (Medina, WA); Warm Beach Free Methodist Church (Stanwood, WA).

A word of thanks is due my colleagues in the School of Theology at Seattle Pacific University. I have no doubt that they in our many interactions have had a decisive role in sharpening my own thinking on this, and other, biblical or theological topics.

Throughout the time I have been working on this project my wife, Dr. Jo-Ellen Watson, has been unwavering in her support. I offer her heartfelt thanks.

Finally, I would be remiss not to mention Reinder Van Til of Eerdmans. He is the first one with whom I spoke about the project. From the beginning to the end he made himself available to talk strategy, edit drafts, work over endnotes, and shepherd the book through the requisite publishing processes. As an added bonus, we discovered that we both speak fluent baseball, though with different accents (Chicago and Seattle, with a hint of Pittsburgh respectively). I am profoundly grateful for his professional help and his friendship.

Introduction

There are obviously many stories in the Old Testament, but they are virtually all related to and contextualized by one main, singular Story. The latter has sometimes been called a *metastory,* referring to a sweeping narrative that reflects a fundamental worldview and thereby subsumes all of the smaller stories. Essentially, the Old Testament metastory is that God created everything good, including the earth, for whose care God commissioned human beings who were made in the divine image (Genesis 1–2). But corruption and evil entered the world as a result of the sinful actions of humans; once sin appeared, it tragically increased exponentially (Genesis 3–11). To reverse the terrible state of affairs into which the world had fallen, God took the initiative and formed a specific community through which the world was eventually to be restored (Genesis 12 and following).

God's formation of the community through whom the restoration of humankind would be accomplished is arguably the most prominent and pervasive feature of the Old Testament metastory. This election resulted in the people who were (eventually) called "Israel," a group that throughout the Story had a distinct identity as the "people of God" and a never-to-be-ignored mission that was divinely mandated. Indeed, so pronounced is the Old Testament theme of God's election of a particular people that both Jews and Christians, for all their other differences, have historically assumed it as a given in their interpretation of the Old Testament and in their respective religious self-understanding.*

---

*Jews do not, of course, refer to their Bible as the "Old Testament." The latter is a dis-

1

This unique election on God's part clearly gives heavy accent to the notion of exclusivity. And that may be a difficult idea to swallow in an era that promotes inclusivity, multiculturalism, and the willing acceptance of religious diversity as supreme values, not to mention as requisite for an enlightened social, political, or religious outlook. Whether we like it or not, however, those who put religious stock in the biblical tradition cannot get around the prominence of the exclusivity theme in the Old Testament. After all, this is no minor development; rather, it is a central and unambiguous feature of the metastory in which God selects one and only one people to accomplish the goal of blessing and reconciling the whole world (Gen. 12:1-3). For this reason, the "chosen people" is presented in every nook and cranny of the Old Testament as God's very own special community, designed and destined to be used exclusively for God's purposes. The biblical claim is astonishing, even audacious. What else is one to make of the insistence that Israel was chosen at God's initiative and for God's own purposes? Indeed, the metastory puts into the boldest possible relief the point that, apart from God's election, there would never have been an Israel in the first place. Nor can Christians run from this idea and hope to find refuge in the New Testament, because the New Testament has its own version of exclusivity, though it has a somewhat different nuance than its Old Testament counterpart (as we shall come to see).

So Israel's exclusive divine election is replete throughout the biblical tradition. Many narratives treat Israel's role as God's own people directly; others do so indirectly by assuming this crucial relationship between the deity and the community. Whatever the circumstances, this concept is virtually always present in one form or another. A sampling of texts illustrates this basic teaching. Two critical examples occur in the Book of Deuteronomy. In the first instance, Israel is asked a rhetorical question about its unique status as an elect people:

> "For ask now of the days that are past, which were before you, since
> the day that God created man upon the earth, and ask from one end

tinctively Christian term, adopted after the inclusion of a "New Testament." Judaism refers to its Bible as, simply, the Bible, or the Scriptures, or TANAK (an acronym referring to the three main sections into which the Hebrew Bible is divided: Law, Prophets, and Writings [the Hebrew terms for Law, Prophets, and Writings begin with the equivalent of a "T," an "N," and a "K"). Sometimes the terms *Hebrew Bible* or *Hebrew Scriptures* are used to designate what Christians call the Old Testament.

of heaven to the other, whether such a great thing as this has ever happened or was ever heard of. Did any people ever hear the voice of a god speaking out of the midst of the fire, as you have heard, and still live? Or has any god ever attempted to go and take a nation for himself from the midst of another nation, by trials, by signs, by wonders, and by war, by a mighty hand and an outstretched arm, and by great terrors, according to all that the LORD your God did for you in Egypt before your eyes?"

This quote (Deut. 4:32-34) closely parallels another from the same book (7:6): "For you are a people holy to the LORD your God; the LORD your God has chosen you to be a people for his own possession, out of all the peoples that are on the face of the earth." This same sentiment is reflected later in a famous text from the prophet Amos (3:2): "You only have I known of all the families of the earth." The word translated "known" here betokens God's relationship by special agreement (a "covenant") with the people in question. Clearly, this text states forthrightly that God "knows" Israel in a manner different from any other people. But this is not chiefly a matter of God's mere factual knowledge; rather, it is a matter of God's specialized relationship. In light of Israel's position as divinely chosen, no fate was worse than forfeiting that status. The prophet Hosea named one of his children "Not My People" as a way of denouncing Israel when it refused to act in accordance with its divine election (Hosea 1:9). Many more texts with the same teaching could easily be mustered, for the plain fact of the matter is that Israel's chosenness is at the very heart of the Old Testament message.

In light of this paramount teaching, it is hardly surprising that Israel is consistently presented as the quintessential "insider" community, made abundantly clear by the Amos and Deuteronomy texts just quoted. In the former, God says *you only* have I known"; in one of the Deuteronomy texts (7:6), ". . . your God . . . has chosen you . . . *out of all the peoples that are on the face of the earth.*" While it is true that God has chosen Israel for the ultimate benefit of all the world's peoples, that does not change the fact that Israel remains God's specially elected people. This community is truly an insider community; even more importantly, it is the only insider community.

It is instructive to observe this accent on Israel's exclusive insider status from the very beginning. The idea does not develop over time: it is foundational. Without this guiding concept, the Old Testament metastory would never have gotten off the ground. Thus, at the outset of the biblical story, in response to the terrible predicament into which humanity has gotten itself — as portrayed in Genesis 1–11 — God summoned two individuals, Abraham and Sarah (Abram and Sarai before God changed their names), to turn around the dire situation (Gen. 12:1-3). And by selecting these two, God did not select anyone else.

But this divine exclusion actually goes deeper than that. We eventually discover that only those descended from Abraham and Sarah together were considered part of the elect, insider group (Gen. 17:15-21; 18:9-15; 21:1-7). One had to be the offspring of both ancestors: having Abraham as your father (with another mother) or Sarah as your mother (with another father) was insufficient. But making things even more complicated, being descended from Abraham and Sarah was not sufficient either, because not all those biologically descended from these two ancestors were to be incorporated into the chosen community through which God planned to effect the world's salvation. More than a blood relationship to Abraham and Sarah or their descendants was required for membership in this select group. Indeed, the divine promises made to these forebears — that their offspring would become a great people and possess their own land — were very restrictively applied.

This may be seen in the fact that Abraham had children who were exempted from the ancestral promises (Gen. 16:1-16; 25:1-6). An even more poignant illustration is seen when Isaac, the only son Abraham had by Sarah, fathers twins. Though both children are obviously equally related by blood to their parents (Rebekah is the mother), only one of the twins is destined to become the bearer of God's future promise. The other will be, by definition, left out of the special, insider community (Gen. 25:23). Seen from this angle, the Old Testament seems to say that God's election is not only maddeningly exclusive, it is apparently arbitrary as well — at least from a human standpoint. Regardless of human designs, machinations, and manipulation, God has the initial and the final say about what people would eventually constitute God's particular community of Israel. That community, and only that community, was mandated to be a "light to the nations." No one else need apply. Israel was God's only insider community. One may be uncomfortable with this emphasis, but one cannot expunge it, for it is a core feature of the story.

As I have noted, Israel's divine election and God's exclusive commitment to this community remain in focus throughout the whole Old Testament. When the elected ancestors' descendants become enslaved by an Egypt that has gone from being benevolent (Genesis 37–50) to malevolent (Exodus 1–12), God rescues them by devastating their oppressors. Subsequently, God leads the people through a hostile wilderness and cements the divine relationship with them by means of a covenant (Exodus 20ff.). In time, God gives Israel the promised land (Joshua) and later establishes Israel as a great people (Samuel-Kings). As this story unfolds, it becomes ever so clear that it is a story with a capital *S*, whereas all the other lowercase stories of all the other peoples in the world are of interest only in their relationship to Israel. Apart from Israel's exclusive story, none of the other people's stories would be mentioned at all. Theologically speaking, Israel is the only game in town! At least, that's the way the Old Testament consistently presents the picture.

But it would be a mistake to construe Israel's exclusive election as a function of its superiority. On the contrary, Israel's exclusive status is completely a function of what might be called God's exclusive status. This may be seen best in the realization that referring to the Old Testament deity simply as "God" does not actually do justice to the exclusivity theme. Israel's God has a name: YHWH.* Now, by according God a personal name, Israel was no different from any other ancient Near Eastern people; all the gods of that ancient world had distinctive personal names. But the difference for Israel, as it is portrayed in the Old Testament, was the radical belief that its god, YHWH, was the only living god and therefore the only divine being deserving of worship and obedience. Those who acknowledged an array of gods might have been willing, at least in theory, to include YHWH in their pantheons. In that sense, such people might be legitimately considered "religiously inclusive." By their lights, every god was to be acknowledged and at least feared, if not accorded respect. But Israel rejected this approach. Its god was a "jealous God" (Exod. 20:4-5; Josh. 24:19) who brooked no rivals. YHWH would either be worshiped and acknowledged exclusively or not at all (Josh. 24:14-15). It follows that Israel's exclusivity was parallel to YHWH's exclusivity. To be sure, Israel often strayed

---

*These consonants have conventionally been vocalized as *Yahweh*, the pronunciation of which is uncertain. Typically, in English Bibles the name of God has been rendered as LORD. In this book I use the unvocalized YHWH to indicate the distinctive, personal name of Israel's deity. In the quote from Deuteronomy above, the word LORD in all capital letters is a rendering of YHWH.

from this ideal, but whenever it did, the prophets were adamant in calling for repentance and announcing judgment for such an egregious breach of loyalty. Refusing to serve YHWH exclusively is portrayed as perhaps the greatest sin in the Old Testament; in fact, properly understood, it is the *only* Sin — all the other "sins" are commentary on that one great Sin. This is why only YHWH can be "blamed" for Israel's insider status. Israel could not elect itself, after all.

Equally, it would be erroneous to think of God's electing Israel as a divine action calculated to benefit the chosen people to the exclusion of everyone else. While Israel's insider status as a result of its divine election is never in doubt, it has to be kept in proper theological perspective. God did not choose Israel in order to preserve Israelites while condemning all others. That is not the way either election or exclusion works in the Old Testament. Israel was not chosen to keep everyone else out of God's fold; Israel was chosen to make it possible for everyone else eventually to be included. Remember that YHWH selected Abraham and Sarah in the first place for the express purpose of blessing *all the families of the earth* (Gen. 12:3). Ironically, Abraham and Sarah are exclusively chosen so that everyone else might be embraced in God's plan for blessing. This means that Israel's antecedents were culled out of all potential candidates not primarily for their own advantage, but to be the vehicle through which YHWH would act favorably toward the whole earth's inhabitants. The election, though by all means exclusive, was designed to be inclusive in terms of its ultimate goal. God chose Israel as the means by which all the other peoples of the earth could be reconciled to that same deity. That is the primary thrust of the biblical story of salvation.

In light of the broad placement of this theme throughout the Old Testament, the emphasis on Israel's divinely engendered exclusivity and its unique role in God's plans is neither coincidental nor is it an aberrational concept that may be dismissed as a sidelight. It is part of the Old Testament's warp and woof. There is the one and only one God and one and only one people through whom God will accomplish the divine purpose for all of humanity. There is no way to avoid this "scandal of particularity"; it is as transparent and prominent a datum as appears in the pages of the Old Testament. One may not like it, or understand it, or agree with it. But it cannot be removed from the Old Testament's thought structure without risking a complete collapse of the whole edifice.

Besides, excising this central teaching from the Old Testament would undercut one of the most significant biblical teachings, namely, the doctrine of the grace and sovereignty of God. It must always be kept in the forefront of our thinking that Israel's special election by God is a function of God's inscrutable will and immeasurable grace. This is why neither Israel's ancestors nor Israel itself in any period was ever presented as particularly worthy of having been divinely chosen. On the contrary, over and over the "chosen people" are described as being totally undeserving of any special divine favors. Abraham and Sarah both doubted the Lord at times or even dubiously took matters into their own hands when they were unsure of God's timing and methods (Gen. 12:10-20; 15:1-3; 16:1-6; 17:15-22; 18:9-15). Jacob became ascendant over Esau through the most questionable of means (Gen. 25:27-33; 27:1-29); nothing in the story suggests that he was a suitable candidate for selection. Subsequently, the whole elect family was preserved from perishing by famine through the transparent evil of brothers selling a brother into slavery (Gen. 37–50). Why should such a "dysfunctional" family have been singled out for special favor? Also, the descendants of those early ancestors had to be virtually dragged "kicking and screaming" out of Egypt, where they were state slaves (Ex. 1–15; see especially 5:21; 14:10-12). Once in the wilderness, instead of being grateful to YHWH for their rescue, they complained every step of the way and even yearned, unbelievably, for the "good old days" in Egypt (Ex. 16–18). During the period of the "judges," Israel was caught up in a vicious "cycle of disobedience" in which God put them under judgment time after time (Judges; see especially 2:11-23). Then, once they became a "great people" during the time of the kings, Israelites collectively were so disobedient that finally YHWH removed them from the very land that had first been given them as part of the divine promise (Samuel-Kings; see especially 2 Kings 23:26–25:26). Had God been looking for a "good" people to select for blessing the world, then God made a singularly poor choice!

Because Israel's selection has to do with YHWH's grace and sovereignty, there's no figuring out why Israel was called. The deity explicitly notes that the choice of Israel had nothing to do with its suitability or superiority (Deut. 7:7; 9:6). It remains a mystery why Israel was selected, as it would remain a mystery why anyone else might have been selected. This explains why Israel is portrayed in the Bible in such stupendously unflattering ways. If someone were going to invent a story designed to make a people look good and therefore deserving of divine election, the result would never have been the Old Testament depiction of Israel. More often than not, Israel comports itself as though it had *not* been singled out by YHWH for a special vocation. As hard as the Old Testament judgments are on "the [outsider] nations," they are equally hard on the (insider) people of Israel. The most cursory scanning of the prophetic writings bears that out.

Nevertheless, even though Israel did not necessarily deserve to be God's exclusive people (nor did anyone else "deserve" such a designation!), and even though being God's exclusive people provided no exemption from divine wrath, the fact remains that Israel and only Israel was the chosen people of YHWH. For reasons known only to God, Israel was chosen to be the means for the world's salvation and blessing. This means without question that God's goal of getting the whole world eventually blessed through Israel had to do solely with God's grace as well. Just as Israel did not deserve to be divinely elected, the world did not deserve to receive the benefits of God's grace either; but in both cases God's limitless and amazing grace was operative. Again, from a biblical standpoint, YHWH's determination to elect and use Israel as the vehicle for the whole world's blessing and ultimate salvation was totally due to the divine character. God's love, grace, inscrutable will, sovereign design, and holy determination to save humanity from itself are key to biblical understanding. It goes without saying that neither Israel nor the world deserved God's grace, but that is because grace *by definition* is undeserved; it can never be merited.

I intimated above that there is also a New Testament version of this election and exclusivity theme. But the New Testament take is a little different because the identity of the "insider" community is not as straightforward. To be sure, the Israel that had been elected by God is still God's own chosen people in the New Testament and therefore by all means the "insider" community. But the New Testament teaches that the grace that God manifested in choosing Israel and then expressed through Israel to the rest of the world had its completion and ultimate expression in Jesus Christ. When the New Testament promotes Jesus as Israel's messiah, or anointed one ("messiah" is the Hebrew term for anointed, "Christ" is the Greek term), it is to show that the messianic age has been inaugurated and the reign of God instituted. In other words, what God began in Israel has been fulfilled in Jesus. Just as there was a "scandal of particularity" in YHWH's exclusive election of Israel, so there was a similar scandal when YHWH completed Israel's mission in the incarnation, death, resurrection, and exaltation of Jesus, who, the New Testament unabashedly claimed, was Israel's anointed one (i.e., Christ).

It follows that Israel's identity as an insider community is central in the New Testament just as it is in the Old Testament. But that is not the end of the matter, because the New Testament presents an enormous struggle over the very identity of "true Israel," that is, the Israel that was true to its original election. Keep in mind that every single one of the earliest Christians was a Jew who thought of himself or herself as a member of elect Israel. This is why the earliest Christians, who saw Jesus as uniquely sent by YHWH and the very embodiment of YHWH, did not believe they were starting another religion. They believed with all their hearts that the very God who selected and planned to save the world through Israel had acted in Jesus to complete that very same mission. Were it not for that irreducible belief, there would have been no point in arguing with other Jews. Likewise, those other Jews who saw themselves as part of the chosen people would have seen the "Christians" (that designation took some time to catch on) as one more pagan religion were it not for their irritating and even blasphemous claim that they were more attuned to Israel's selection and mission than most of the Jewish religious leaders were.

In short, the New Testament presents us with an intramural debate. The nub of that debate has to do with the makeup and purpose of God's insider community, Israel. The New Testament makes the case that those Israelites who recognized what YHWH was doing through Jesus, Israel's messiah, turned out to be in effect "more Israelite" than those who failed to see or refused to see what God was trying to accomplish through Jesus.

Thus, in either its Old Testament or New Testament guise, the emphasis on exclusivity as a function of God's inscrutable elective will for Israel is pivotal and pervasive. This is not a subpoint or a minor motif; it is key to the whole biblical witness. In the Bible's macro-story, that is, the story of Israel and Jesus writ large, exclusivity is at the heart of the biblical message. No amount of tinkering or tweaking can hide what is so profound and conspicuous a teaching. Were one to remove this theme, the only thing that would remain would be a pale and truncated version of the original, powerful message. God had a reason for exclusively electing Israel and, so Christians believe, continuing the Israelite purpose and mission in Jesus the Christ.

Yet it is precisely this extraordinary emphasis on Israel's exclusive election and its indisputable insider status that makes it so surprising to come across a number of Old Testament texts that prominently feature *outsiders* of one kind or another. In this context, an "outsider" is any person or group that has not been especially chosen by God to be the vehicle of the world's restoration and reconciliation. Remarkably, there are several narratives where outsiders are not only explicitly presented as such, but where they are in a variety of ways actually shown to be superior to God's elect, the insiders. Sometimes these outsiders show more faith in, a greater sensitivity to, or a greater understanding of Israel's deity; on other occasions they do something that promotes the agenda of Israel's God, their outsider status notwithstanding. There are even times when outsiders become insiders, so much so that they become indistinguishable from the chosen people Israel. Given the Bible's pronounced emphasis on Israel's exclusivity as a function of God's providence and grace, such outsider stories warrant the closest scrutiny if for no other reason than that they have great value in providing context, nuance, and texture for the important election theme. More importantly, these stories actually magnify the emphasis on God's sovereignty and grace.

Just as the election emphasis is found throughout the Old Testament, so texts in which the outsider motif is present occur in every major section of the Old Testament, especially in its Hebrew version, which consists of Law, Prophets, and Writings. Two of the stories I will treat in this book, those dealing with Esau (Gen. 25–36) and Tamar (Gen. 38), are found in Torah.* This is significant because Torah is foundational to the rest of the Old Testament. Another two stories, those dealing with Rahab (Joshua 2) and Naaman (2 Kings 5), are found in the Former Prophets. The story of Jonah comes from the Latter Prophets. And the last Old Testament outsider narrative is that of Ruth, which is part of the biblical section known as the Writings.† At the very least, this spread of texts underscores the contention that

---

*Torah is conventionally translated "law." This is certainly acceptable, since the Torah (Pentateuch) contains the many laws that are part of God's covenant with Israel (Ex. 20 through Num. 10:10). But *Torah* also means more than "law." It means "teaching," "instruction," "story," and "narrative."

†In English Bibles it has been customary to refer to the books of Joshua, Judges, Ruth, Samuel, Kings, Chronicles, Ezra, and Nehemiah as "historical books." But in the form of the Old Testament that the Christian church originally inherited from Judaism, i.e., the Hebrew Bible, there was no category called "historical books." Instead, Joshua through 2 Kings (excluding Ruth) was called Former Prophets. The "prophets" designation has to do with the prophetic perspective from which these stories are told. The Latter Prophets consist of Isaiah, Jeremiah, Ezekiel, and the Book of the Twelve (Minor Prophets); the distinction between "major" and "minor" prophets has to do with size, not importance. The Writings consist of Psalms, Job, Proverbs, Ruth, Song of Songs, Ecclesiastes, Lamentations, Esther, Daniel, Ezra, Nehemiah, and 1-2 Chronicles.

outsider stories are neither incidental nor haphazard in the biblical witness. They are part of the essence of the tradition, especially to the extent to which they provide further insight into the exclusivity theme.

In every single instance, as I hope to show, the outsider stories provide sophisticated insights into that Old Testament theme. Such stories prevent the exclusivity theme from being construed as a one-dimensional, simplistic feature of Old Testament theology. Instead, these stories enhance the exclusivity theme by making it possible for us to view it from a variety of angles, by illustrating its multivalent character, and by demonstrating how rich and complex the Old Testament's view of grace truly is. Considered by itself, the Old Testament's emphasis on divine grace as manifested in God's exclusive election of Israel for the ultimate benefit of the whole world is virtually beyond calculation. But when this emphasis is viewed in light of the several outsider stories, then the accent on God's grace becomes almost impossible to comprehend.

Similarly, attending to the insider-outsider polarity in the New Testament will enhance our understanding of the sweep of the biblical tradition. The famous story of the "woman at the well" in John 4 not only gives us a window into that important Gospel but also helps us understand the roles of insiders and outsiders in the other Gospels as well. As I hope to demonstrate, both the Old Testament and the New Testament are more or less on the same page regarding this crucial topic. Though we will treat only one New Testament story in detail, a brief summary in that chapter will, if nothing else, make us sensitive to how widespread and significant is the insider-outsider motif in that biblical corpus as well.

In the succeeding chapters I will treat each of the outsider stories in detail. This is as it should be, for the Bible generally does not "do" theology with declarative statements and carefully reasoned, systematic treatises. More than anything else, the Bible tells stories. These are narrated in a highly artful manner, resulting in stories that are colorful, dramatic, ironic, surprising, clever, subtle, tantalizing, and almost always extremely interesting. We can grasp the essence of the stories by attending to the exquisite detail with which they are constructed. Often what we are not told (a character's name, for instance) is as important as what we are told. Or the difference between what the *narrator* knows or tells us and what a *character* knows or tells us is decisive in how we understand the story. The bottom line is that the story itself and the manner in which it is told are determinative for getting the meaning of the narrative.

In each of the following chapters we will engage in a "close reading" of the text, so it will be especially helpful for readers to have a Bible close at hand. Even though I will more or less tell each of the stories as I engage the material, there is no substitute for a close reading of the actual text. None of the stories we shall examine takes up much narrative space. The Esau material unfolds over the most extensive biblical text, about twelve chapters (Genesis 25–36); Jonah and Ruth take up four short chapters each; Rahab and the counterpoint Achan episode involve two chapters; and the Tamar and Naaman stories, along with the Woman at the Well, take up only single chapters of the Bible. In short, it is not a burden to keep one eye on the biblical text as we read each of these narratives. Perhaps the best strategy would be to read the pertinent biblical text and then the analysis, referring again to the text as the chapter proceeds.

I have written this book with college and seminary students, pastors, Bible-study groups, and interested laypeople in mind. To that end, I have decided to relegate most of the more technical and bibliographical notes to the back of the book. They are there for any who are interested in the more scholarly discussions, but they may be ignored without any sacrifice of understanding the thematic discussions. I have reserved the footnotes for explaining terminology unfamiliar to nonspecialists or elaborating on strategies I have adopted to treat the material. But I have tried to keep these to a minimum. When it is necessary for the integrity of the story to point out nuances in the original languages, I have used transliteration and, I hope, user-friendly explanations.

For over a decade I have been lecturing on the material found in this book to my own university students and to many congregations. In my judgment, because the material presented is so crucial to comprehending a major biblical teaching, it lends itself to being used as a supplemental text for introductory Bible courses at the university or seminary level or as a study manual for adult Bible education in the church. Though it is not written in a textbook style or format (which some will undoubtedly consider an advantage!), it touches on countless strategic issues in biblical teaching and theology. In any case, I have used this material to great advantage in my own university classrooms and in the churches where I have been privileged to lecture.

More than anything else, I have attempted to concentrate on the stories themselves in this book. The story is, after all, the issue. By allowing the stories to speak for themselves, we give the biblical material in all its richness an opportunity to surface. The great biblical scholar Hans Frei once decried what he termed the "eclipse" of biblical narrative, by which he meant, in part, that the church had lost sight of a crucial aspect of the biblical tradition that is supposed to inform and enlighten it. I have tried in this little book to demonstrate to those who read these stories their power and their ability to address the most significant of theological issues.

CHAPTER 1

Esau: The Face of God

The biblical figure of Esau is a character we love to hate, so to speak. He is known famously for selling his familial birthright for a bite of lunch (Gen. 25:29-34). Why should we not regard such colossal stupidity and impulsiveness with outright disdain? Since we are told that "Esau despised his birthright" (v. 34), it seems only fair to hold him in contempt. No wonder Esau has been a standard negative role model in church and Sunday school. It is difficult to think of another biblical character more deserving of the designation "outsider."

At the same time, Esau's outsider status could hardly be more anomalous, because he begins his life with an unparalleled opportunity to be an insider par excellence. To use a racing metaphor, not only did he begin at the pole position, he was allowed to start running before any of the other horses even got out of the gate. After all, Esau was the son of Isaac and Rebekah, not to mention the grandson of Abraham and Sarah. These ancestors were quintessential insiders as far as the (future) people of Israel were concerned. Without them, there would have been no Israel in the first place. Thus, Esau had the enormous good fortune of being related by blood to Israel's founding mothers and fathers. Even more important, Esau was the older son of Isaac and Rebekah. According to the rule of primogeniture, Esau was in line to inherit not only his family's wealth and social position but any loftier claim they might have on the future as well. Given that this particular family's hold on the future was a function of divine election and promise, Esau's prospects could scarcely have been brighter.

Yet the three most common names found together in the Old Testament are Abraham, Isaac, and Jacob — emphatically not Abraham, Isaac, and Esau. When people bring up the prominent story in which Esau is a main character, typically they refer to "the Jacob and Esau story," not the other way around, even though Esau is the older of the brothers. In point of fact, even before Esau's birth, events have already conspired to undercut his prior advantageous position. What makes his lot perhaps most galling to Esau and any defenders he might have is that his position in the family is altered by the witting actions of his God, his brother, and his mother, not to mention the unwitting actions of his hapless father. Considering all that, it is not the least bit surprising that Esau is depicted in starkly pejorative terms in a variety of biblical narratives.

Adding insult to injury, the nation that claimed Esau as its eponymous ancestor, namely Edom, is likewise relentlessly vilified in the biblical tradition. So intense is the prophetic condemnation of Edom that one scholar posits a "Damn-Edom theology." That may seem to be an exaggeration until one considers the startling prophetic pronouncement in Malachi 1:2, where YHWH expresses the divine relationship to these two brothers in the harshest of terms: "I have loved Jacob but I have hated Esau." It appears that people who do not like Esau are in good company, for God does not like him either!

In light of the preceding, the two questions I will address in this first chapter are: 1) how did Esau the insider get to be Esau the outsider? and 2) is Esau in fact presented as negatively in the biblical story as has generally been presumed? The second question has to do with more than trying to salvage Esau's reputation; rather, it involves an assessment of the theological importance of the Esau character as a strategic segment of the ancestral saga. While there is no denying that Esau did, in the final analysis, become an outsider, we still have to determine from what perspective we should understand his outsider status. More pointedly, it is instructive to study Esau's story to ascertain whether this insider-who-eventually-becomes-an-outsider has anything to teach the insider, namely Jacob, who was destined to bear the divine promise into the future.

The birth of the twins: "the first shall be last"

From the very beginning, the relationship between the elder Esau and his (barely) younger twin, Jacob, is, to say the least, complex. This complexity is revealed first in the irony reflected in the birth account. Though the twins' birth results from divine intervention, they are to experience radically different futures. Their father, Isaac, has prayed in response to Rebekah's failure to conceive, and God has granted his request (Gen. 25:21). During her troubled pregnancy, a distraught Rebekah learns from God that she is carrying twins and that the younger child and his descendants would be ascendant over the older child and his descendants (Gen. 25:23). One aspect of the irony is that Rebekah seeks YHWH in the first place because of the distress triggered by the struggling going on in her womb (Gen. 25:22). But immediately she — and we — may gather from YHWH's statement that the struggle indicates that the twins are engaged in a bizarre prenatal contest to emerge first so as to claim the privileges of the first-born. Yet, according to YHWH's prediction, it turns out to be a disadvantage to be born first. Esau would actually have been better off had his brother, who was still vying for position up to the very last moment, won this initial contest (Gen. 25:25-26). Recall that God has named no names: the deity has only said that the younger — whoever that turns out to be — will end up being preeminent over the elder.

Another aspect of the irony in this story is that Jacob is hardly presented as morally superior to Esau once they have both become adults. Esau is referred to as "a man who knows hunting — a man of the field" (Gen. 25:27). Some interpreters think that this description is subtly unflattering, hinting that Esau is crude, uncultured, and instinctual. The plausibility of this reading may be buttressed by the assertion that Isaac loves Esau because "game was in his [Isaac's] mouth," a less than elegant way of saying that Isaac is fond of the wild game Esau kills and prepares (Gen. 25:28). Also, in the famous birthright incident, when Esau returns hungry from the field, finds Jacob cooking, and blurts out, "Let me cram my mouth with this red stuff," he exposes himself as the epitome of "inarticulate appetite." After the fateful and hurried negotiations over the birthright, a succession of verbs further betrays Esau's ill-mannered ways: "he ate, drank, got up, and left" (Gen. 25:34). One interpreter attempts to capture Esau's behavior in this scene by calling him simply "the crude hunter." But even if we concur that Esau is pictured as bereft of any social graces, and clearly rash, we have to ask whether he is beyond the moral pale as well.

A final verb in this string seems to answer that question unambiguously: "So Esau *despised* the birthright" (Gen. 25:34). It is difficult not to construe this as moral failure. Granted, Esau is truly hungry (Gen. 25:29);

still, it's not clear why he thinks he's at death's door (Gen. 25:32). In any case, his hunger pangs appear to have completely clouded his judgment, making the birthright worthless in his eyes — at least momentarily. In sum, Esau is lacking not only in etiquette but in virtue. At the moment he returns from the field, nothing but food has any value, so he foolishly cedes his sociolegal rights and squanders his future. Having no sense of restraint, proportion, or priority, Esau has indeed "despised" the birthright, thus treating that most precious gift as trivial and making the first fateful move toward becoming an outsider.

Nevertheless, as bad as Esau comes off in this encounter, his brother does not exactly dazzle. Though he is as shrewd as Esau is foolhardy, Jacob is far from commendable. In fact, the narrator fairly invites us to surmise that Jacob has been waiting for an occasion when Esau might be susceptible to his exploitation. Demanding the transfer of a birthright is not a natural response to a brother's request for food — manners or no manners! Without question, Jacob has his eye on the future, is apparently schooled in legal procedures ("swear to me today"), and has been careful not to let a golden opportunity slip through his fingers. Thus armed, Jacob thoroughly outwits his intemperate brother. Certainly, Jacob is superior in this exchange in the sense that he runs circles around the ridiculously careless Esau; still, Jacob is not his brother's *moral* better. Jacob is more wily than Esau, more manipulative, and without question more attuned to the future; but he is no exemplar of brotherly love. If Esau is crass and stupid, Jacob is coldly extortionary. Esau is condemned by the explicit verdict that "he despised the birthright"; but there is an implicit negative estimation of Jacob as well. As J. P. Fokkelman comments on this text, "Morally speaking, there are only losers."

It is important for us to remember that the moral makeup of the twins is hinted at when they are initially described, and irony is evident here as well. As already noted, Esau is identified in terms of his occupation: a hunter, a man of the field. What is said about Jacob, however, is curious. He is identified with the Hebrew word *tām* as well as being called a tent-dweller (Gen. 25:27). Being someone who lives in tents seems straightforward enough: perhaps it is meant to contrast with the portrayal of Esau as an outdoorsman. But how should *tām* be understood? Translators have often regarded the word as indicative of an unassuming disposition and therefore translated it as "quiet," "mild," or the like. But other instances of *tām* in the Old Testament connote moral innocence or integrity (e.g., Gen.

6:9; 20:5-6; Job 1:8; 2:3). What evidence do we have that *tām* does not imply moral excellence in this case as well? This is where irony is likely in play once again, since *tām* may be an antonym of the root *('qb)* from which Jacob's name is derived. If this is so, then perhaps we are meant to see Jacob as simultaneously morally bankrupt and morally upright, at least potentially. He is a "supplanter," as his name implies and his actions confirm, but he also figures to be a moral exemplar in his eventual role as the bearer of the divine ancestral promise. So far, Jacob the morally questionable man overwhelms Jacob the morally compelling man (cf. Gen. 27:36). For this to be reversed, profound changes will have to occur in Jacob. Though Esau is far from moral or *tām* himself — and will never be described as such — he may have more to do with Jacob's pending reversal than seems evident at this point. With this possible transition in view, it may turn out that the outsider will be far more influential on the insider's moral transformation than these early episodes in the story indicate.

Deception in the tent

Any hopes Esau may have harbored about regaining his insider status within the family are cruelly and decisively dashed by the plot hatched against him by his mother Rebekah and his brother Jacob (Gen. 27:1-45). Notwithstanding his previous loss of the birthright, Esau is now poised to receive his aged father's blessing. All Esau has to do is follow his father's simple instructions to hunt game, prepare a meal, and present himself to his father for the coveted prize (Gen. 27:1-4). At this point in the story it is unclear whether Esau's procuring of the paternal blessing would result in nullifying the effects of his having already relinquished his birthright. At the very least, one would think that getting his father's blessing, which presumably belongs to the firstborn no less than the birthright itself, might even the score a little. If one brother claims a birthright and the other claims a patriarchal blessing, then perhaps mediation would be required, thus giving Esau a sporting chance. But alas, when the dramatic episode comes to a close, Esau has lost both birthright and blessing. He's a two-time loser.

Seen from one angle, this turn of events simply fulfills the future that God has predicted for the elder scion (Gen. 25:23). But seen from a slightly different angle, Esau ends up being the only sympathetic character in the whole scene, primarily because all the others are so seriously flawed. To be sure, Isaac the patriarch does nothing consciously or obviously immoral. Still, he comes across as incompetent, confused, and at times almost pathetic. As for Rebekah, her actions are as morally dubious as they are brilliant. Without any hesitation or qualms whatsoever, she lets Jacob in on her strategy and urges his complete cooperation (Gen. 27:6-10), brushing aside any potentially negative consequences of being caught (Gen. 27:11-13). Because we are never told whether Rebekah's efforts to promote Jacob at Esau's expense are a function of her knowledge of the divine oracle or of blatant maternal favoritism, or both (Gen. 25:23, 28), her motives remain shrouded. Regardless of her motives, though, her actions cannot be justified on moral grounds.

Jacob's behavior is no less reprehensible. Though he initially protests his mother's proposed tactics, his primary concern is the chance of being discovered and incurring his father's wrath (Gen. 27:11-12). Indeed, once he agrees to follow his mother's instructions, he has no trouble lying coolly and without compunction when he stands before his father. No matter how sacred the occasion, the first time Jacob — the very one destined to become one of Israel's vaunted patriarchal triumvirate (Abraham, Isaac, and Jacob) — is asked his name, he tells a bald-faced lie: "I am Esau your firstborn" (Gen. 27:19). And when pressed by Isaac, he reaffirms the lie (Gen. 27:24). As if that weren't enough, the first time Jacob mentions God in the story, he is manipulatively dishonest. Asked how he has caught and prepared game so quickly, Jacob says, "Because YHWH your God gave me success" (Gen. 27:20). In fact, the only time Jacob tells the truth in the entire episode is when he reminds his mother that he is a "smooth man" and thus likely to be detected (Gen. 27:11). There is a definite *double entendre* in this phrase: it means the obvious, that he is literally not hairy, but also, metaphorically, that he is "smooth," "slick," or "slippery" in the sense of being untrustworthy. In addition to these examples of self-incrimination, Jacob's character is revealed by other narrative voices: Isaac later informs Esau that "your brother came with guile and took your blessing" (Gen. 27:35). And Esau's own verdict is even more damning: "Is he not well named Jacob, since he has supplanted me these two times: my birthright he took and now my blessing he took."

However, in spite of the fact that Jacob is fully complicit in his mother's scheme and robs Esau of something incalculably precious for a second time, he remains the privileged son who will carry forward the promises made to the ancestors (see Gen. 28:2-4, 13-15). To be sure, not once does the narrative downplay Jacob's mendacity; but neither does it ever come close to suggesting that his unconscionable behavior disqualifies him from fulfilling his divinely appointed destiny. No matter how unfair it appears, God's promised future will be brought about by Jacob. Esau is simply out of luck or, more pointedly, on the wrong side of Providence.

At the same time, there is more to Esau's own future than is commonly perceived, both in terms of his personal fortunes and the difference he makes in Jacob's future — and thus in the ancestral promise itself. Though he has inexorably been demoted to outsider status, he cannot merely be dismissed. Indeed, he still has a vital role to play in the story, without which Jacob's understanding of God's ways would have been greatly impoverished. This vital role becomes evident initially when we compare the two futures Isaac announces for his sons.

There can be no question that Jacob receives from his father the primary blessing, while Esau receives at best a secondary blessing. This is communicated in two ways. One is the manner in which the language of blessing "surrounds" Jacob. Except for Isaac's preliminary arrangements (Gen. 27:4), virtually every reference to blessing in the rest of the episode is aimed at Jacob (Gen. 27:19, 23, 25, 27, 30). This obtains even when Isaac *thinks* he is speaking to Esau, though the reader knows that he is really addressing Jacob. And even when Esau's return brings the deception to light, Isaac proceeds to confirm Jacob's blessing (Gen. 27:33, 35). As for poor Esau, he is reduced to repeating his father's bad news and begging for his own blessing, even if "only one" (Gen. 27:31, 34, 36, 38). But even after all this, Isaac still does not *bless* but only *answers* Esau (Gen. 27:39).

The second way the primacy of Jacob's blessing is emphasized is in the content of the blessing itself: it is simply beyond challenge that Jacob's future is to be preferred to Esau's. Nonetheless, though Esau has no choice but to be satisfied with something less than a full-fledged blessing compared to Jacob's, what Isaac offers his elder son is rather more positive than is usually assumed. In fact, in the part of the blessing that refers to future prosperity, Esau's prospects are as good as Jacob's. This has been obscured by translators and interpreters who insist on taking Isaac's statements to his two sons as complete antitheses, regardless of what the text actually says. The simple fact is that Isaac promises that both his sons will enjoy the benefits of "the dew of heaven" and "the fat of the land" (Gen. 27:27b-28, 39). The Hebrew grammar supports this reading, which is well reflected in the translation of the Jewish Publication Society:

In Jacob's case:

"May God give you of the dew of heaven and the fat of the earth,
    Abundance of new grain and wine."

In Esau's case:

"See, your abode shall enjoy the fat of the earth
    And the dew of heaven above."

It's true that, when all is said and done, Jacob's blessing is surely greater than Esau's; but that does not negate the fact that both brothers are promised prosperous futures. The extended narrative corroborates this understanding when it reveals that Esau has subsequently become wealthy in his own right (see Gen. 32:6[Heb. 7]; 33:1, 9; 36:6-7).

But in the second part of the brothers' blessings, they have completely opposite futures laid out for them. Isaac promises Jacob service and deference from — even lordship over — not only "peoples and nations" but his brother as well (Gen. 27:29). Conversely, Esau is "promised" — if such a positive word is appropriate with such a negative future on the horizon — that he will live "by the sword" and, in addition, serve his younger brother (Gen. 27:40). About the only positive aspect of Esau's future is in Isaac's puzzling statement that one day he (Esau) will break free by removing Jacob's yoke from his neck. Having the yoke of another around one's neck, of course, is an ancient metaphor for slavery; Isaac intimates that this condition will not be permanent, but we have to wait for the story to unfold to see how the change will come about.

There is no doubt that Jacob gets the better bargain from Isaac's dual blessing. Yet the distinction is not that Jacob is blessed and Esau is cursed; rather, the twins have been issued different sorts of blessings. At worst, it's fair to say that Esau gets half a blessing and half a curse. To be sure, Esau will never attain Jacob's role and status; and he certainly will never be considered the "child of promise" who bears Israel's glorious future (see Gen. 28:3-4, 10-15; 35:9-12). But there are indications that Esau's prospects for the future are better than a man whom God has not elected and whom his brother and mother have utterly exploited might reasonably have expected.

There are glimmers of a potential turnaround for Esau even before the story relegates him to the background and concentrates exclusively on Jacob for the next twenty years in the narrative chronology. One of these glimmers comes to light when Jacob is forced to flee his brother's ire. We cannot help but be struck by the irony that Jacob, who is now the "child of promise," has to vacate the "land of promise," while Esau, now bereft of birthright and primary blessing, is able to remain in that same land (Gen. 27:41–28:5). Another irony involves Esau's marital situation: just before he drops out of the story for an extended period, he is shown trying to make amends for the consternation his Hittite wives have been causing his parents (Gen. 26:34-35; 27:46). Though it seems an irrelevant detail, there is in fact significance to Esau's taking a third wife from *within* the divinely elected family, which he has done as a direct response to the disappointment registered by his parents (Gen. 28:6-9). This time Esau marries none other than Abraham's granddaughter (by Hagar). If nothing else, it shows that there is more to Esau than has met the eye up to this point.

Jacob's dreaded reunion with Esau

As the narrative spotlight concentrates on Jacob's conflicted encounters with his Uncle Laban, Esau fades from the story (Gen. 28:10–31:54). But once Jacob has negotiated a peaceful separation from Laban, he and his large family, along with his vast holdings in servants and property, leave for Canaan. The "land of promise" is once more in view for Jacob, and for him that is indeed the good news. Unfortunately, there is also bad news: in moving toward Canaan, he will have to confront Esau. Jacob's preparations for the inevitable encounter turn frantic when his messengers bring him word that "your brother Esau is coming to meet you and four hundred men are with him" (Gen. 32:6[Heb. 7]). Jacob had ordered his servants to locate Esau and inform him that he has become fabulously wealthy and would be interested in an accommodation (Gen. 32:3-5). But the messengers' report is apparently not what Jacob expected to hear. His sudden panic (Gen. 32:7[Heb. 8]) underscores his assumption that the "men" with Esau are armed and spoiling for a fight.

At this point in the drama there are compelling reasons to sympathize with Jacob and to be concerned about Esau's motives. Can there be any doubt that Esau, just as he threatened so long ago (Gen. 27:41), is determined to avenge Jacob's heartless theft of his birthright and blessing? Granted, Jacob has been informed that Esau has said he will not harm his brother while their father is still alive. But at this juncture Jacob has either forgotten that pledge or chosen to ignore it — unless he now figures that Isaac has surely died (Gen. 27:41-45). Don't forget that, twenty years before, Isaac had summoned Esau for the blessing ceremony precisely because he felt his death was going to be sooner rather than later (Gen. 27:1-2).

Every single thing Jacob does as he braces for Esau's dreaded arrival is telling. Before he even learned that Esau was coming his way with four hundred men, Jacob has had messengers inform his brother of his fabulous wealth and desire for an accommodation (Gen. 32:3-5[Heb. 4-6]). It is more than revealing that Jacob has mentioned nothing about extending an apology, offering reparations, or wanting to establish a mutually beneficial fraternal relationship. As a matter of fact, the message Jacob is most anxious that his brother receive is little more than a thinly disguised bribe. Jacob seems to be hoping that Esau's realization that his nefarious twin is fabulously wealthy and shamelessly interested in an "accommodation" will blunt any lingering desire for revenge.

Once he surmises that Esau's barreling toward him with four hundred men in tow is surely ominous, Jacob moves to cut his losses by dividing his camp. He figures that Esau will not be able to attack both parts of a separated camp. The worst that could happen, he seems to reason, is that his wealth and holdings will be reduced by 50 percent, an absorbable loss (Gen. 32:7-8[Heb. 8-9]). Jacob has only one motivation here: he wants to retain as much of his wealth as possible. However, he is still apparently worried that this particular strategy could fail, and he takes an even more desperate measure — he prays. But this is a quintessential "foxhole" prayer (Gen. 32:9-12[Heb. 10-13]): though stress and fear have driven Jacob to his knees, his prayer contains no remorse at all, let alone a hint of confession. There is no acknowledgment of wrongdoing whatsoever. True, Jacob does admit that he is unworthy of the divine benefits extended to him; but this is not, strictly speaking, a confession. There may even be a whiff of irony here in that Jacob is only being "appropriately humble" while, without realizing it, he is also being as truthful as he has ever been. In the final analysis, Jacob's desperate petition to be rescued from Esau seems based entirely on an appeal to YHWH's presumably unconditional promises, not on any expression of regret for the way he wronged his brother (see Gen. 28:15).

At this point, Jacob pulls out all the stops to avert the disaster he sees coming with Esau's approach. He arranges for a lavish present of livestock to be offered to Esau: the number of animals involved is nothing short of staggering (Gen. 32:14-15[Heb. 15-16]). This is no house-warming gift but a shameless bribe of an overwhelming and presumably (in Jacob's mind) irresistible amount. Jacob obviously is convinced that any gift this magnificent will be all but impossible to refuse. After all, everyone has his price. But the reader does not have to guess at Jacob's motives in arranging for this present, because we are invited by the storyteller into Jacob's mind: "For he thought, 'I will cover his face [i.e., appease him] with the present advancing before me; thus, afterwards when I see his face perhaps he will lift up my face [i.e., forgive or accept me]'" (Gen. 32:20[Heb. 21]).

What Jacob does next is not parallel to the other actions he has taken preparing for Esau's arrival, because in this instance he does not initiate the action. Instead, when he is alone for the first time since he fled his brother in the first place, a "man" appears out of nowhere and engages Jacob in a wrestling match. Still, this mysterious event serves as the culmination of Jacob's just-concluded preparations to meet Esau. For that matter, this strange incident is the culmination of Jacob's entire life up to this point: this unnamed man seems to symbolize every person with whom Jacob has ever struggled — Esau, Isaac, or Laban. More than that, Jacob's wrestling evokes not only his conflicts with other people but with God as well, for the "man" at the beginning of this puzzling episode is almost surely God at the end of it, as the ineffability of the divine name and Jacob's recognition of the divine face suggest. This most peculiar encounter blends Jacob's "wrestling" with people and God into a single event. In any case, after this final, enigmatic episode, Jacob can no longer avoid coming face to face with his long-estranged and, we may assume, long-seething and still-outraged sibling.

At the very beginning of the tension-filled encounter between the twins, the prophecy that Jacob was to be lord and master over Esau is reversed, at least temporarily (Gen. 33:3, 6-7). Perhaps the most poignant way this reversal is illustrated is when Jacob bows low in anticipation of a reunion whose outcome he hopes will be benign but fears may be catastrophic (see Gen. 32:11, 20[Heb. 12, 21]). At last, the dramatic tension that has been building ever since Jacob heard that Esau was heading toward him with the four hundred men reaches the breaking point. However, instead of leading up to an explosive confrontation, Esau's actions as he approaches his brother let us know immediately that this reunion will not only be peaceful but conciliatory and constructive. Four verbs occurring in succession with Esau as the subject make this abundantly clear: "Esau *ran* to meet him, *embraced* him, *fell* on his neck, and *kissed* him" (Gen. 33:4). A fifth verb in the series, this time with Jacob and Esau as joint subjects, puts an exclamation mark on this moving and unexpected scene: "They wept" (Gen. 33:4). We will recall that the last time Esau wept, he wept alone out of the disappointment of losing his blessing to his brother's trickery (Gen. 27:38).*

A great deal is revealed about Esau in this astonishing encounter. For one thing, we discover that he has completely forsworn revenge: he comports himself as a brother, not as an avenging enemy who would stop at nothing to even the score. The text offers no explanation for this change of heart, but there is every indication that Esau is completely sincere. We also learn that Esau himself has become quite wealthy in the time he has been separated from Jacob, while the latter was with Uncle Laban. This is first hinted at when Jacob's messengers report that four hundred men are with Esau; only a man of significant means could afford to have so many at his disposal or in his employ. More significantly, Esau's response to Jacob's offer of the enormous gift of animals calls attention to his impressive holdings: "I have plenty, my brother; keep what you have for yourself" (Gen. 33:8-9). Naturally, when we hear of Esau's impressive wealth, we remember Isaac's pronouncement that Esau would at least have a prosperous future (Gen. 27:39). Later on in the story we discover that Esau's vast wealth is the reason he is moving to Seir, since the land that he and Jacob previously occupied could not support the two brothers' accumulated wealth.

However, what is surely most important and revealing about Esau in this reunion scene is his extraordinary graciousness. His refusal of the gift — which, we must keep in mind, was actually a bribe — gives concrete expression to his unconditional acceptance of Jacob. The elder brother does not so much as ask for an apology from the younger brother who has so callously and outrageously cheated him. Jacob's own reaction to Esau's refusal of the gift provides a most fitting commentary on the exchange: "No, please, if I have found favor in your eyes [i.e., have been regarded graciously by you], then take the gift from my hand, for truly seeing your face is the same as seeing God's face, because you have treated me so favorably" (Gen. 33:10). Fittingly, in the early part of Rebekah's story, where we are informed that the children are struggling in their mother's womb (Gen. 25:22), the Hebrew word for "struggle" contains the three root consonants

---

*Jacob wept one other time in the story, when he met Rachel for the first time (Gen. 29:11).

rṣṣ. Now, when Jacob describes for himself how graciously Esau is acting, he uses a Hebrew word with the consonants *rṣh.* This is a play on words, since the two words have two of three consonants in common. It is a way of emphasizing that the twins' relationship that began with "struggle" concludes with "grace."

In an amazing turnabout, Jacob, the recipient of God's elective grace and thus the one destined to bear the ancestral promise into the future, begins to understand the very essence of that divine grace by experiencing the munificent forgiveness and generosity of Esau, the very one whom God has bypassed (even despised) — at least in terms of the coveted ancestral promise. Furthermore, it should not escape our attention that, in this reunion with Esau, Jacob has for the second time seen, by his own admission, the "face of God." The first time was in the wrestling match with the "man" who turns out mysteriously and inexplicably to be God (Gen. 32:22-32[Heb. 23-33]). The second time is in this encounter with a brother from whom Jacob has rightfully expected only animosity and aggression but instead has received abounding and amazing grace.

Though Esau is so magnanimous in this scene that he expects no compensation and turns down Jacob's proffered gift/bribe, in the end he gets a most surprising reward. With only one exception, every reference to Jacob's gift in chapters 32–33 uses the Hebrew word *minḥāh.* This is a common word meaning simply "present" or "gift." The one exception is right after Jacob responds to Esau's refusal of the gift — "I have enough my brother, keep what you have for yourself" (Gen. 33:9) — by imploring his brother to reconsider and accept what he has offered: "If now I have found favor [i.e., 'grace'] in your eyes, take my gift *[minḥāh]* from my hand, for my seeing your face is like seeing God's face, because with such graciousness you have received me" (Gen. 33:10). Jacob's final effort at persuading his reluctant brother involves a stunning change of vocabulary: at this point he offers Esau something more than a "gift"; he offers him "my blessing" (Gen. 33:11: *birkātî*). In effect, Jacob now symbolically returns to Esau the very blessing he previously stole. To be sure, this exchange will not alter God's elective plan for the twins, but it serves to relativize and contextualize Jacob's crooked machinations in gaining the upper hand over Esau. This move accents Jacob's ascendancy as an act of sheer grace — for all the human efforts involved were completely suspect and patently immoral — and also illuminates the fact that Esau's future is itself a function of Providence.

There is another strange twist to this scene that requires comment. Thinking back to what Isaac said to Esau that fateful day when his brother maneuvered to acquire the primary blessing for himself, we remember the father's statement that Esau would live by his sword and one day break Jacob's yoke from his neck. This vocabulary certainly evokes thoughts of physical violence. At the same time, while the repetition of the word "neck" in the reunion scene seems to allude to Isaac's prophecy and the potential for its being fulfilled, the manner of fulfillment is not quite what the language leads us to expect. Esau does not use a sword to remove Jacob's yoke, even though Jacob fears that his brother and his four hundred men are undoubtedly armed to the teeth. Instead, with a gesture that is the very antithesis of violence and can only be described as an act of blithe acceptance and reconciliation, Esau falls compassionately on his brother's neck, embracing and kissing him (Gen. 33:4). And that is how Esau frees himself. Forgiveness, not the sword, is his preferred "weapon" in his dealings with his brother. This is why it's entirely appropriate that Jacob view his brother's remarkable display as comparable to divine grace. Jacob could find no better way of expressing himself in this moment than to acknowledge that seeing Esau's face is tantamount to seeing God's face.

However, as impressive as the reunion between these two previously estranged brothers is, there remains a nagging sense that something is missing. In light of the fact that Jacob and his Uncle Laban finally settled their differences over a meal (Gen. 31:44, 46), might we not expect the two brothers to dine together as a conciliatory gesture? Does this failure to break bread together hint at unresolved issues in the reconciliation? What happens next may suggest the answer to that potentially disturbing question. Jacob is reluctant to follow his brother to Seir, even though Esau offers assistance and, tacitly, hospitality in this his home territory. Jacob certainly gives the impression that he and his company will join Esau there in a little while, allowing only for the slower pace required by nursing animals and easily fatigued small children. At this point, we actually look forward to the brothers once more living in proximity, where their new relationship can be nurtured and strengthened.

But Jacob does not follow through with that plan and makes no move to head toward Esau's territory (Gen. 33:12-17), in spite of the impression he has left with Esau. Instead, he buys land from Hamor the Shechemite. Jacob prefers this to settling down with Esau or even being close to his brother's home (Gen. 33:18-20; cf. 34:1-31). Granted, this move makes good sense from the perspective of the story's direction. Still, at this juncture there is no hint of nobility or awareness of an ultimate providential purpose on Jacob's part. Are we to gather from this that Jacob does not quite trust Esau to continue in the gracious mode he exhibited at their reunion? Is it true that Jacob has perhaps begun to understand the nature of God's grace on the basis of his brother's forgiving posture, but that comprehending fully the property of such radical grace will be some time in coming?

However we answer such questions, the brothers get together only one more time in the course of the narrative, when they bury their aged father (Gen. 35:27-29). When the two men get together at their father's funeral, one can't help but remember Esau's previous determination to kill Jacob as soon as the mourning period for Isaac has passed (Gen. 27:41). But a gracious Esau has long since moved beyond that threat. Whether Jacob has by now fully grasped graciousness of this magnitude is less than clear, despite the fact that he, by his own admission, saw God's face in his brother's face.

Esau: blessed and a blessing

The very last part of this story is designed to put in perspective the proper relationship between Jacob and Esau. If we step back and take a look at the overall narrative, we discover that the saga begins with a genealogy (Gen. 25:12-18) and concludes with one (Gen. 36:1-5). The former is the genealogy of Ishmael, Abraham's son by Sarah's maidservant Hagar (Genesis 16); the latter is the genealogy of Esau. While we modern readers are not enamored of biblical genealogies — does any part of the Bible have a worse reputation? — they often function in strategic ways. In this case, both of these genealogies feature sons who end up outside of God's elective purposes for Israel's future. Consequently, the main story, bracketed as it is by the genealogies of Ishmael and Esau, underscores that Jacob alone is the bearer of the ancestral promise. Nevertheless, Ishmael and Esau are still destined to enjoy excellent futures despite the fact that they do not fit into God's primary plans for Israel. In Esau's case, his claim on the future derives from his father's pronouncements after he bestows the primary blessing on Jacob (Gen. 27:39-40). As we have seen, by the time of his reunion with Jacob, he has already become wealthy, thus fulfilling one feature of the paternal blessing.

But Esau's "blessed" future includes more than wealth. In addition to wealth, and possibly more significant than wealth, Esau also becomes a country: Edom. As though we are inclined to forget, Genesis 36 says it three times: "Esau is Edom" (vv. 1, 8, 19). These assertions make explicit what is only implicit in the twins' birth story, where we recall that Esau is associated with "Edom" and "Seir" with puns about his complexion and hairiness (Gen. 25:25, 30). Now, however, Esau's connection with Edom and Seir is abundantly clear. Add to this the fact that Esau is now referred to as the ancestor of the country Edom (Gen. 36:9, 43). Is there any lingering question that, in the biblical rendering, Esau's future is much more positive than the impression we get from the "negative press" he has typically received?

The story even goes so far as to emphasize that Esau/Edom had kings before Jacob/Israel did (Gen. 36:31; see 1 Chron. 1:43). Even though God expressly promised that kings would issue from Jacob (Gen. 35:11; see also 17:6 [Abraham], 16 [Sarah]), Esau's country Edom ends up boasting of kings first, despite the fact that Esau has never received such a promise. And even though the Bible is ambivalent on the subject of kings and kingship in many passages (e.g., 1 Samuel 8), the concept of kings was generally viewed as a positive feature in the ancestral texts (see Gen. 49:10; Deut. 17:14-20). Thus YHWH's mentioning that there were to be kings in Israel's future should surely be seen as an enrichment of the overall promise. That Esau/Edom gets to enjoy this benefit before Israel will once again highlight the fact that there is much that is positive about Esau's life and future that is not negated by his failure to be the coveted bearer of God's promise.

Furthermore, the story doesn't allow us to forget for a moment that Esau's future is no less a function of divine providence than Jacob's future is, though obviously directed toward different ends. According to Deuteronomy, Esau/Edom's nation and territorial holdings are an explicit function of God's provision. Israel is expressly forbidden to confiscate any of Edom's land, precisely because YHWH is the one who bequeaths it (Deut. 2:5, 12, 22). As a matter of fact, there is a striking similarity of vocabulary when the text describes Jacob/Israel's and Esau/Edom's providential fortunes. Esau/Edom's land is a "possession" that YHWH "gave" (v. 5). Also, Esau/Edom experiences its own version of a "conquest" of its "promised land," which includes dispossessing the previous inhabitants (v. 12). This parallel between Jacob/Israel's and Esau/Edom's respective conquests is explicitly noted (v. 12). Furthermore, a similar emphasis is found in Joshua 24:4, where Joshua asserts that Esau received his territory from God, while

Jacob and his children had to postpone their reception of the land by first diverting to Egypt.

In the end, of course, nothing can compensate Esau for missing out on being the bearer of the ancestral promise. Had the "natural" order of things been allowed to unfold, Esau would naturally have been the insider who bore the chosen people's promise into the future for the benefit of "all the families of the earth" (Gen. 12:3). But as a result of YHWH's inscrutable will, Esau becomes an outsider, with the prime insider role reserved for Jacob. Nonetheless, despite this outsider status, Esau is blessed with excellent prospects for the future: progeny, prosperity, land, statehood, and kings. Most importantly, his outsider status does not prevent him from expressing the gracious magnanimity that serves as the impetus for reconciliation with the brother he once despised and vowed to murder. Indeed, Esau's "amazing grace" provides the means whereby the insider Jacob begins to comprehend the divine grace ultimately responsible for his role in God's salvific plan for the whole world.

By blood, and eventually by deportment, Esau and those descended from him were to have a special relationship with God's chosen people. This is codified in Deuteronomy: "You shall not abhor an Edomite, for he is your brother" (23:7[Heb. 8]). Highly negative assessments of Esau/Edom will still appear in later biblical texts, but they should not be allowed to cloud the positive evaluations that are demonstrated in the strategic story in Genesis.

It follows from the above analysis of the story that we should resist the temptation to view Jacob and Esau as one-dimensional characters who are "good" and "bad" respectively. A closer look at the narrative reveals that Jacob is less than elected, blessed, favored, and righteous; conversely, it makes clear that Esau is more than rejected, cursed, disadvantaged, and evil. In acknowledging the strategic importance of Jacob's ultimate election to fulfill the salvific role YHWH has in mind for all humanity, we should not lose sight of the fact that Esau's future is enviable in many ways and that his gracious behavior turns out to be exemplary. Though an outsider in terms of divine purpose and election, Esau displays as much grace as any Israelite insider ever did.

Our reaction to the way the people of Edom are so unmercifully vilified in the prophetic texts surely needs to be balanced by the compelling depiction of Esau in Genesis. After all, Esau does not permit his life's circumstances to keep him from expressing uncommon grace toward the very brother who has so thoroughly wronged him. Why, then, do the later prophets so unrelentingly condemn Edom? Many have suggested that there is a simple correlation between biblical texts that treat Esau positively and periods of amicable national relationships between Israel and Edom; on the other hand, negative texts are correlated to times when there were presumably tensions between the two countries. This is certainly a possible explanation, but is it convincing? At the very least, one difficulty with this approach is that the historical record is so spotty. Another problem is that nothing in the historical record adequately explains how Edom attained such a distinct "most hated nation" status. In strictly historical terms, what justifies Edom's becoming the archetypal Israelite enemy in so many prophetic passages? One can more readily understand other countries attaining that dubious honor, countries such as Egypt, Assyria, Babylon, or even Syria. What accounts for a historical bit player such as Edom becoming part of this biblical "axis of evil"? In my judgment, most of the standard historical explanations do not satisfactorily answer this question.

Rather than trying to explain the Bible's attitude toward Edom on the basis of ancient Near Eastern *Realpolitik* (which is in any case all but lost to us), I have proposed in this chapter that Esau/Edom is presented in the biblical material in the light of two salient factors: 1) Esau is, after all, Jacob's brother, and any tension between Esau/Edom and Jacob/Israel is, at the end of the day, a "family affair"; 2) the way the story of Esau/Edom is told in its relationship to Jacob/Israel has the effect of relegating any primarily historical considerations into the "deep background," while bringing to the fore prominent theological perspectives. Regarding Esau's fraternal relationship to Jacob, we have seen that early on in the story the elder brother is portrayed in most unflattering terms. Nonetheless, before he finally fades from the scene, Esau not only acts in an unselfish and conciliatory manner toward Jacob, but is so gracious that his brother confesses to seeing God's face in his face (Gen. 33:10). Is there any more brotherly behavior in the whole Bible? Without question, what makes Esau's brotherly love toward Jacob so remarkable is the awful fate he suffered because of his brother's deceit. Given Esau's model behavior in this compelling account, there surely is no reason not to expect that Edom's posture toward Israel would always be similarly gracious. Should not the memory of Esau's running toward Jacob, falling on his neck, kissing him, and weeping with him, always inform Edom's posture toward Israel and vice versa? In short, despite Esau's being forced to become an outsider from the point of view of God's providence and election, he has insisted on being brotherly. Is there

31

any reason why the country that later bears his name should not pattern it-self after its exemplary ancestor?

This question is obviously rhetorical, and perhaps that's the rub. When Edom is later perceived to have departed significantly from the gracious footsteps of its eponymous ancestor Esau, it is all but predictable that this will elicit the most negative of responses from Jacob/Israel's descendants. It is bad enough to deal with any pernicious enemy who seeks or delights in one's downfall; it is beyond the pale when that enemy is a brother, especially one who once displayed incomparable fraternal love and lavish grace. Quite simply, the nation of Edom, as depicted in the biblical stories, did not follow in the footsteps of Esau the man. The later prophetic condemnations of Edom, therefore, are a function of an appalling (from Israel's point of view) transition from a most gracious brotherhood to a most malignant sibling rivalry expressed at the national level. Again, from the biblical standpoint, this egregious shift is blamed not on "politics" but on religion. It is as though Edom no longer honors the gracious fraternity with which Esau so long ago honored Jacob, and has turned its back on its brother.

Indeed, one of the prophetic texts that so bitterly condemns Edom expresses its disappointment precisely in these terms. In the prophetic Book of Obadiah, Edom is subjected to a scathing denunciation for looking the other way as Israel was being attacked. Again, it is one thing for just another country to do that, but it is quite another when that country is a "brother." Obadiah says:

> For the violence done *to your brother* Jacob,
>   shame shall cover you,
>   and you shall be cut off for ever.
> On the day that you stood aloof,
>   on the day that strangers carried off his [i.e., Israel's] wealth,
> and foreigners entered his gates and cast lots for Jerusalem,
>   you were like one of them.
> But you should not have gloated over the day *of your brother*
>   in the day of his misfortune;
> you should not have rejoiced over the people of Judah
>   in the day of their ruin;
> you should not have boasted in the day of distress.
>
> (vv. 10-12 [RSV]; emphasis mine)

In summary, as I believe the biblical story makes clear, theological perspectives predominate in the depiction of Esau in Genesis. At first, it appears that the choice YHWH reveals to Rebekah (Gen. 25:23) is justified by Esau's being so unbelievably rash, crude, stupid, and shortsighted. These characteristics make it rather easy for him to be taken advantage of by his exploitative brother and scheming mother. Thus, early on in the narrative, one gets the first impression that Esau, though an insider by birth, actually deserves to become an outsider; little commends him to us. Yet, in the end, Esau utterly surprises us by acting exactly the way one would have supposed the ancestor of God's "chosen people" should have acted: with acceptance, forgiveness, and graciousness.

We recall that right off the bat Jacob is identified as "upright"/*tām* (Gen. 25:27), but his actions do not correspond to such a lofty characterization, at least not until Genesis 35 (where he is featured as a kind of religious reformer). Granted, Esau is never referred to as "upright"/*tām*, but he in fact comports himself in such a morally exemplary manner that characterizing him with such a lofty term seems almost natural — emphatically by Jacob's own testimony (Gen. 33:10). Had personal merit been the criterion for being selected as bearer of God's promise to bless the world — which, of course, it wasn't — Esau could have held his own with Jacob.*

There seems to be no way to escape the conclusion that Esau's transition from an insider to an outsider is completely a function of divine choice and human complicity that he was powerless to change. This meant that at best he could only be Jacob/Israel's brother and never the bearer of the glorious ancestral promise. Nevertheless, this person who could not prevent his becoming an outsider — for reasons that remain as inscrutable as God's initial election of Abraham and Sarah — acted in a way that would have made any insider justifiably proud. At the moment of crisis, when Esau might have vented a vengeful rage against the brother who had so terribly wronged him, he instead accepted that brother unconditionally. Nothing that had been done to him — by his brother, his mother, his father, or his God — kept him from finally acting in a remarkably gracious way. By Jacob's own admission, Esau's behavior made it possible for him to glimpse the "face of God." We should never lose sight of the fact that the possibility of seeing God's gracious face in the gracious actions of a forgiv-

---

*The Apostle Paul makes this point in Romans 9:10-13.

ing, accepting human being was the purpose God had in mind for the chosen insider community in the first place. How wonderfully ironic and reflective of God's "amazing grace" that Jacob the insider saw God's face so clearly in the face of his outsider brother Esau.

CHAPTER 2

Tamar's Resolve, Judah's Family, Israel's Future

We saw in Chapter 1 that Esau ended up being an outsider not because he was unrelated to the family of promise but because he was not elected to be the bearer of that promise. In point of fact, if family connections had been the sole issue, Esau would easily have had top billing as an insider: he was, after all, the firstborn of Isaac and Rebekah, who were both themselves primary recipients and bearers of the insider promise. Unfortunately for Esau, a combination of the inscrutable will of God and the machinations of his brother and mother robbed him of his natural privileged position within the family, at least in terms of the divine promise.

When we move from Esau's story to the Judah and Tamar story (Genesis 38), however, we discover a very different kind of outsider. Right away we are struck by the curious juxtaposition of one of the most famous biblical characters, namely Judah, and one of the most obscure, namely Tamar. Not only that, the story that shows their two lives coming together is hardly a mainstream biblical episode. Genesis 38 is usually left out of lectionaries, almost never used as the text for a sermon, and is studiously avoided in Sunday school. Given the story's depiction of an extremely bizarre custom regarding a widowed sister-in-law, plus some indelicate, almost salacious sexual details, this is scarcely surprising. Indeed, on reading Genesis 38, one might call to mind the old quip, "If the Bible were read in Boston, it would be banned!" We might emphasize how strange this account truly is by noting that it has been neglected in spite of being situated in the middle of one of the Bible's most familiar and endearing narratives — the story of Joseph and his brothers.

Even though Genesis 38 has been virtually ignored, I hope to show in this chapter that it is not only an integral part of the Joseph story but an excellent outsider story as well. Still, Tamar is not an outsider on the order of Esau: not only is she completely unrelated to the ancestral family of promise, she belongs to one of those groups whom the chosen family was supposed to go to great lengths to avoid — at least in terms of familial relationships. The ancestral narratives take great pains to emphasize the importance of marrying within the extended family. Abraham tried to ensure that his son Isaac married a close relative (Genesis 24). Likewise, Jacob was dispatched to his mother's kinfolk so that he could find a wife (or wives) among his relatives (Gen. 28:1 — 30:43). In both situations, Abraham and Isaac respectively stressed the importance of their sons' not marrying outsiders, especially Canaanite outsiders (Gen. 24:3; 28:1; cf. 26:34-35; 27:46). Thus it was all but unimaginable to think that a foreign woman of Tamar's ilk could have had such a decisive impact on the very family YHWH had chosen to be the vehicle for blessing the world. There's no getting around the fact that Tamar represented those who were never to be allowed into the familial fold.

However, despite her pronounced outsider status, Tamar had a dramatic effect on the direction in which one prominent member of the elect family was headed. But her actions had an impact on more than this single member with whom she was most immediately involved. Indeed, she ended up preserving the whole family's future and thus managed to keep its divine mission intact.

Tamar is only one of the outsiders who surround Judah in this episode. He befriends an Adullamite named Hirah and marries an unnamed woman whose father is the Canaanite Shua (Gen. 38:1-2). We are never told what is going on in Judah's mind when he decides to take a Canaanite woman as his wife; but he is clearly violating the family norms for marriage when he does so, at least as those norms are represented in the narratives leading up to this point. Later on, the rules for marrying within the family (mainly for religious reasons) would be codified in Israelite law; but at this juncture the nonexistence of such a law is no excuse for Judah's violating the mandate. Both Abraham and Isaac, of course, had been adamant about their offspring marrying within the family (Gen. 24:3; 28:1). But Judah obviously sees things differently. It is one thing to hobnob with folks outside the family. But Judah goes beyond hobnobbing: his interactions are not simply economic or social, but are personal — highly personal.

They seem to have been casual as well, for there is not the slightest degree of anguish indicated in the narrative when Judah marries a Canaanite woman "at first sight." In the space of a single sentence (and only two verbs) Judah "sees" and "marries" a Canaanite woman as though the two actions are one. Judah has met three outsiders and married one of them before the main outsider in the story, Tamar, has even set foot on the narrative stage.

Though she is late in appearing, we find out that Tamar actually has the leading role soon after she shows up. At the very least, she is co-protagonist with Judah in the episode (though Judah could also be seen as the antagonist of the story), for it cannot be denied that he initiates the action(s) to which she eventually responds. Still, her responses are not of the passive kind; instead, they are very active responses, tied as they are to calculated risks, bold counter-moves, and anticipations of Judah's likely reactions. This woman is no bit player.

From one vantage point, the prominence of the outsider motif in Genesis 38 should not be so surprising in light of the Joseph story that surrounds it. Whatever else may be said about the famous account in Genesis 37–50, outsiders are found throughout. Ishmaelites, Midianites, and, of course, Egyptians have decisive parts in the Joseph drama (Gen. 37:25, 28, 36). Curiously, for a long time scholars saw virtually no relationship between Genesis 38 and its surrounding context, so the twin outsider motifs went unnoticed. More recently, however, scholars have observed not only linguistic links between Genesis 38 and the Joseph story but thematic ones as well. While these are welcome new insights, the role of the outsiders in these tandem stories has not been given due emphasis. As I hope to demonstrate, outsiders are a major theme in both narratives.

Failure to appreciate the outsider theme in Genesis 37–50 may explain partially why the importance of Genesis 38 was missed until very recently, or at least relegated to narrow interests that did not appreciate the story's strategic importance. Some mention the chapter only in passing as an "interruption" of the Joseph account. Others have attempted to mine the chapter for details concerning the strange custom of a brother-in-law being required to impregnate a widowed sister-in-law, which is called "levirate marriage." Still other researchers have been interested in the extent to which Genesis 38 provides information about the tribal history of Judah. Finally, those investigating Genesis 38 from the newer literary and sociological perspectives have tended to view this chapter as reflecting complex cultural dynamics, especially those that reveal the difficult and arduous role of women in a patriarchal society. In this last view, Tamar's efforts are to be understood in the context of a woman asserting herself and her rights in a misogynist social setting where her only resources are a resolute will along with clever and subversive tactics geared toward getting what is rightfully hers.

Analyzing Genesis 38 from these angles has certainly yielded a number of helpful insights. Nevertheless, I will argue that the primary value of Genesis 38 in its present biblical context has to do with the story's placement in the ancestral stories in general, and in the story of Jacob the ancestor in particular (see Gen. 37:2). The Jacob/Joseph and Judah/Tamar stories are equally crucial even though they are not given equal narrative space. More to the point, I maintain that the outsider motif is the most helpful rubric for comprehending an important aspect of the theological thrust of this segment of the ancestral narratives, though that rubric is explicit in the Judah/Tamar account while only implicit in the Jacob/Joseph account.

Judah leaves his brothers

The Judah-Tamar story begins "at that time" when Judah "went down from his brothers" (Gen. 38:1). Several crucial temporal aspects are suggested by what appears at first glance to be simple background phrasing. One is that the chapter is situated between the period when Judah was complicit in his younger brother Joseph's being sold into slavery (Genesis 37) and his subsequent trip with his brothers to Egypt, where they encounter Joseph after he has become a powerful public official (Genesis 42ff.). Another is that in this temporal sequence the fortunes of the family of promise are dramatically altered by what happens when two of Jacob's sons "went down" after leaving the family. Judah "went down" (Hebrew root *yrd*) from his brothers (Gen. 38:1); his departure from the family was voluntary. Conversely, Joseph is "taken down" (Hebrew root *yrd*) to Egypt (Gen. 39:1); his departure is obviously involuntary, a result of fraternal rivalry and premeditated cruelty. A third aspect is that the fortunes of both brothers, while they are absent from the family, is determined in large part by the outsiders they encounter on the way. "At that time" is, therefore, a phrase signaling that Judah's and Joseph's futures at this point are developing along parallel lines. This is one of the reasons why the two stories should be read together.

Away from his brothers, Judah immediately engages outsiders: he encamps with a certain Hirah (Gen. 38:1), an Adullamite. It is less important to know precisely what an "Adullamite" is ethnically than to remember that such a person is clearly outside Judah's family. Almost simultaneously, Judah sees the daughter of Shua, a Canaanite man (38:2); Shua is significant not only as the second outsider Judah encounters but also because he immediately becomes Judah's father-in-law. Thus, in the blink of a narrative eye, Judah is at once entangled with three outsiders: Hirah the Adullamite, Shua the Canaanite, and Shua's daughter — also obviously a Canaanite.

As though to emphasize the degree and speed of Judah's engagement with these outsiders, three sequential verbs occur in rapid succession: "he saw . . . took . . . and went in to her. . . ." Judah moves ever so quickly from observation to matrimony, from neighborly contact to intimate involvement with an outsider group. His marriage to an outsider, as we have seen above, is in stark contrast to two previous accounts of marriage among the ancestors. Both Abraham and Isaac have harped on the importance of their sons not marrying outsiders, specifically Canaanites (Genesis 24:3; 28:1; cf. 26:34-35; 27:46). This is what makes Judah's actions so startling. He does not show an ounce of the concern that Abraham and Isaac have shown in the significant matter of marriage outside the extended family. To make matters worse, his new wife belongs to the very group that his grandfather (Isaac) and great-grandfather (Abraham) have explicitly said was to be most assiduously avoided. If Judah's marriage to the Canaanite's daughter is the first hint of something gone awry while Judah has been away from his brothers, the fact that she is unnamed — and remains unnamed — is perhaps the first indication of a misogynist overtone in the narrative. Indeed, the succession of verbs leading to Judah's marriage ("saw . . . took . . . went in to . . ."), in which Judah is the subject of all the verbs and his wife the object, adds to this flavor of misogyny, especially since the reader never does learn his wife's name.

Once they are married, Judah's wife bears three sons in quick "grammatical" succession, and the way each of these children is named is instructive. At the first son's birth, we read, "He named him Er" (38:3); without question, the "he" is Judah, that is, the father names his firstborn son. But Judah's wife does the honors when the next son is born: "She named him Onan" (38:4). And she names the third son as well: "She named him Shelah" (38:5). At one level, this pattern is unremarkable, for in the Bible both mothers and fathers name children (for example, Gen. 21:3 [fathers]; 29:32, 33, 35; 30:11, 13 [mothers]). But two details are noteworthy in this case. One is the fact that Judah names the first son, his wife the next two. Is this mere happenstance or is something else suggested by the pattern? Is this a subtle hint that Judah is beginning to distance himself from his family ever so slightly? Is he interested only in his firstborn? How one answers these questions may be suggested by a second detail in the naming pattern.

A literal translation of the text on the occasion of the third child's birth is as follows: "Yet once again she bore a child; she named him Shelah. He was in Chezib when she bore him" (38:5). The first part in the naming sequence is straightforward: the mother obviously has done the naming. But the second part is problematic, since it is not clear who the "he" in Chezib is. Given the ambiguity, some translations (e.g., the RSV and NRSV) follow the Greek Old Testament (called the Septuagint and abbreviated with the Roman numerals LXX) and render the phrase as, "She was in Chezib when she bore him." Phrasing it that way places Judah's wife in a certain town at the time of the birth of the third child. But why would we need to know where the mother is for the birth of the third child when we have been given no such information about the first two? The issue is even more complicated than that. Adopting the Greek reading presents a problem, for this version says, "She was in Chezib when she bore *them*." Thus, the mother was in Chezib for the birth of all three babies, not just for the third one. Not only is the Greek perfectly consistent on this score, but the naming pattern is not the same as in the Hebrew in any case, because in Greek there is no way to tell whether the mother or father is doing the naming: the verb *(ekalēsen)* can mean either "he named" or "she named." The point I want to make is that the Greek version and the Hebrew version are both just fine, so that it is a mistake to conflate them.

In fact, if we take the Hebrew at face value, it pictures Judah becoming more and more distant from his family, something that is reflected elsewhere in the story. The fact that he names only the first child while his wife names the next two is not sufficient by itself to demonstrate that; but if Judah *is* the person in Chezib when the third child is born, that is another matter entirely. It is true that it is grammatically possible that the pronoun refers to the baby. But would not such a statement be absurdly redundant? Why would we need to be told that the baby was with his mother at the time of birth? Newborns are always where their mothers are upon delivery. Thus the narrative tells us that it was Judah who is in Chezib when his wife delivers the third child, Shelah. If this is so, the sequence runs as follows: Judah names the first son (Er); the mother names the second (Onan); the mother names the third (Shelah), and Judah is not even in town when the last baby is born.

Perhaps the best argument that Judah's being out of town at such an important time in his family's life represents his blithe lack of interest is the name of the town itself. The town Chezib is derived from a Hebrew root *(kzb)* that denotes deception or falsehood. Later in the narrative we will see that Judah is, without question, a deceptive man, which the name of the town cleverly foreshadows during this episode. So Judah is not only out of town when his third son comes into the world, he's in "Liarsville" at the time. Out here in the Pacific Northwest, there is an apt geographical name that evokes untrustworthiness: Deception Pass. That is the semantic equivalent of this place Chezib, which signals simultaneously Judah's distance from his family on the momentous occasion of a son's birth and something disturbing about Judah's character that the story will later confirm. There is no escaping the fact that a man who should be with his wife when Shelah comes into the world is most conspicuously absent by visiting a place with a most suspicious name. Judah is obviously no model family man. Given that his family just happens to be part of the larger "family of promise," Judah's posture and attitude are most worrisome.

Enter Tamar

In the compressed chronology of the story, just one verse after Judah's third son is born, his firstborn son is ready for marriage. Tamar appears on the scene for the first time, being the woman Judah "takes" as a wife for Er (38:6; see v. 2). But the marriage ends dramatically when Er is struck down by YHWH, in whose eyes he is wicked (38:7). In another clever linguistic ploy, the text may foreshadow this severe measure of YHWH in Er's very name. The consonants making up his name *('r)* are the exact reverse of the consonants making up the word "wicked" *(r')*. In any case, once Er's death has left Tamar a widow, levirate custom dictates that it is up to Er's brother Onan to perform the duty of a brother-in-law, which Judah exhorts his second-born son to do: "Approach your brother's wife and perform the duty of a brother-in-law for her, namely, raise up progeny for your brother " (38:8). Judah carefully refers to Tamar as "your brother's wife." Onan is not required to marry Tamar, only to impregnate her. Whatever we modern people may think of such a custom, its applicability to this situation is simply assumed by the narrative.

However, we are apparently not the only ones to find this custom distasteful. Onan is not happy about the situation either. He is quite aware that any offspring brought forth by his coupling with Tamar will not be his except in a biological sense, so he makes sure that his sister-in-law will not get pregnant by practicing *coitus interruptus* (38:9). We can sympathize with the man; yet, at the same time, his behavior seems rather less than a principled refusal to take part in a social custom he finds repugnant. After all, he could have forthrightly told his father that he was unwilling to carry out his obligation and then accept any consequences of his bold refusal. But he doesn't do that. Somehow, his disaffection with the brother-in-law custom is not so strong and principled that he avoids Tamar altogether. Onan does not want Tamar to have his child, but he is not above using her for his own sexual gratification. The cynical nature of Onan's transgression is underscored even more boldly if, as some contend (and the grammar does allow it), he has intercourse with Tamar not just once but regularly over an extended period. Onan's selfishness and willingness to satisfy himself at Tamar's expense add to the undercurrent of misogyny in the unfolding drama.

Like his brother Er before him (38:7), Onan has offended YHWH, and he loses his life (38:10). But this time the text declares up front the reason for the divine sanction: "What he did (that is, preventing Tamar from getting pregnant) was evil in YHWH's eyes. . . ." But the evil deed is more than a creative and illicit method of birth control. By withholding "seed" from Tamar, Onan is in effect squandering the family's future. The Hebrew word "seed" (*zera'*) may mean "seed," "semen," "offspring," or even "grain." In the setting of the ancestral narratives, more than anything else "seed" indicates future offspring without whom the divine promises are abrogated. Destroying "seed" in this context pits one against YHWH's agenda for the future, not only regarding Israel as the people of promise but regarding "all the families of the world" as well (Gen. 12:1-3).

It is interesting that, even though YHWH summarily eliminates Judah's first two sons, many interpreters have viewed the deity as essentially absent from this story. For example, Coats says, "No important theological observations can be made about YHWH, the God who kills levirate dodgers." On the contrary, I maintain that references to the reasons for the two brothers' deaths — they did evil in YHWH's eyes — requires the reader to keep YHWH in mind throughout. It's true that, but for those two instances of ultimate judgment, YHWH is not in public view, so to speak; but the fact that YHWH is directly responsible for the untimely demise of Er and Onan makes us aware that YHWH is "around," albeit in the background. Beginning with Genesis 37, YHWH's involvement is generally much more indirect than it was in Genesis 12–35. In the narrative featuring Joseph, YHWH operates more or less behind the scenes: thus God is "with" Joseph (Gen. 39:2, 3, 21), blesses what Joseph does or makes it successful (Gen. 39:5, 23), is seen to have been behind events after the fact (Gen. 41:25, 32), and is revealed through dreams (Gen. 40:8, 16; cf. 37:5-11). In the end, this mode of divine interaction hardly shows that God's providential hand is missing. Twice Joseph confesses that God's will is to be discerned in the mix of unfolding human actions (Gen. 45:7; 50:20). Likewise, YHWH's role in the deaths of Er and Onan in the Judah-Tamar story is scarcely incidental; it serves to remind the reader of a lurking providence.

In any event, in the wake of Onan's death, the brother-in-law custom means that it is now Shelah's turn to impregnate Tamar. Judah confirms this when he reminds Tamar that Shelah is too young to perform his duties; and so he orders Tamar to return to her father's house and stay there as a widow until Shelah becomes an adult (Gen. 38:11). But Judah is being dishonest: what really worries him is that his one remaining son will meet a fate similar to that of his first two sons. Even though Er and Onan died as a matter of divine judgment, Judah blames their deaths on Tamar. Once again the element of misogyny emerges. And if Judah's deceptive character is only hinted at in the reference to his presence in Chezib/"Liarsville" when his third child was born, all doubt is removed at this juncture in the story. The narrator leaves no doubt that Judah is lying through his teeth.

As for Tamar, she accepts her father-in-law's orders and goes home without a word of protest (v. 11). Presumably, she believes that her father-in-law is being straightforward with her. Why should she think otherwise? Though the narrative has been extremely economical, even cryptic, up to this point, we may reasonably infer that she has been a compliant wife, a receptive sister-in-law, and a dutiful daughter-in-law. There is not much else to say about Tamar's development as a character so far because her fate has been entirely in the hands of the male characters who surround her, and she has been completely amenable if not altogether passive. But that is about to change dramatically.

Judah's foolish dalliance

In yet another telescoped narrative time frame, Judah's wife dies (Gen. 38:12). The text does not indicate how much time passes between Tamar's return to her father's house and Judah's wife's death; but we do know that enough time has elapsed for Shelah to become an adult (38:14). Once Judah is finished grieving his wife's death, he and his friend Hirah the Adullamite travel to Timnah to check on the flocks at shearing time. Tamar somehow hears about Judah's journey (38:13) and springs into action. No longer the least bit passive, she positions herself so that she can orchestrate events.

First, she removes her widow's garments (38:14). Though our attention is focused on Tamar's change of demeanor as well as her clothes, we can't help noticing that she has been wearing mourning clothes all this time. At least formally and publicly, Tamar is still grieving. In contrast, Judah seems barely to have missed a day's work after his wife's death (38:12). Indeed, we are never told that Tamar has been comforted about the death of Er, only that Judah has been comforted about his wife's death. Having taken off her widow's clothing, Tamar veils herself before stationing herself at the entrance of Enaim, which is on the way to Timnah, Judah's destination. Her intentions are clear: she has realized that, with the passage of time, Shelah has long since grown up and Judah has not kept his promise to her — that she would be given to Judah's third son as his wife (Gen. 38:14). Soon the plot she is craftily hatching will come to light.

As planned, Tamar manages to make herself plainly visible — though she is disguised — to Judah on his way to Timnah. When he looks her way, the veil leads him to assume that she is a prostitute (38:15). With no hesitation whatsoever, indeed with transparent resolve, Judah propositions her (38:16). At this point we might ask what has led Tamar to conclude that her father-in-law will rise so readily to her bait. Are we to assume that Tamar figures males in general are easy marks for a prostitute's wiles, Judah being no exception? Or does she correctly guess, once she learns that Judah's wife has died, that he will be ready for sex the first chance he gets?* Or do the overtones of misogyny and careless family relationships found elsewhere

---

*Some scholars have posited that sheep-shearing was not only a time of work but a time of celebration in which alcoholic beverages would have flowed freely; and promiscuity may have been part of such a bacchanalian atmosphere.

in the story inform Tamar's intuition? That is, given the events surrounding her life, has Tamar gotten the insight that the men in this family would have no compunction about using a woman whenever they are presented with the opportunity?

Perhaps all three possibilities are pertinent to our reading of this episode. No man in this story is portrayed sympathetically; ironically, only Hirah the Adullamite and Shua the Canaanite are depicted at least neutrally. Shelah plays no active role: he is only acted *upon* in the account. But Judah, the main male character, is at best casual about his family and its future, if not utterly irresponsible about it. He bothers to name only his first son and is in "Liarsville" when the third is born. Moreover, because he has wrongly blamed Tamar for the deaths of Er and Onan, he callously neglects his own family's future by refusing to allow Shelah to perform the duty of a brother-in-law to Tamar. He jeopardizes the future of his family even further by tending only to economic matters after his wife's death. It's easy to see how a man with this history might be less than resolute in his resistance to the lures of a prostitute. When we contemplate Judah's blatant hypocrisy and double standard later in the story, our negative evaluation of him is sadly confirmed (38:24).

Other males in this story fare no better. Er is wicked and loses his life due to divine judgment, as does Onan, in his case because he refuses to perform his family obligation. The men who report Tamar's illegitimate pregnancy do so without any due process or deliberation (38:24). Just as the reader is able to discern this pattern of misogyny in both the background and the foreground as the drama unfolds, it is legitimate to conclude that Tamar's actions are a function of the same discernment. Indeed, Judah falls for Tamar's trap in a way that shows how accurately she has seen into his character and anticipated his behavior. Perhaps Tamar's risk is not a sure bet, but the odds are certainly stacked in her favor considering Judah's behavior throughout the progress of the story.

As the story moves forward, Judah's eagerness to have sex with the prostitute leads him to drop his guard and agree to a stupid and potentially disastrous arrangement. Whereas Tamar leaves the payment for services completely up to Judah — "What will you give me?" (38:16) — he carelessly leaves the matter of collateral up to her (38:17-18). How much smarter it would have been to let her name the price for the encounter while reserving to himself the choice of security items. Given Judah's extreme foolishness, nothing prevents Tamar from requesting his ring, cord, and staff — all personal items that would identify their owner beyond question. Agreeing without a whimper of protest, Judah unwittingly supplies Tamar with a foolproof way to identify the person with whom she is about to have sex. Her charade works perfectly: not only does she become pregnant in this single encounter, but she also knows that it will be all but impossible for Judah to deny his paternity when the matter becomes public. Further underscoring Judah's distance from his family — and especially his attitude toward women — is the fact that he manages to have sex with his daughter-in-law without recognizing her. Though she is veiled, surely her voice is recognizable. Apparently, Judah's strong sexual appetite has dulled all his other senses.* One further irony lies in the fact that Judah makes no effort to keep from impregnating the woman he thinks is a prostitute. On that score, he would have been better off had he imitated his son Onan.

After this sordid transaction, Tamar returns home and dresses in her mourning clothes once again (38:19). But Judah has a debt to pay; and, more importantly, he has to retrieve the personal effects that could blow his cover. So he sends his friend Hirah to find the prostitute so that he can make payment to her. Naturally, Hirah finds no woman at the entrance to Enaim (38:20), leading him to make inquiries about the prostitute's whereabouts. At this point, there is an intriguing change of vocabulary in the text. Recall that when Judah first sees the veiled Tamar, the text says that he takes her to be a prostitute (Hebrew *zônāh*, 38:15); the term might be rendered in English with several more or less parallel terms — hooker, whore, streetwalker, working girl, lady of the evening, and so forth, that is, an ordinary woman in the business of selling her body. But when Hirah makes his inquiries, he does not ask the townspeople if they have seen a *zônāh*; instead, he asks if they have seen a "cult prostitute" (Hebrew *qᵉdēšāh*). They respond that they know of no such person (38:21). This switching of terms is hardly accidental, since *qᵉdēšāh* refers to a woman who engages in sexual intercourse as a function of religious beliefs and formal fertililty ceremonies.

What explains Hirah's use of *qᵉdēšāh* instead of *zônāh* in this situation? One explanation may be that a *qᵉdēšāh*-prostitute is potentially a less offensive term than *zônāh*-prostitute; somehow, consorting with the former is not as reprehensible as being with the latter. A second and potentially

---

*Of course, this had also happened to Judah's father, Jacob. He spent his honeymoon night with a woman not his wife and did not realize the mistake until morning (Gen. 29:21-25).

more significant explanation may be that, from Hirah's perspective, having sex with a *qᵉdēšāh*-prostitute is not only not blameworthy but actually praiseworthy in that it shows religious commitment and participation in a religious rite. If this is true, it says that the narrator at this point means to emphasize the fact that Judah has become indistinguishable from the Canaanites/Adullamites whom he has befriended and in whose circles he now moves — at least from their point of view. Ironically, from a strictly Israelite standpoint, consorting with a *zônāh*-prostitute would have been less abominable than engaging a *qᵉdēšāh*-prostitute. To be sure, being with a *zônāh*-prostitute was a blatant violation of one of YHWH's commandments; nevertheless, this transgression did not necessarily negate one's relationship, however sinned against, with YHWH. But consorting with a *qᵉdēšāh*-prostitute was more than a sexual sin, for it presupposed a relationship with a deity other than YHWH: thus it was an act of worship directed toward another god.

The story reveals even more about Judah's character when Hirah returns with the news that he has been unable to locate the prostitute. Hirah uses the term *qᵉdēšāh*-prostitute in his report, with Judah making no effort to correct him (38:22). It is as though Judah, once he hears it, prefers Hirah's choice of terms and his "spin" on the situation, even though the narration leaves no doubt about Judah's initial assumption that the woman was indeed a *zônāh*-prostitute. The Canaanite flavoring of the *qᵉdēšāh*-prostitute designation does not seem to trouble Judah in the least; apparently he has become completely comfortable in this outsider environment.

Equally revealing is Judah's next move. Even though the woman with whom he has had the sexual encounter still holds the personal effects that can identify him, Judah decides to let the matter drop. She can keep the ring, signet, and staff (38:23), he says. What prompts Judah to drop the search? The text is clear: he is worried about being made a laughingstock. Judah is satisfied that he has made a good-faith effort to pay the woman what they had prearranged, so that continuing the search — which would no doubt necessitate more embarrassing questions of local townspeople — would surely only subject him to ridicule. He adamantly refuses to take that chance.

Judah's concern about coming off as ridiculous is decisive. That's because his concern for his reputation — among "outsiders," no less — has become pronounced. What is most interesting about Judah's posture here is that he expresses virtually no concern about the status of his family. Yet a brief review of family matters shows that their future is in extreme jeopardy: he has lost his wife and his first two sons, both of whom died childless; with his wife dead, Judah is unable to beget any more children, at least morally and legally; his family's only hope lies with Shelah and Tamar (whose coming together is mandated by the brother-in-law rule), but Judah has withheld Shelah, wrongly blaming Er's and Onan's deaths on Tamar rather than on YHWH. Given the social structures that define Judah's situation, the future of his family has run into a dead end. Presumably, Shelah cannot marry another woman as long as Tamar is alive and prepared to have a child by him (the story does not mention whether Judah has tried to figure out how to obtain a wife for Shelah). Likewise, Tamar is not free to remarry as long as one of her deceased husband's brothers remains available, as Shelah certainly is. Despite these serious threats to Judah's family's future, the only concern he expresses is for his public reputation. He utterly ignores the implications of not having a wife, and he expresses no misgivings about keeping his one remaining son and his daughter-in-law locked in their present social positions. Judah has simply failed to attend to his or his family's future. This has serious implications, of course, for Israel's future as the people of God as well. But Judah appears unmoved by or perhaps even unaware of that sobering reality.

Tamar's upper hand

Three months after the fateful encounter, the drama heads inexorably toward resolution when we learn that Tamar is pregnant. Just as previously "it was told" (Gen. 38:13) to Tamar that Judah was on his way to Timnah, so now "it was told" (38:24) to Judah that Tamar is with child. Both "tellings" precipitate major turning points in the story. At this juncture, for the very first time, an actual character in the narrative mentions Tamar by name; in fact, it now dawns on us that up until this point only the narrator has referred to her by name. It should not be lost on us that, the first time another character (as it happens, a male) uses Tamar's name, it is to accuse and condemn her. As a widow she has only one licit way to become pregnant, namely, by her one remaining brother-in-law. And since that option has been foreclosed by Judah's refusal to allow Shelah to perform his duty, Tamar's pregnancy is without question illegitimate. Indeed, when the report is made to Judah, the messenger specifies that she is pregnant because she has been a whore (Gen. 38:24; terms relating to being a *zônāh*-prostitute are used here). Thus Tamar's being named by another character in the drama constitutes no elevation of her status whatsoever. On the contrary, now that she has been finally named by another character, she finds herself immediately in mortal danger, and the misogynist flavor of this episode comes to the fore once again.

The misogyny becomes even more blatant in Judah's response to Tamar's condition. Regardless of the fact that he himself was with a *zônāh*-prostitute only three months ago, Judah summarily pronounces ultimate capital judgment: "Bring her out and let her be burned" (38:24). Could any action have illustrated a more egregious double standard than this one? Regardless of whether Judah is strictly within his legal rights to render such a grave decision outside a judicial proceeding, the fact remains that he rules with alacrity and without deliberation in Tamar's case. Had it not been for her clever planning in obtaining objects that would identify her "john," she would surely have been doomed.

But as she is being brought forward for swift, merciless execution, Tamar sees to it that Judah first receives the personal effects she secured from him as collateral for payment on their sexual encounter (see 38:17-18). Along with these damning items she sends a twofold message: the first part says simply that the man to whom these things belong is the man by whom she is pregnant; the second part of her announcement is an imperative: "Recognize now to whom these, namely, the ring, the cord, and the staff, belong" (38:25). Interpreters have suggested, correctly in my view, that the use of "recognize" here and in the scene where Jacob is shown Joseph's garment (37:33) is one of several linguistic markers that tie the two stories together (it is the same Hebrew word in both instances). Indeed, when Judah recognizes the objects, he has no choice but to admit that he is their rightful owner. He also immediately implicates himself and exonerates his daughter-in-law: "She is more righteous than I since I did not give her to Shelah my son" (38:26).

Generally, the phrase "she is more righteous than I" is taken in either an ethical/moral sense or a juridical one. In the ethical/moral sense, Judah's confession is tantamount to saying that Tamar is simply more morally upright than he is, despite her deceit and willingness to have sex with him. In the juridical sense, Judah's confession announces that, in the context of the legal status of his behavior vis-à-vis Tamar's, she is more likely

49

to be exonerated, and he is more likely to be indicted. Either of these interpretations is possible; perhaps it is best to allow both meanings to stand
side by side, since there is no reason to regard them as mutually exclusive.
If we view this episode from a moral perspective, Tamar's actions are the
more defensible; and even if we view it from a legal perspective, Tamar's
actions are the more defensible. Judah, the insider, has been bested in
moral and legal terms by Tamar, the outsider.

The emphasis of the story finally falls squarely on the family of promise and its future. Judah has put himself in a situation where his hold on
the future is tenuous in the extreme. His first two sons have died at
YHWH's hand and obviously cannot contribute to Judah's future. Judah
has withheld Shelah, his one remaining son, from Tamar due to an irrational fear that she has had something to do with the deaths of his first two.
When Judah's wife dies, his prospects for more family — and consequently
the future — have come to an absolute standstill. Nevertheless, in spite of
this dire circumstance, Judah's energies are directed to business concerns,
dalliance with a prostitute, and his reputation.

But Tamar does what she feels she has to do to secure her own — and
by extension, Judah's — future. When she finally deduces that Judah has
placed her in an impossible bind, she undertakes desperate measures.
Using deceit and cleverness, she manages to produce children, and at the
same time she ensures that she will be spared. Ironically, this Canaanite
woman, this marginalized outsider, has acted in such a way as to save Judah's family and future. Judah's actions have actually placed his future in
Tamar's hands, a circumstance to which she has responded with utterly determined resolve. Only later do we learn just how important this particular
future becomes: Judah's family is destined to be the source of Israel's kings
(Gen. 49:10).

Viewed in simple moralistic terms, Tamar's actions would lead us to
conclude that she is, in the final analysis, no better than Judah. Both have
much for which to answer. But viewed in theological terms, Tamar's willingness to go beyond social convention and even to risk her life results in
her creating the conditions where her own future, Judah's future, and even
Israel's future fit providentially into God's plan for getting the whole world
blessed. Whether Tamar was more self-serving than altruistic is less important than that her actions are oriented to the future, a future in which
YHWH is deeply invested. As was the case with Joseph, Tamar is used to
"preserve life" (Gen. 45:5). Likewise, regardless of what might have been

"meant for evil" in the story featuring Tamar and Judah, God "meant it for good" (Gen. 50:20). With the birth of her twins, Tamar has done her part, so to speak, for her own, Judah's, and Israel's futures; YHWH would be able to bless the world in large part through the actions of this outsider woman. Indeed, this outsider, whose legal and social resources were very meager, does more for the future of God's people and therefore the whole world than does the insider Judah, who — theologically speaking—has had everything at his disposal.

Later in the Old Testament (as we shall see in the next chapter) we learn that the descendants of one of Judah and Tamar's twin sons comes to an inglorious end. Achan, whose ancestry is explicitly and pointedly traced to Judah (and therefore Tamar), "broke faith" by keeping proscribed materials in Israel's defeat of Jericho (Josh. 7:1). This breach of loyalty leads eventually to the elimination of his entire family (Josh. 7:25). But the other twin, Perez, is mentioned in the genealogy of David's ancestors (Ruth 4:18-21). This seemingly modest genealogical note informs the reader that, had there been no Tamar, there would have been no David either. Beyond the Old Testament, and from the perspective of the whole Christian Bible, Tamar's actions are also indispensable, for she ends up in the genealogy of none other than Jesus, whom Christians believe was Israel's messiah and therefore the one through whom God would finally fulfill all the past promises made to Israel (Matt. 1:3). Could any Israelite insider ever claim to be more crucial to the future God envisioned for Israel and the whole world? The answer must surely be a resounding "No." It was Tamar, who as an outsider is still obscure in many religious quarters today, who acted in a manner that was decisive for the future of God's people and God's world. She was not originally an elected insider, but she saw to it that the chosen people's mission stayed on course. God used her to ensure that the insiders and their mission had a future.

CHAPTER 3

Rahab and Achan: Role Reversals

The Book of Joshua, which features the dual episodes of this chapter's title characters (Rahab: Joshua 2; Achan: Joshua 7), is arguably more self-consciously geared to the insider-outsider theme than any other biblical narrative. This is because Joshua tells the story in which the Israelites are under a divine mandate to dispossess, conquer, and even — horrifyingly — annihilate the inhabitants of the land they are about to enter. These inhabitants, since they occupy a land that God long ago promised to Israel's ancestors (Gen. 12:4-7), have to be removed in order for the divine agenda to go forward. Yet there is an ironic twist, for at this point in the drama the Israelites, who naturally are the ultimate insiders from the point of view of the sweeping biblical epic, are actually outside the land God promised them; and the outsiders (relative to Israel) are inside that same land. A complete reversal must take place for the insider community, Israel, now temporarily outside the promised land, to take up residence within it. Conversely, the outsider Canaanite community, now currently inside the land, will have to be exterminated or removed. The Book of Joshua tells the story of this necessary reversal between Israelite insiders and Canaanite outsiders.

Stated this baldly, the story's meaning is difficult to fathom and morally reprehensible to boot. At the same time, the story's complexities and nuances, as I hope to show, are designed to bring out other issues besides the ones that seem so obvious on a superficial reading. Indeed, it is precisely the strategic roles played by Rahab and Achan that relativize what comes across as gratuitous violence, and in the process they enhance the complex, ironic flavor of the overall story. Rahab and Achan are much more than bit players, or "walk-ons," whose parts can be removed without affecting the larger drama. Rather, they are central to the dramatic themes and key to understanding the complexities of the full narrative.

Initially in the Book of Joshua, YHWH's promise to Israel centers on the land rather than its current inhabitants (Josh. 1:2-4, 6, 11, 12-15). So far the only allusion to those residing in the land comes in God's reassuring remark that "no one" (that is, of those who currently dwell in the land) will be able to resist Joshua and Israel (Josh. 1:5). However, though the land is often in the foreground in references to God's promise of the sacred territory, its present inhabitants are never far from view. The Book of Joshua mentions these inhabitants in a number of configurations, perhaps the most prominent of which is the various lists of the "seven nations." In three instances the listing includes all seven groups: Canaanites, Amorites, Hivites, Hittites, Girgashites, Jebusites, and Perizzites (Deut. 7:1; Josh. 3:10; Josh. 24:11). In other occurrences, all but one or two of the seven nations are included, though the names omitted are not constant. Once or twice, names crop up even though they are not a regular part of the standard seven. Nonetheless, there is little doubt that the purpose of these lists is to draw the strongest possible contrast between Israel (the insiders) and the nations about to be dispossessed (the outsiders).

Sometime earlier in the chronology of the biblical epic, in the famous episode where God promises the land to Abraham in the context of the patriarch's "deep sleep," the internal population in question in the Book of Joshua is referred to collectively as Amorites, though a much fuller listing is appended (Gen. 15:12, 15, 18-19: Kenites, Kenizzites, Kadmonites, Hittites, Perizzites, Rephaim, Amorites, Canaanites, Girgashites, and Jebusites). Conventionally, however, the shorthand for referring to the inhabitants of the promised land is Canaanites: from the Bible's bird's-eye perspective, these are the dreaded outsiders.

Rahab's house

As the story gets under way, the general opposition between Israelite insiders (who are still outside the land) and Canaanite outsiders (who are still inside the land) puts in bold relief Rahab's significance in Joshua 2 and Achan's significance in Joshua 7. At first, Rahab seems to be simply one of the many outsiders targeted for removal; thus she apparently receives special attention only because the Israelite spies just happen to encounter her before they do any other outsiders. However, a close reading of the text reveals that Rahab is hardly just another nondescript and doomed inhabitant of the land. On the contrary, she is a virtual *representative* of these outsider inhabitants. It is hardly an exaggeration to say that Rahab is the quintessential outsider in the whole Book of Joshua. She is as Canaanite as they get!

What is the evidence for this? There are any number of clues that Rahab represents the collective outsiders in this story. Perhaps the reader gets the very first indication on reading that the spies Joshua has sent to Jericho have gone immediately to the house of a prostitute named Rahab and "lodged there" (Josh. 2:1). The text supplies no reasons for what appears to be curious, perhaps dubious, behavior. Are we to assume that the spies figured that a house of ill repute was the best place to uncover information? Was Rahab's house the only available lodging? Did the spies surmise that no one would think to look for them in such a place? Or, more suggestively, were they mixing a little pleasure with their business of spying, so that information was not all they were attempting to "uncover"?

Answers to these questions are not obvious because of the story's penchant for suggestive and teasing language. "They lodged there" is a perfectly acceptable translation of the Hebrew verb, which elsewhere means "to lie or sit down, stay, dwell, or inhabit." But context is decisive: a verb that is innocuous in one setting may be provocative in another. An analogy in English is the word "sleep." Sometimes it simply means "to slumber"; but in a different context — "I heard that John is sleeping with Mary" — sleeping is hardly the activity being referred to. Thus the phrase "the spies lodged" at the house of a prostitute likely is a *double-entendre:* one can't be sure whether they simply "lodged" there or whether they — ahem — "lodged" there.

There is no doubt that this ambiguity is purposeful in the text, because this first mention of the spies' involvement with a brothel is only one of a number of sexual innuendoes. As we shall see, the reasons why these innuendos are present go beyond efforts to spice up the narrative. The story is not full of sexual hints primarily to increase the ratings of the Book of Joshua. If the declaration that the spies "lodged" in the house of a prostitute is intended to evoke a sexual image (and since it was a bordello, perhaps we should think of Rahab as a "madam"), the second sexual allusion is surely Rahab's name itself. Readers who understand Hebrew will immediately wonder whether Rahab's name is meant to be risqué: in etymological terms, Rahab's name connotes something "broad" or "wide," hardly bold in describing a path, say, but having an entirely different sense when applied to a woman engaged in the "world's oldest profession." It may not be too far-fetched to consider Rahab's name the equivalent of the English slang word "broad" when applied to a female who is known to be sexually experienced and has a notorious reputation. But even that is probably more sanitized than is warranted. In a language related to Hebrew (Ugaritic), the same word refers to the female genitalia. Granted, this is not a proper translation of the Hebrew word; but given the explicit description of Rahab as a prostitute (a *zônāh*-prostitute — see the discussion in the previous chapter) and the general meaning "broad" or "wide," which is sexually suggestive for a woman of this métier, the name is almost surely to be taken as a not too subtle symbol of both her occupation and reputation.*

The sexual references are even more blatant in the scene where the king sends his men to Rahab's house after hearing that spies have infiltrated the land (Josh. 2:2). When the king's agents demand that Rahab produce the spies they believe she is entertaining, if not harboring, their language is lewd and crude: "Send out the men who entered you . . . er, who entered your house." The combination of the Hebrew verb for "enter" and the preposition "unto" sometimes means to approach someone with sexual intent (e.g., Judg. 15:1). So the king's agents incorporate a well-aimed barb into their insistence that Rahab bring forth the men they believe she is hiding. But Rahab gives as good as she gets, for she uses the same linguistic combination to acknowledge that the men indeed "had come to/entered me." Once again, the *double entendre* seems unmistakable.

As we shall see later, there is at least one more interesting sexual allusion in the story, this time involving the scarlet cord. Leaving that aside for the moment, we should investigate the connection between the sexual allusions and bawdy humor and Rahab's designation as a representative of the entire Canaanite population. Though her representative status becomes virtually undeniable in her "confession" (Josh. 2:9ff.), at this point it is a function of the sexual references themselves, because one of the most prominent metaphors for idolatry in the Old Testament is sexual promiscuity, sometimes expressed in the phrase "whoring after other gods." In the Book of Joshua itself, primarily in the important speeches Joshua makes at

*One Jewish commentator (Tikva Frymer-Kensky) refers to Rahab as "this biblical Suzie Wong. . . ." She also picks up on the "broad" allusion by calling Rahab the "broad of Jericho."

the conclusion of the book, the potential for idolatry is the explicit rationale given for (1) eliminating the population and (2) not intermarrying
with any inhabitants remaining after the conquest (Josh. 23:6-9, 11-13, 15-
16; Josh. 24:14-18, 23). Rahab's name and occupation, plus the sexual innuendoes scattered throughout the story in which she appears, all call to
mind the strongly "Canaanite" character of the episode, not so much in
ethnic terms but in religious terms. Canaanite ethnicity (whatever that
might be) was not Israel's worry, but its religion was. Thus Rahab represents one of the tempting features of Canaanite religion, which is why the
narrative is so tantalizing in reporting that the Israelite spies went straight
to a Canaanite prostitute's house and "lodged" there. That fact in the narrative calls attention to Israel's being in a situation where it has to be careful about even flirting with the temptations of Canaanite religion in the
land. In this sense at least, Rahab not only speaks for the Canaanites but
epitomizes them in terms of being a seductress: this is a sexual metaphor
for one of Israel's most besetting and persistent sins, namely, worshiping
gods other than its own.

There are other indications of Rahab's status as representative of the
Canaanites collectively. For example, when she tells the spies that she
knows YHWH has given Israel the territory in which she resides, she mentions the "land" (2:9), not merely Jericho. This echoes the promise that
YHWH has reiterated in Joshua 1 (vv. 2, 6, 11, 13, 15). Rahab also claims to
know the Canaanite state of mind sufficiently to anticipate the official reaction to the presence of the spies (2:2-4, 6); she knows how they have cow-
ered before Israel's anticipated assault (2:9, 11); and she knows what the
population thought about YHWH's actions in Israel's behalf (2:10).

From this initial encounter, the spies' first interactions with Rahab are
potentially disastrous from a couple of religious perspectives. First, we
might certainly question Joshua's wisdom in sending out the spies. Already
in Joshua 1, YHWH makes perfectly clear to Joshua that taking over the
land is a function of divine promise; furthermore, there is no possibility of
a Canaanite victory (Josh. 1:2-5, 10-11, 15). Joshua later explicitly tells the Israelites that their victory has had nothing to do with their military prowess
— it was not "by your sword or your bow" (Josh. 24:12). So comes an insistent question: Why send spies at all? Presumably, spies are supposed to
gather information about an enemy's strengths and weaknesses, ascertain-
ing, if possible, their counter-strategies. Apparently, the Israelites figured
that this "intelligence" was necessary in order to neutralize Canaanite

strength and outwit Canaanite strategy. But none of this mattered in light of God's promises. Sending spies is at least a failure of nerve, if not of faith, on Joshua's part.

Second, the spies are so utterly incompetent that they not only endanger their lives but put themselves in a position of having to accede to Rahab's demands, as we shall see. What's most serious about this is that it involves a direct violation of God's Torah (law) as expressed in Deuteronomy 7:1-5: Israelites were to make no covenants of any kind with Canaanites — whether marriage covenants or any other kind. But that is exactly what the spies are forced to do once they've been found out. In Deuteronomy 20, Israel was told that it should always offer terms of peace to the inhabitants of any lands on their way toward — but still outside — Canaan; but the inhabitants of Canaan were to be offered no such terms. They were to be put to the Ban or proscribed, that is, completely eliminated. This is because the land of promise was in the process of being "purged" of all idolatrous religious elements and influences (Deut. 20:10-18). Nonetheless, the spies' agreement with Rahab made it necessary for them to violate Torah at precisely this point. We shall soon see that this turn of events underscores one of the most radical features of the story.

Rahab has a plan, but before she can execute it, she has to get rid of the king's agents who have come to intercept the spies. Incidentally, we may gather from the way the story unfolds that the clever strategy she uses to save herself and her family suggests itself to her when she sees that she is caught between the menacing Israelites and the defensive-minded people of Jericho. After all, had the spies not "lodged" in her establishment, she would have had no opportunity to play a role in the developing drama. In any case, Rahab manages to send the king's operatives on what amounts to a wild goose chase. She makes no effort to lie about the presence of the spies, though she isn't forthcoming about their origins: "Yes, the men came to [or had sex with] me, but I did not know from whence they came" (2:4). Then she fibs that the men left before the city gate was closed, and she has no idea in what direction they headed. But that doesn't prevent her from encouraging the agents to pursue the fleeing spies: "Hurry after them, for you will overtake them" (2:5). Even though they are clueless about what direction they should take in pursuing the spies, the agents are off after their quarry with dispatch. And even though the Israelite spies have been shown to be hopelessly bumbling operatives by being immediately found out, the agents of the king of Jericho are depicted as equally inept for not demanding to search Rahab's premises, and then for scurrying after the spies even though there is no way to know their escape route. As we take in the hilarious incompetence of both the spies and the king's agents, it becomes clear to us that the only competent person in the whole narrative is Rahab.

Indeed, it would be a mistake to dismiss Rahab as a "common" prostitute or a run-of-the-mill madam, given her extraordinary perception, even prescience. How is it that she so quickly and effortlessly discovers spies in her midst? Who leaks word to the Jericho authorities? Is it Rahab herself? One of the women who works for her?* Then again, how does Rahab have the foresight to hide the moles? Depending on how one translates, Rahab either hides them prior to the arrival of the king's agents ("Now she had taken them up to the roof and hidden them . . .") or when they get there. The latter scenario would mean that she would have had to dash into the house, hustle the two men upstairs, hurriedly cover them with the flax stalks, then breathlessly reappear at the door and announce, "They're not here!" This second possibility is delicious to contemplate, since it makes for a riotous Monty Pythonesque scene (2:6). Either interpretation — hiding the spies before or after the king's agents arrive — is grammatically plausible.

Also noteworthy is the deftness with which Rahab handles the government's men and her ability to strike such a favorable bargain with the Israelite spies. As the only named actor other than Joshua in this episode (the spies, the king of Jericho, and the king's agents are all nameless, and the only other personal names are Sihon and Og, mentioned in Rahab's "confession"), Rahab is presented as larger than life. This befits her representative status as the quintessential Canaanite outsider.

On the roof

What transpires once Rahab has managed to get rid of the king's search party is truly astounding. Turning her attention exclusively to the spies whom she has hidden under the flax on the roof, she launches into what

---

*It is tantalizing to contemplate that the Israelite spies were discovered because they were circumcised, something that might have been revealed in a house of prostitution. Of course, we need to remember that a common way to refer to the "other"/outsider from an Israelite point of view was as someone "uncircumcised" (e.g., 1 Samuel 17:26). However, at least in the final form of Joshua this would be a stretch, for the Israelite males were said to be uncircumcised until *after* the spy episode (Josh. 5:2-9).

may be taken as nothing short of an Israelite confession of faith. When she says she "knows" that YHWH has given Israel the land, she has no trouble invoking the distinctive name of the Israelite deity. She adduces this as the reason that all of Jericho's inhabitants have "melted" at the prospect of Israel's imminent assault (Josh. 2:9). Rahab's admitting to Jericho's collective fear is not necessarily remarkable, for one expects a city to be anxious about a military force deployed on its outskirts, regardless of how formidable it believes its own defenses are. But what is remarkable is Rahab's forthright perception of reality: "YHWH has given you the land." This Canaanite prostitute not only knows the name of Israel's deity, she knows what the deity has promised and is about to accomplish; and she acts as though God's gift of the land to Israel is a *fait accompli*. Incredibly, it looks as if Rahab is more confident that YHWH will deliver as promised than Joshua is. If Joshua had been that certain, would he have dispatched spies in the first place?

Rahab goes on to explain why she holds this view: "For we heard that YHWH dried up the waters of the Yam Sûp from before you when bringing you out of Egypt and what you did to the two kings of the Amorites who were in Transjordan, namely Sihon and Og, whom you utterly annihilated" (2:10). It is astonishing that Rahab is acutely aware of the principal example of YHWH's salvific activity in Israel's behalf — the exodus from Egypt. No single divine action in the Old Testament is more prominent in emphasizing God's gracious and providential care of Israel. But there is more than Rahab's general awareness of the exodus from Egypt: she specifies the exact name of the body of water that YHWH dried up, the Yam Sûp, or Sea of Reeds. Even though this phrase is conventionally rendered in English Bibles as the Red Sea, the Hebrew text does not support that designation. The great exodus miracle took place at the Yam Sûp, not the Red Sea, and Rahab is fully aware of that. In fact, she is the only non-Israelite ever to use this geographical name. We might contrast her detailed knowledge of this geography to that of the Philistines in 1 Samuel 4:8. When that particular group of outsiders speaks of the fact that Israel's God afflicted the Egyptians with plagues, they cite the location as the wilderness (as opposed to Egypt proper). The Philistines are partly correct, that is, that YHWH did punish Egypt mightily with plagues; but they get the geography all wrong. In contrast, Rahab is 100 percent correct about both YHWH's actions and the site where these took place.

Even Rahab's use of the verb "dried up" (2:10) emphasizes her close acquaintance with the specialized language of Israel's salvation history. This verb in this particular form is found only in Joshua 4:23 (twice) and Joshua 5:1 as explicit references to YHWH's actions during the rescue from Egypt (nonverbal references are found in Ex. 14:16, 22, 29; Ex. 15:19; Josh. 4:22; Ps. 66:6; Neh. 9:11). The point is that this verb in this form evokes one of the main events in Israel's storied experience of YHWH's power and willingness to save. Nevertheless, Rahab, a Canaanite prostitute, is familiar with this Israelite theological language as though she has graduated from an Israelite religious academy!

The woman's mind-boggling familiarity with the details of Israelite history is also manifest in what she says about the defeat of the two Amorite kings. When she describes their defeat, she uses the verb meaning "utterly annihilate." This word is a technical term that is used in very specific contexts in the Old Testament; it is almost never used to describe conventional military action. Scholars have long considered it part of the distinctive vocabulary of "holy war." Whether the concept of "holy war" is the proper rubric for understanding this term, the fact remains that it has a most specialized use. Tellingly, Rahab is the only outsider who uses this word in this distinctive way. At this point in her "confession," she presents herself as fully and comfortably conversant with information that would typically characterize an Israelite insider completely knowledgeable about Israel's religious thought patterns.

This contention is strengthened by what Rahab says next. She elaborates on her thoughts and the Canaanite state of mind (she speaks unselfconsciously for the Canaanites throughout, emphasizing her representative status) with a startlingly unambiguous affirmation: "For YHWH your God is God in heaven above and on the earth below" (Josh. 2:11). The second part of this acclamation — YHWH is God on the earth below — is found only three times in the entire Old Testament. In fact, later Jewish scribes known as Masoretes saw this phrase's triple occurrence as sufficiently noteworthy to mark the other two uses in the margin of this text. It turns out that Moses and Solomon are the only other characters who make the same acclamation (Deut. 4:39; 1 Kgs. 8:23). It is nothing short of astonishing that Rahab utters this formula and in so doing puts herself in the same company with those two biblical heavyweights, managing to become a member of one of the most unusual threesomes in the whole Bible: "Moses, Solomon, and Rahab" does not exactly roll off the tongue when one thinks of the Bible's obvious heroes of the faith. Part of this particular expression involves the seemingly innocuous phrase "God is." But this sentence, also marked by the Masoretes, occurs three other times in the Bible (Jer. 10:10; Ps. 100:3; 2 Chron. 20:6), and in each instance it involves a positive confession about the Israelite deity.

Finally, even Rahab's later invocation of God's name in the swearing formula (Josh. 2:12) is decidedly insider language. Other than the Gibeonites in Joshua 9:18-19 (other outsiders who become part of Israel), the formula is used only by Israelites (Gen. 24:3; Judg. 21:7; 1 Sam. 24:22; 28:10; 2 Sam. 19:7[Heb. 8]; 1 Kgs. 1:17, 30; 2:8, 23, 42). If all one had to go on was Rahab's use of vocabulary and phraseology in her confession, one would have to conclude that she is an Israelite of the first order. It is not even a stretch to say that this woman might have been a strong applicant for a job teaching Israelite catechism.

Given all the elements of this confession, Rahab, the quintessential outsider, has gone a long way toward transforming herself into an Israelite insider capable of making an exemplary Israelite statement of faith. Her recitation comes across as a sort of Israelite "Apostles' Creed." The narration makes no effort to elaborate on how Rahab has acquired this knowledge, only that she has it and is able to express it expertly and forthrightly. Attempts to dismiss what she says as a cynical ploy to save her own skin (and that of her family) are not cogent. The simple fact is that, if she were not convinced that YHWH had in fact given the land to Israel, she would have had no reason to be afraid. She could have trusted in Jericho's defensive capability. Instead, the narration seems clearly and boldly to present her as a confessing Israelite, her occupation as a prostitute and her status as a representative Canaanite notwithstanding. She is, as it were, the epitome of a catechumen thoroughly schooled in all the relevant Israelite texts and concepts. In fact, Rahab's confession is arguably the best one in the entire Book of Joshua, even better than anything offered by the great leader himself, Joshua.

The "red rope district"

After her confession, Rahab begins a serious bargaining session with the spies. As she has done in her credo, she approaches this process with a thoroughly Israelite formula: "Swear to me by YHWH" (2:12). From her perspective, the negotiation is a quid pro quo arrangement: "Just as I have acted graciously toward you, you act graciously toward my father's house; further, you give me a positive sign" (2:12). Her elaboration of the extent of her family ensures that there will be no misunderstanding: "You shall keep alive my father, my mother, my brothers, my sisters, and all who belong to them; you shall rescue them and their lives from death" (2:13). The spies readily agree to this — do they have a choice? — even though their willingness to accept Rahab's demands (2:14) will entail an explicit violation of Torah as stated in Deuteronomy 7 and 20, as we saw earlier. But the spies accept Rahab's terms on the condition that she not disclose their position.

There is one more detail to which the spies need to attend. As Rahab uses a rope to lower her "guests" over the city wall so that they can return to the Israelite encampment (recall that her house is in the wall, 2:15) and gives them instructions about hiding in the mountains before they return to Israel's camp (2:16), they tell her how to assist them in keeping their part of the bargain. First, she is to tie "this scarlet cord" in the window, a signal that will mark her dwelling for the invading Israelites; second, she must be certain that her family remains in the house. Israel will not be able to guarantee their safety if they're out in the streets; in fact, unless the family is inside, the spies' oath will be nullified (2:17-20). Rahab agrees to these instructions and attaches the rope to the window (2:21).

The curious detail about the scarlet cord is interesting for a couple of reasons. First of all, it is potentially one more sexual allusion in the story. In a few places in the Old Testament the color scarlet is associated, at least indirectly, with prostitution, promiscuity, or eroticism. In the story of Tamar and Judah (Gen. 38 — see Chapter 2 above), Tamar pretends to be a prostitute in the hope that her father-in-law will impregnate her. The first of the twins that comes from Tamar's successful ruse is marked as the first-born when the attending midwife ties a scarlet thread around his wrist (Gen. 38:28, 30). A more explicit reference is found in the Song of Songs, an extended erotic poem. In Song of Songs 4:3 the male lover, who is rhapsodizing about the many beautiful features of the object of his passion, extols the woman's sensuous lips, which are "like a scarlet thread." Jeremiah also uses scarlet in an erotic image, except that in his case it is derogatory: the prophet describes a morally wayward Israel as a promiscuous woman who has excessively adorned herself to attract lovers. Along with painted eyes and gold jewelry, this slattern has "dress[ed] in scarlet" (Jer. 4:30). There is a similar usage in Isaiah: the prophet laments that Israel's sins are "like scarlet" (Isa. 1:18); just a couple of verses later (Isa. 1:21), Isaiah explicitly uses the term "whore" *(zônāh)* to describe the once faithful city (signifying God's people). These references combine to suggest that the color of Rahab's cord is not incidental but purposeful.

Considering these other references, it is legitimate to ask why there was a scarlet cord lying around Rahab's house in the first place. Presumably, this was no ordinary household item, but had a specific purpose. In fact, the spies seem to be quite aware that Rahab's use of a scarlet cord to signal the advancing Israelites will alert no one else, certainly no one in Jericho. The reason is simple: that red rope was often draped in Rahab's window. Quite simply, the rope was a sign of her profession and an indication of the sort of "house" she lived in. In short, Rahab lived in the "red rope district."

This emphasizes the second reason the presence of the scarlet cord was so tantalizing. The Hebrew text twice uses the word *tiqvāh* (2:18, 21) to designate the length of rope that was to act as a sign for the invading troops. Like many words, *tiqvāh* means more than one thing. Of course, in this context it clearly means "rope" or "cord"; but its other meaning, "hope," lends itself to the making of a wonderful pun: "the rope was her hope." Whereas the red rope was initially her business calling card, in the turn of events after she confesses her faith in YHWH, which has created the possibility not only of her being spared the fate of the rest of the Canaanites but more significantly of her inclusion in the community of Israel, the rope becomes her hope for rescue. The rope portends even more than mere rescue: indeed, it symbolizes salvation. In the end, Rahab and her family are not only kept alive when the Israelites attack Jericho, they eventually become part of Israel, God's own elect people. For this reason, Rahab (and her family) lived forever after that as part of Israel — "to this day" (Josh. 6:22-25). The reversal of the rope's use parallels the reversal of Rahab's fortunes. She has been the quintessential Canaanite; nonetheless, she becomes an Israelite. And in light of her impressive confession of faith, it is not unwarranted to say that she has become, if not a quintessential Israelite, at least an exemplary one.

Enter and exit Achan

The episode involving Achan is in antipodal relationship to the Rahab pericope; that is, the two stories are polar opposites of each other. If for no other reason, the two chapters need to be taken together because they are the only stories in the Book of Joshua that feature spies. Also, these two stories bracket the conquest of Jericho, with the Rahab narrative preceding and the Achan narrative following the city's destruction. Most important, however, is the fact that Achan is presented as the quintessential representative of Israel, just as Rahab has been presented as the quintessential representative of Canaan. As significant as the two accounts are standing alone, we can assess the full measure of their significance only when we read them in tandem.* What we have in Joshua 2 and 7 are the stories of a representative outsider and a representative insider as literary bookends.

Achan's position as a prime representative of Israel and as a quintessential Israelite becomes clear in the very first verse of the episode in which he appears (Josh. 7:1). Right away we learn that "the Israelites broke faith with regard to the Ban . . . so YHWH's anger grew hot against the Israelites."† This is a most serious violation. The verb "broke faith" or "violated" is found in this same form in 1 Chron. 5:25 (again marked by the Masoretic scribes), where it refers to the tribe of Manasseh; though it does not describe exactly the same sin, the transgression it does indicate is serious enough to call for exile from the land at God's instigation (1 Chron. 5:26). In any event, immediately on the heels of a story in which Israel was almost completely obedient (with the possible exception of Joshua's slight wavering in the sending of the spies and the spies' own questionable behavior), they now find themselves accused of a dreadful moral lapse that has brought them divine wrath.

Something is terribly wrong. Despite the Israelites' being in focus at the beginning and ending of Joshua 7:1, it is Achan, who appears grammat-

---

*Given their placement in the strategic section of Joshua 2–7, these two chapters, along with the material found between them, may actually function as the hermeneutical key for understanding the theological thrust of the Book of Joshua in its entirety.

†Translating Hebrew *ḥerem*, which I have rendered here as "the Ban," is most difficult. There is no English equivalent. The term refers to the practice of proscribing everything of profit that Israel might gain in encounters of this sort and dedicating them entirely to the deity. The verbal form of this word, which I discussed in the context of Rahab's use of the word (translated there as "annihilate"), also speaks to the necessity of eliminating all banned items rather than retaining any of them. The ultimate goal was purification, so to speak, for the purposes of YHWH's larger agenda. If the Ban was violated, that made Israel's activity *conventional* rather than *religious*, at least as seen from the Old Testament's theological perspective. Ironically, Rahab is the first character in the Book of Joshua to bring up the technical term regarding the Ban.

ically and spatially in the middle of the verse, and Achan alone who is the perpetrator of this abominable violation. Yet YHWH reacts as though all the rest of the Israelites have been complicit in his sin. This is true even though at this juncture no one else in the story has the slightest clue about what has happened. This feature of the story involves more than ideas of "collective personality"; rather, it highlights Achan's representative status. As we soon discover, unless the Israelites differentiate themselves from Achan, they will suffer the same fate they would have if they had in fact aided and abetted this sole transgressor. Achan's actions symbolize the whole community's actions.

If there were any doubt at all about Achan's role as the quintessential Israelite, it is utterly removed when we take note of the way he is first introduced in the episode. It isn't simply Achan who has violated the Ban; it is Achan ben Karmî ben Zabdî ben Zerah, belonging to the tribe of Judah — that is, Achan, son of Carmi, son of Zabdi, son of Zerah, of the tribe of Judah. This is by far the most impressive pedigree in the Book of Joshua. Had there been an Israelite equivalent of the *Mayflower,* Achan's ancestors would have been on it. The point being made here is that this is no ordinary, garden-variety, marginal, or nondescript Israelite who is guilty of violating the Ban. This is a man with the most impeccable and prestigious of Israelite credentials. Coming from the lineage of Judah means that Achan belongs to the group from which Israel's kings would eventually be selected (see Gen. 49:10). Without question, Achan is as Israelite as Rahab is Canaanite, which makes his violation, if possible, even more egregious.

As the story unfolds, not only does the enormity of Achan's actions come into sharp focus, but their impact on Israel as a whole as well. The narrative gives us the startling news that Israel is suddenly on the verge of being eliminated as God's people. So what Achan has done does not constitute a little mendacity or a forgivable peccadillo; he has jeopardized the very existence of Israel, though at first the situation does not seem dire. After once again sending spies and receiving their optimistic report (their evaluation of Ai's strength calls for only a modest show of force), Joshua sends a small contingent to attack Ai, the next town on Israel's hit list after Jericho (Josh. 7:2-3). But when the troops encounter Ai, they are routed, and thirty-six men are killed in the process (7:4-5).

While such a defeat may not seem that catastrophic, it certainly is in light of the overall theological perspective of the narrative. Regardless of YHWH's initial promises (Josh. 1:3, 5, 9), the singular success God has given

Israel in the Jericho campaign (Josh. 6:27), and the spies' calculations that Ai would present minimal resistance, Israel suffers an unexpected and ignominious defeat. In addition, from the general perspective of the narrative, this is not merely a military reversal. What happens in the Ai incident threatens the whole enterprise in which Israel is engaged: the taking over of a land that YHWH has promised. The religious aspect of this endeavor has been called into question, and that is far more serious than any military setback, regardless of how concerned Joshua and the elders are about that.

The narration concludes this part of the story with most chilling words, indicating just how traumatic Israel's first defeat is understood to be: "So the heart of the people melted and became like water" (Josh. 7:5). This language goes beyond an initial visceral response to a failed military foray. The "melting" of the people's hearts evokes the same language used to describe the reaction of the Canaanites when they realized what YHWH had done (in Egypt and the *yam sûp;* to Sihon and Og) and realized that this deity is God in heaven above and on the earth below (Josh. 2:9-11). We should not lose sight of the fact that Israel is on the verge of resembling the Canaanites in their response. The Israelites don't know it yet, but they are responding to a circumstance at Ai that has been engineered by YHWH (we later learn). It turns out that when Achan violates the Ban, he — and the Israelites that he in effect represents — have taken a fateful first step toward transforming themselves into Canaanites. In that sense, the melting of their hearts is an appropriate, if terribly ominous, response.

It takes a little time for Joshua and the rest of the elders of Israel to figure out what has caused this inexplicable and frightening turn of events. At first they lament their misfortune by tearing up their clothing, prostrating themselves before the Lord's ark, and putting dirt on their heads — all symbolic gestures of lament, fear, frustration, and anger (Josh. 7:6). At first they see no need to confess or repent, for no one (with the exception, perhaps, of Achan) understands what has prompted YHWH to abandon Israel. This explains why Joshua virtually accuses YHWH of cynically leading the Israelites into the clutches of the Amorites (effectively a synonym for Canaanites in this setting). From Joshua's vantage point, Israel would have been better off had YHWH allowed them to remain in Transjordan. And now that Israel has been forced to turn tail and flee from its enemies, the rest of the Canaanites will seize the opportunity to finish off Israel once and for all. Joshua demands to know what that will say about God and the divine plan (7:7-9).

But YHWH is unfazed by Joshua's rant (7:10). There is no mystery, in God's view (or that of the readers, who have been informed from the beginning what is going on): "Israel has sinned" (7:11). It will not be necessary for Joshua to guess at the nature of the transgression, for God provides details. As YHWH begins the litany of Israel's misdeeds, we should notice that the verbs have plural subjects even though, literally speaking, Achan is alone responsible. With a succession of connected verbs, YHWH elaborates on what Israel has done: "They have transgressed the covenant which I commanded them; they have taken some of the Ban; they have stolen and lied; and they have placed [the forbidden items] among their own stuff" (7:11).

Unfortunately for Israel, the consequences of these actions could not be more devastating. "The Israelites will not be able [plural] to rise up before their enemies; they turn back in the presence of their enemies. Since they have become subject to the Ban, I will no longer be with them, unless you [plural] destroy the banned object from your [plural] midst" (7:12). What is so unsettling about YHWH's denunciation here is not the pronouncement of judgment per se; throughout the Old Testament, Israel is often the object of divine punishment. But this is punishment of a different kind: Israel has moved beyond being a recalcitrant or wayward people in need of a chastising that is geared toward moral rehabilitation or religious renewal. In light of what God has just declared, the unpalatable fact is that Israel has become Canaanite. Therefore, unless there is a radical and rapid change of direction, Israel will suffer the same fate that is in store for the Canaanites, namely, the Ban (7:12). That means nothing short of complete annihilation. If Israelites act as Canaanites, then God will regard them as Canaanite and treat them accordingly. Israel, God's chosen people, is in danger of becoming *not* God's people; indeed, they are on the precipice of becoming no people at all.

This development involves a strange twist because we readers know that there is only one guilty party: Achan. Again, this issue turns on more than a case of corporate personality, in which the actions of one person have an impact on the group. There are elements of that idea here, to be sure, but that does not get to the heart of the situation. Just as Israel was to put all the Canaanites to the Ban so as to remove any possibility of temptation, and just as they had to be wary of Canaanite seductions (as the Rahab pericope suggests), now it is a matter of a serious and malignant Canaanite presence within Israel. Achan, a person who is as Israelite as one can get, has managed by his violation of the Ban to make a Canaanite out of himself even though he is ostensibly hidden in the very heart of the Israelite community. It is difficult enough to get rid of Canaanites and Canaanitism when these are visible, obvious, and targetable. How much more difficult is it to discover one of their own whose Canaanite behavior threatens to bring ruin to the community and to defy the reasons for which God chose it in the first place?

Israel's immediate and urgent task is to find the offender and take appropriate action; otherwise, they are doomed. YHWH instructs Joshua (and by extension Israel) to engage this emergency project immediately (7:13-15). Unless Israel is successful, the capture of the promised land will come to an inglorious end: "O Israel, you cannot stand before your enemies until you remove the Ban from your midst" (7:13).

Not surprisingly, Joshua moves quickly: using a system of lots, he narrows the search and isolates Achan (7:16-18). As though to retain the emphasis on Achan's status as the quintessential Israelite, the narrator once again gives his full pedigree: Achan, son of Carmi, son of Zabdi, son of Zerah, of the tribe of Judah (Josh. 7:18). At the same time that it does not allow Achan's credentials to fade into the background, the narrative makes it increasingly clear that Achan's impressive background, his family "connections," will not be a factor in getting him off the hook.

For that matter, Achan's violation is so serious and its potential consequences are so unthinkable that not even his straightforward confession makes any difference. After the casting of lots singles Achan out as the guilty party and after Joshua confronts him, Achan readily admits to what he has done: "I have indeed sinned against YHWH, the God of Israel; what I did was this" (7:20). Achan then goes on to explain what he coveted and eventually took for himself: various precious and expensive goods (7:21). Sure enough, messengers sent by Joshua to Achan's tent, where he has hidden his prohibited treasure — again emphasizing the motif of things hidden in Israel's midst that must be removed — confirm the incriminating evidence of his booty (7:22). They bring these goods not only to Joshua but to "all the people of Israel"; the communal nature of this drama is constantly kept before the reader (7:23). Achan's confession gives Israel the opportunity to find the offensive goods and punish the offending party. However, as harsh as it may seem, his confession is not destined to be a step toward forgiveness or reconciliation. Achan has endangered Israel and God's plans to save the whole world through Israel. In effect, Achan has committed the unpardonable sin, and though he is the quintessential insider, he is about to suffer the ultimate outsider's fate.

It would probably be a mistake to conclude that that ultimate punishment is to be death. After all, every Israelite would eventually die. Even if an Israelite's death was brought about by divine judgment, it was still possible to die as an Israelite, regardless of the opprobrium that might be heaped on any individual Israelite or any larger entity within Israel. But given the tenor of this story, and its antipodal relationship to the Rahab episode, Achan is about to die as a Canaanite. No punishment could be greater, no ignominy more pronounced.

This particular take on the story is attested by Joshua's words, Israel's actions, the specifics of the execution, and finally the memorialization of Achan's offense. First, "Joshua and all Israel" act as one as they take Achan, his ill-gotten treasure, his children, his animals, his tent, and "everything that belonged to him" to the Valley of Achor (7:24). Achan's sin is not against Joshua as a leader, or against any individual family, clan, or tribe in Israel; it has had an impact on the very heart and essence of Israel, all Israel, as God's elect people. Second, just as Rahab and her family and all that belongs to her and to them are saved from destruction (Josh. 2:12-13, 18; 6:22-23), so Achan and his family and all that belongs to him and to them are consigned to destruction—that is, effectively, the Ban. Third, in a most chilling pronouncement, Joshua declares that just as Achan has brought "trouble" on us (that is, Israel), so YHWH now brings "trouble" on you (that is, Achan and his family — Josh. 7:25). Joshua's use of the word "trouble" is an obvious wordplay on the name of the valley where this is all taking place — Achor (Hebrew root *'kr*) — quite simply, the Valley of Trouble, as Achan's actions have troubled (*'kr*) Israel. As a geographical location, the Valley of Achor, which also evokes the name of the man (Hebrew *'kn*) whose actions have almost spelled Israel's doom, will be a constant reminder of the dire consequences of violating faith (7:26).

Fourth, not only does "all Israel" stone Achan and his family, but they burn them as well (7:25), which was the fate inflicted on Jericho, the first city of the Canaanites to be destroyed. To be sure, the "stoning" in Jericho was metaphorical: the walls came down so that the inhabitants were in effect stoned (Josh. 6:20). After the stoning — metaphorically in Jericho's case and literally in Achan's — both are burned (6:24; 7:25), that is, the Canaanites and the quintessential Israelite-turned-Canaanite suffer the same end. Finally, the people pile up a great heap of stones to mark the sordid incident and its aftermath, which remains "to this day" (7:26). Early on in the march toward Jericho, Israel erected stone monuments to mark YHWH's leading the people over the Jordan on dry ground. Such stones would not only be a testimony ("to this day") of God's mighty actions but would also be a means of telling subsequent generations when they would ask, "What do these stones mean?" (Josh. 4:1-24, esp. v. 21). But that stack of stones, which memorialized the positive message of God's deliverance of his people, was not the only one Israel had to contemplate in future years. Even more telling, the body of the King of Ai was later placed under a "great heap of stones" — the same phrase that occurs in the Achan story — and also remains "to this day" (Josh. 8:29). Thus Achan's treatment is the same as that of a Canaanite king. His incomparable Israelite pedigree ironically affords him the "opportunity" to be infamously memorialized under a "great heap of stones" after the manner of someone who also had impressive credentials — a Canaanite king.

Both scholars and laypeople have traditionally read the Book of Joshua from the standpoint of ethnicity and militarism: Israel as an ethnically homogeneous social group inflicting its will by force on other ethnically homogenous groups, which are known collectively as Canaanites. Thus the theme of the book is little more than an ancient version of genocide. Even those who regard the Book of Joshua as part of their Scripture — whether in the context of Judaism or Christianity — find little religious or theological value in it. A moralistic treatment of the figure of Joshua, God's giving Israel the promised land, divine judgment visited on the immoral Canaanites — these were the basic themes gleaned from this otherwise apparently barren part of Scripture.

But I would argue that the Book of Joshua is a highly charged theological narrative in which the first seven chapters serve as an interpretive key to the whole book. In these chapters, the motif of insiders and outsiders forces us to completely rethink what it means to be Israel and to remain Israel. The fact that a quintessential Canaanite — not only "non-Israelite" by definition but one whose occupation evokes Canaanite religion and all its temptations — can become part of Israel "to this day" completely changes the equation. Rahab's inclusion in Israel further required defying explicit instructions in Torah, which underscores the importance of this "conversion." "Converting" to Israel, to God's people, and to God's means for the world's redemption takes precedence over strict adherence to the directives in the Torah. Achan's story completely reverses the Rahab story. It demonstrates that ethnicity, regardless of its purity, is no guarantee for remaining part of God's people. Just as Rahab's confession of faith got her and her family included, Achan's violation of faith got him and his family excluded. The outsider came in, and the insider was ousted; confessing faith and violating faith were the variables.

As Scripture, this text is addressed to every successive generation of the believing community that regards it as part of Scripture, whether Jews or Christians. The import of this text is that the community of faith must be constantly aware that outsiders are only a confession away from being included, while insiders are only a violation away (when it is a violation of Achan's magnitude) from being excluded. This story is not one that merely reports brutal and gory war stories from the past, nor is it an affirmation of an ethnic understanding of religion. It is a story in which the interplay of insiders and outsiders requires a reevaluation of the very nature of what it means to be God's people. Rahab should give all "outsiders" hope; Achan should make all "insiders" cautious and attentive to keeping the faith.

One final note is in order. As was the case with Tamar (see Chapter 2), Rahab also shows up later in the genealogy of Jesus, Israel's messiah, or "anointed one" (according to the New Testament; see Matt. 1:5). There can be no more powerful affirmation of the role of an outsider than that Rahab, by means of her strong Israelite confession of faith and her ultimate saving of the spies (see James 2:25), not only becomes (along with her family) part of the elect people Israel "to this day" but also has a crucial part in the birth of that people's messiah (according to the Christian point of view). A woman who was an outsider of the lowly level of a Canaanite prostitute becomes an insider of the magnitude of a mother of the faith. She becomes the ancestress of both the great Israelite David (Ruth 4:18-22) and Jesus Christ. Rahab's story is a conversion story of the first order.

CHAPTER 4

Naaman's Cure, Gehazi's Curse

The story told in 2 Kings 5 demonstrates the biblical outsider-insider theme in a most straightforward and accessible way. At the beginning we are introduced to Naaman, a high-ranking Aramean military officer,* who, we are amazed to discover, eventually confesses his singular belief in the Israelite God YHWH. When the story concludes, we learn that Gehazi, servant of the great Israelite prophet Elisha, suffers an ignominious fate as a result of his seeking to profit from Naaman's eagerness to leave a gift in gratitude for his newly found faith. On the surface, the story almost seems to function as a simple morality tale: even Arameans may come to believe in Israel's God, while Israelites, even a prophet's aide, may fall victim to greed and cynicism.

Compared to the first three stories of outsiders we have analyzed, this one certainly doesn't appear to measure up to their depth, complexity, and drama. Does it possess the irony, intricacy, stunning reversals, and development of the concept of radical grace that comes through in the Esau narrative? Is there anything of the cleverness, courage, and sheer will of Tamar, who acted completely on her own to do what was necessary to ensure her future—and with it Judah's and Israel's — regardless of great personal risk? Does it compare to the racy and humorous, yet gravely serious, account of Rahab becoming part of Israel though she was a quintessential Canaanite, at the same time that her counterpart, the quintessential Israelite Achan, was subjected to the dreaded Ban?

*Many modern translations use Syria or Syrians for Aram and Arameans. I have chosen to retain the nomenclature as it appears in Hebrew.

One is tempted to give a negative answer to each of the above questions. Somehow, 2 Kings 5 does not seem to be quite on a par with the other stories we have examined. But that may be a premature evaluation. It's true that the surface theme of the Naaman-Gehazi account is rather obvious. At the same time, there are details in this story that bring out aspects of the outsider-insider subject that we have not seen before. More than that, close attention to the nuances of the text reveals a number of issues that are extremely important in the Bible's treatment of this topic. It turns out that this business of insiders and outsiders is a complex theological matter. As we shall see, some of these complexities may be observed in a story that has long been considered interesting but hardly compelling.

Naaman's impressive credentials

On one level, it may seem strange that 2 Kings 5 starts out by introducing an Aramean military officer; but on another level, it makes perfectly good sense. Arameans have been prominent in the biblical narrative for some time before 2 Kings, and their presence will be felt in subsequent stories. During the time of the judges, the Israelites worshiped Aramean deities, along with the gods of several other foreign countries (Judg. 10:6); thus the Aramean outsiders represented one of Israel's perennial temptations. Later, Aram became one of Israel's major enemies and was one of the countries King David had to subdue to consolidate his power (2 Sam. 8 [esp. vv. 5, 6, 12, 13]; 2 Sam. 10 [esp. vv. 6, 9, 11, 13, 14-19). Absalom was a fugitive in Aram before he returned to Israel to overthrow temporarily his father's kingdom (2 Sam. 15:8). By the time of Solomon, there are peaceful trade relations with Aram; they are still outsiders, of course, but there has been a cessation of hostilities (1 Kgs. 10:29). Nevertheless, before Solomon's death, Aram has again become an adversary (1 Kgs. 11:25). Long before this story turns its focus on the prophet Elisha, Aram is depicted as constantly embroiled in Israel's military and international affairs (1 Kgs. 15:18; 20:1, 20-22, 26-29). The most recently we have heard of Aram in the biblical narrative before the Naaman story, Aram has been responsible for the death of the Israelite king Ahab (1 Kgs. 22 [esp. vv. 1, 3, 11, 31, 35]). Therefore, when this account begins by introducing Naaman, an Aramean officer, it is not nearly as unusual as we might have thought at first blush.

At the same time, there are peculiarities evident in the introduction of this character. It becomes clear that no other Aramean has "gotten so much press." Furthermore, the coverage has been positive, even glowing. After pointing out Naaman's military rank, the narrator all but gushes that he was "a great man *('îš gādôl)* before his lord" (that is, the Aramean king) and highly praised (2 Kgs. 5:1).* The question is: Why would an Aramean military officer, no matter what his rank and accomplishments, be introduced in this text with such admiration? After all, he is not only an outsider but an enemy outsider. Once in a while an Israelite is described in such superlative terms (e.g., 1 Sam. 16:18), but what accounts for introducing the foreigner Naaman this way? Was this a matter of grudging Israelite respect for a highly talented enemy soldier and officer? The answers to these questions will be supplied by the unfolding story.

As though Naaman has not yet been sufficiently lauded, the text adds a detail that is all but incomprehensible. It turns out that his success — and thus his rank and status — has been a direct result of the military feats he has performed in Aram's behalf, which were brought about by YHWH, Israel's own deity. There is no ambiguity at all about this assertion: "For YHWH had given victory to Aram by him" (that is, Naaman). How did this piece of unabashed Aramean propaganda find its way into the biblical text? What was YHWH thinking, aiding and abetting one of Israel's archenemies in this way? Wouldn't it be obvious that Israel could count on support from its own God? Aram was a serious enough adversary as it was, without YHWH's support.

In point of fact, this notation about YHWH's positive involvement with Naaman and Aram has the effect of reorienting the reader. At the very least, it means that no facile conclusions can be drawn about what "side" YHWH is on, regardless of the special relationship between Israel and its God. Israel was always fundamentally in error believing that its interests, regardless of how they were defined or who defined them, were always commensurate with YHWH's plans for Israel and the world. As a matter of fact, whenever Israel was not fulfilling its role as God's covenant people, its presumption of YHWH's favor might be construed as an attitude of sinful arrogance and folly. In the biblical tradition, not only was YHWH occasionally not pitted against Israel's enemies, whoever they might be; very of-

---

*It is difficult to know whether any of our modern military designations are the equivalent of Naaman's rank as a *śar ṣᵉbā'*, literally "captain," or "chief" of "armies." Given his role in this story, "general" or even "defense secretary" may be appropriate.

ten YHWH used those very enemies as an instrument of judgment against Israel. In the case of Aram, for example, its most recent victory against Israel was the result of a prophecy that Micaiah ben Imlah had delivered against Ahab (1 Kgs. 22:17-23, 28-36). Thus, in at least one sense, saying that Aram's victories were a function of YHWH's help is more a matter of Israelite theology than Aramean propaganda. In short, if the Arameans ever won their battles as a result of divine aid, from an Israelite point of view, the aid had to come from YHWH: there was no other deity who could have helped them, for there was no other deity, period.

Actually, this statement about YHWH's giving Aram victory through Naaman is somewhat less startling than a previous story, in which Israel's God expressly instructs Elijah to anoint Hazael king of Aram (1 Kgs. 19:15). As part of the same instructions, Elijah was also to anoint Elisha as prophet in his place and then Jehu king of Israel. Anointing Jehu and Elisha makes perfect sense: they are both Israelites; but Hazael is another matter altogether. From the theological perspective of the biblical story, however, this merely underscores YHWH's sovereignty and universality. Thus, if in one setting YHWH can order an Israelite prophet to anoint an Aramean king, then it is scarcely inconsistent if in another setting YHWH facilitates an Aramean military victory, regardless of whether that victory is a function of divine judgment or not. In either case, a sovereign, universal God is at work.

But back to Naaman. We realize that, at least in part, his considerable credentials are the result of YHWH's orchestration. It doesn't matter that neither Naaman nor Aram are aware of this; indeed, not only are Naaman and other Arameans oblivious to what YHWH is doing in their behalf, almost surely they would be expected to attribute all their successes to their own gods and religious activities. But from the point of view of the narrative, this only highlights the irony of the point being made. Naaman is an outsider, a highly accomplished outsider, and an enemy outsider at that. Nevertheless, to some degree his position has been bolstered by the invisible hand of Israel's deity, even though Israel is one of the nations against whom Aram's military prowess has been directed from time to time. In sum, Naaman is a great man before his lord (the Aramean king), and he is further highly praised because of the victory granted to Aram by YHWH. Whether or not any Israelites like that fact — or even know that fact— that's the way things stand.

One more fact provided in Naaman's introduction sets the stage for the subsequent narrative. Despite being a valorous hero (Hebrew "mighty man"), he has a grievous skin condition. The operative Hebrew word has typically been understood as "leprosy"; but that translation is certainly debatable. What the modern medical community refers to popularly as leprosy is almost surely not the condition reflected by the Hebrew terminology. In fact, it may fairly be questioned whether leprosy as commonly conceived even appears in the Old Testament. It's true that the nature of Naaman's disease is important (though not primarily for medical reasons), and we should not dismiss the precise nature of that disease as though any disease would do — we shall soon see why the disease is so very important.

Still, we need to bear in mind, from the very first verse, that this story is first and foremost about the prominent outsider Naaman, which is why his name comes first in the sentence, a feature of Hebrew syntax suggesting emphasis. Naaman was more than just any old outsider who lived beyond Israel's borders. He was part of Aram's military machine. Whether he had ever actually been involved in military operations directed against Israel, we are not told.* But his role as a highly decorated military officer in a country constantly at odds with Israel made him an extraordinary outsider, an enemy par excellence. None of this is mitigated by the reminder that YHWH had helped Aram and Naaman achieve victory. Israelites would not have been aware of this any more than Arameans were.

This is where the disease comes in, for Naaman's outsider status is underscored precisely by his disease. This is why translating the pertinent Hebrew term as "leprosy" is unfortunate: when modern people hear the word leprosy, they think of a highly contagious and dreaded disease that emaciates and debilitates those who suffer from it. Even worse, lepers are thought of as social pariahs and are shunned by society.† But it is clear that Naaman does not have a disease of this kind at all. He is in contact with his king (v. 4), the Israelite court (vv. 6-7), Elisha's servants (v. 10), and his own

---

*2 Kgs. 5:2 may indicate that Naaman had, in fact, conducted military campaigns in Israel. After all, his wife benefited from an Aramean military raid by getting an Israelite lass as a slave. Still, we are not told specifically that Naaman either took part or even ordered the raid himself.

†One need only recall the depiction of leprosy in the classic film epic *Ben Hur* (1959). In any number of movies on biblical themes, leprosy is presented in a similar manner. While seeing leprosy in these terms may be more appropriate to New Testament times (though actual leprosy — Hansen's disease — is not in fact extremely contagious), retrojecting such ideas into Old Testament times appears unwarranted.

military entourage (vv. 9, 13). No character in any of these settings reacts in a stereotypical way to a person whose very diseased presence would ostensibly constitute all but a certain death sentence. Granted, Naaman's disease is a very serious problem, but not primarily for medical reasons. There is little question that Naaman himself initially believes his problem to be primarily medical; but that is not the standpoint of the narrative.

The main issue having to do with Naaman's ailment is religious and theological, not clinical. The most serious consequence of being afflicted with this malady was being cut off from God's people and, more particularly, not having access to the temple for worship. Two full chapters in Leviticus are devoted to the diagnosis and treatment of this disease, precisely so that those so afflicted will again have access to YHWH during temple worship and also be able to participate fully in God's elect community once again. It is not clear why some conditions render one ritually unclean and others do not. Nonetheless, it is clear that this particular disease keeps one from worship and involvement in the community until it is dealt with properly. Impurity cannot be allowed to infect God's holy temple. John Hartley summarizes the issue well when commenting on Leviticus 13–14:

> His [i.e., the priest's] purpose is to regulate those who have access to the sanctuary in order to keep it and the congregation from defilement by entrance into the area of the sanctuary by one who is unclean.

Jacob Milgrom also insists that we are dealing in this instance with "ritual, not medicine." There were undoubtedly many diseases in the ancient world to which Israelites would have been susceptible. But none of them would have been more feared than those that made the afflicted ritually unclean, for that meant that access to God in the temple would be denied, and normal interaction with God's community Israel would be impossible until the person was made ritually clean once again (see Num. 12:14-16; Deut. 24:8). No Israelite could have suffered a worse religious fate.

Now, if an Israelite with this grievous skin condition was kept from the temple and ordinary interactions with the covenant community, how much more would it be true for an outsider like Naaman? His outsider status comes out in bold relief in the very first verse: he is a highly placed Aramean military officer, apparently with immediate access to the king himself, and, most significantly of all, he has the sort of disease that would deny him access to Israel and Israel's God even if he had been an Israelite. At first Naaman does not care in the least that he is denied such access; but the time will come in the development of the story when he comes to covet that access. For now, it is enough to know that Naaman is an outsider at the farthest remove from Israel and Israel's God.

Medical attention for Naaman

Naaman's disease is not only in focus as the story proper gets under way, it is the principal element in the story. His disease is what prompts a number of actions in the first major scene. In one of the military raids that they have conducted against Israel, the Arameans have captured a young girl; she is subsequently placed in the service of Naaman's wife (2 Kgs. 5:2). There is something of a redundancy in the way this girl is described, which perhaps is meant to underscore her low status, at least with respect to the household of Naaman: she is a "young woman" or "little girl" *(naʿărāh)*, which may indicate both age (low to middle teens perhaps) and her position as a servant (a *naʿar* is often a male servant; a *naʿărāh* is a female one). However, not only is she called a "young woman/little girl"; the noun is further modified with the adjective "little." Thus she is a "little little girl." Whatever one makes of this phrase, it stands in stark contrast to the description of Naaman as a "great man." The juxtaposition in the same household of a "great [Aramean] man" and a "little little [Israelite] girl" rivets our attention.

Yet despite her lowly status, this little Israelite girl deigns to offer advice to her mistress, or at least expresses the hope that her husband ("my master," as the little girl says) would be healed of his bad skin condition, if only he were with the prophet in Samaria (5:3). Regardless of any fear or loathing she might have toward her captors, she volunteers information that she thinks will result in Naaman's cure. She even correctly names the disease, though she does not name the prophet, referring to him only as "the prophet." Evidently, not just any prophet will do; she has a particular one in mind. Neither Naaman nor his wife has any idea which prophet this may be. Considering the unfolding of events, this lack of information is not an impediment, for the prophet will find Naaman, not the other way around.

At this point, a couple of curious elements crop up in this scene. For one thing, no questions whatsoever are posed to the little girl, such as, "What kind of prophet do you have in mind?" "What makes you think Israelites rather than Arameans have this power?" "Who are you to give us advice?" "Arameans have sufficient resources for dealing with this, thank you." Or one might have expected simple questions about the basic information: "Where might we find this prophet?" "What are his credentials for effecting such cures?" "Has he had experience with this particular disease?" "Does the prophet require a fee for his services?" The little girl has uttered her only line in the whole story, but she gets no follow-up questions of any kind.

It is also curious that we are never told that Naaman's wife has reported what the little girl said. After the girl's remarks in verse 3, Naaman is the subject of the verbs in verse 4, indicating that he knew the message and hastened to inform "his lord," the king. Has Naaman simply overheard the little girl speaking to his wife? Has the wife in fact relayed the message to him (a detail the narrator chooses to omit)? Or, in light of Naaman's immediate reaction ("he went and told his lord . . ." [v. 4]), are we to understand that Naaman is sufficiently desperate that time is of the essence? Not only is there no time to waste asking the little girl relevant questions, there apparently is no time in this narrative to waste having Naaman's wife repeat the message. A bit more time is allotted when Naaman reports the contents of the little girl's remarks to his king, but not much. Instead of the common practice of repeating the message verbatim or at least summarizing it, the narrator has Naaman blurt out, "Thus and so the girl who is from the land of Israel said" (v. 4).

Now the Aramean king seems to suffer from the same lack of curiosity afflicting Naaman and his wife. Without asking a single question or probing for any more details, he tells Naaman to head out for Israel. Why haven't any of these three Aramean principals said, "What does a little Israelite girl know about such things?" Why has no one asked the name of this presumably vaunted prophet? Amazingly, if the little girl had not mentioned Samaria as the prophet's residence, the Arameans would not have known where in Israel the prophet could be found. Again, it is likely that the narration has been framed in this way to emphasize Naaman's (and perhaps his wife's) desperation and the king's acknowledgment that there are no Aramean resources available to deal with this situation.

Another curious fact is that the Aramean king informs Naaman of his intention to send a letter along with him to be delivered to his counterpart, the Israelite king. Why should there be an audience with the Israelite king at all? Is this a matter of diplomatic courtesy? Or is it an attempt to signal peaceful intentions? Naaman is, after all, a renowned military figure. Perhaps more telling, the Aramean king has no categories for believing that a prophet might be independent of a king's power and directives. If the royal office is the wielder and arbiter of all meaningful power, then any power at a prophet's disposal must surely be derivative of such royal power. This modest detail has the effect of emphasizing all the more the outsider perspective of the Arameans. They have no grasp of the prophetic office from an Israelite perspective; rather, they have recast Israelite prophecy in thoroughly Aramean terms. Kings talk to kings, not lesser officials; furthermore, if Israel has any power at its disposal, surely their king controls it. The reader will recall that when the little Israelite girl makes the comment to her mistress that sets all these actions in motion, nary a word is said about the Israelite king. Her remarks about a "prophet who is in Samaria" have been completely misconstrued by the Aramean king.

That Naaman is in full accord with his king's perspective is illustrated by the lavish gift he brings with him to Israel and the Israelite king: ten measures of silver, six thousand units of gold, and ten changes of clothes (v. 5). This is a state visit for Naaman, regardless of its personal dimension. Though in another setting Aram might still be in the business of conducting the occasional raid against Israel (v. 2), this situation apparently calls for the full range of diplomatic and political gestures. Perhaps more than protocol is in view as well. Is Naaman thinking in terms of inducing the Israelite king with an impressive present rather than the more usual military threat? In any case, he is not about to go to Israel empty-handed.

Naaman's state visit to Israel

When Naaman arrives at the Israelite court and presents his king's letter, we are flabbergasted by its contents. The misconception of the Aramean king and Naaman is worse than we expected. Completely ignoring any mention of a prophet, the letter is directed squarely at the Israelite king: "Now, when this letter comes to you, you will realize I have sent my servant Naaman to you. Heal him of his grievous skin condition" (v. 6). At first, the Israelite king's response to this demand shows that he believes he sees through to the true purpose of the letter: after tearing his clothing as a gesture of lament, wondering aloud whether the Arameans have taken him for a deity with the power to kill and make alive, he accuses his counterpart of provoking a confrontation (v. 7). Unfortunately, the Israelite king's actions indicate that he has no more insight into the nature of the situation than do the Arameans. He never once thinks of "the prophet who [is] in Samaria"; he doesn't even think to invoke YHWH. From the Israelite king's vantage point, neither he nor Israel is any more capable of dealing with Naaman's condition than are the Aramean king and the Arameans. He and Israel are equally devoid of sufficient resources. But considering what he's done with his own clothes, he'll find it helpful that Naaman has brought with him a few changes of clothing as part of the diplomatic gift. Were this not so tragic, it would be humorous: the insider king is just as clueless as the outsider king is.

Finally, we get the name of the prophet whom the little girl has mentioned at the beginning of the episode: Elisha. Somehow he has heard of the pitiful scene taking place at the Israelite court, and he reacts. Rebuking the Israelite king for his disappointing reaction ("Why did you tear your garments?"), he goes on to request that "he" — studiously avoiding any mention of Naaman's name or office — come to me so that "he might know there is a prophet in Israel" (v. 8). We should note that the little girl's reference to a "prophet in Samaria" has now been transformed by Elisha himself to a "prophet in Israel." He does not belong to Samaria, especially since Samaria is the political seat and the location of the king's palace. He is a prophet in Israel.

Fortunately for the Israelite king, Naaman responds at once and goes to Elisha's home. It is still in the nature of a state visit for him, even though the venue is no longer the palace. Naaman arrives with the appropriate pomp — "with his horse and chariot" (v. 9) — but it does him no good. He gets no farther than the front door. Standing there, doubtless waiting breathlessly for Elisha to appear, the great military man gets only Elisha's unnamed messenger. Isn't this a most egregious breach of protocol? Apparently, Naaman's office and status don't even warrant a private audience with the prophet himself. To make matters worse, what the prophet orders Naaman to do through the messenger seems absurd: wash seven times in the Jordan River (v. 10). It appears that he isn't even to be accompanied by prophets or priests or anyone else. Washing in the Jordan is enough, he's told, and "your flesh will be restored and you will be clean."

This snub is more than the great man can take. He stomps off in a huff. The reader is then given a glimpse of Naaman's interior dialogue and thus the reasons for his anger. Basically, his thinking is that the pomp and circumstance he has shown in coming to Elisha's home could have been met in kind. The prophet wouldn't have had to respond with military or political gestures, but prophetic regalia and rituals sure would have been nice. Naaman's fuming thoughts are most revealing: "I figured he would by all means come out to me, stand [in a ritually appropriate manner?], invoke the name of his God, YHWH, wave his hand over the place, and heal the grievous skin disease" (v. 11). Naaman's seething thoughts continue when he sputters about the superiority of Aramean rivers to Israelite waters (v. 12). He has no idea why he might not have washed in rivers at home to become clean. His interior dialogue begins with him stomping off angrily, and it ends the same way: "So he turned and left in anger."

Were it not for Naaman's servants, part of his military entourage, the story would end on this unhappy note. But servants play important roles in this episode. The little girl is designated by another term *(na'ărāh qᵉṭannāh)*, but there is no question that she is a servant; after all, she is "before the wife of Naaman" (v. 2: *lipnê 'ēšet Na'ămān*), who is also "her mistress" (v. 3: *gᵉbirtāh*). Likewise, at this point Naaman's servants step to the foreground. As the little girl has done, they speak prudently and helpfully. Addressing the commander with a strange title, "My father" (presumably one of the servants speaks on behalf of the group), the servant suggests that Naaman would have done any "great thing" *(dābār gādôl)* the prophet ordered (v. 13). That's just the problem: a great man like Naaman wants only to do a great thing, but in his eyes he's been asked to do a "little thing." And he's not about to stoop to that level. He has his dignity, and he has a reputation to uphold. But his servants are inclined to nudge him a little. If he's willing to do a great thing, whatever that might be — and Naaman has given a glimpse of what that might look like in his interior dialogue — then why not give in a little. Maybe if he relents and washes *(rḥṣ)*, then he might end up clean *(ṭhr)*. Considering Naaman's mood (the text uses two different words to describe his anger in verses 11 and 12), these servants deserve credit for their willingness to approach him, regardless of what their motivation might be.

Much to our surprise, and without a word of explanation, Naaman does exactly what they suggest, that is, what Elisha has prescribed: "He went down and dipped in the Jordan seven times." More importantly, he does this "according to the word of the man of God" (v. 14). The results are exactly what Elisha has predicted: Naaman's flesh is restored; indeed, it becomes like that of a little child, and he is made clean *(ṭhr)*. The story has come full circle. And it all started because of what a "little girl" *(na'ărāh qᵉṭannāh)* has said; it comes to fruition when a "great man" *('îš gādôl)* becomes like a "little boy" *(na'ar qāṭôn)*. Between the little girl and the great man who becomes like a little boy is the prophet, who is not only in Samaria but in Israel.

Naaman's confession and strange requests

After his restoration, Naaman heads to Elisha's home for a second time. This time, however, he meets Elisha himself — without the house as a barrier or a messenger as a mediator (2 Kgs. 5:15; compare 5:9-10). He is still accompanied by his entourage, but the pomp and circumstance of the previous visit is downplayed when this passage does not mention "his horse and chariot" specifically. Also, whereas previously he "stood" (*wayya'ămōd;* 5:9) only at the door of Elisha's house, on this second encounter he "stood *(wayya'ămōd)* before him" (that is, Elisha). The audience that Naaman coveted in the first instance has become a reality in the second instance. But the circumstances have changed radically: his flesh has been restored like that of a little boy, and he has become clean (v. 14).

The result of Naaman's first visit to Elisha, when he got only as far as the door of the house, was a display of anger — and the reader was able to get inside his head. Since his restoration, however, we are given no indication of his mood or interior thinking. Instead, his state of mind on this second visit must be inferred from what he has to say. And what he has to say is not a profusion of thanks; instead, remarkably and unbelievably, it is a straightforward confession of faith. In fact, as though Naaman can't wait to articulate what he now thinks about the whole affair, there is not even a minimally requisite expression of gratitude, no apology for his rant, not even a concession that what the prophet's messenger has ordered him to do has turned out to be efficacious. He has no time for such pleasantries. He has a confession to make, and he wants to get on with it.

His confession is as profound as it is brief: "Look, now I know that there is no God in all the earth except [the one] in Israel" (v. 15). In a sense, Naaman now makes verbal a confession he made implicitly and unwittingly by traveling to Israel in the first place. Had there been a deity or deities to rely on for his problem back in Aram, there would have been no need for the trip to Israel and the embarrassing situation the "great man" finds himself in. It's pretty clear that both Naaman and his king have been thinking more along the lines of political power or perhaps even magic. At the same time, despite their muddled thinking and the detour to the Israelite king, the only reason for Naaman's journey has to be a tacit admission that there is a God in Israel — or at least a prophet who has access to one. That Naaman now realizes that this is the only God in all the earth — including Aram — merely makes explicit what has been subtly indicated before. And Naaman's overt expression of faith is not generic. He has mentioned the name of Israel's God (YHWH) during his angry mutterings (v. 11) and later, when he affirms his intention to offer sacrifices exclusively to that same God (v. 17).

Thus, having affirmed his conviction that the world has only one God — Israel's — Naaman is now ready to offer a gift (the contents of which are given in v. 5), presumably as a gesture of appreciation (v. 15). Naaman's sincerity and humility are highlighted by the way he refers to himself: "your servant." Before his conversation with Elisha is over, he uses this designation for himself four other times (vv. 17-18). This Aramean general, whom Aram's king has called "my servant" (v. 6), has been transformed by his own chosen terminology into the servant of an Israelite prophet. He is evidently offering both the confession and the gift in good faith; furthermore, the gift, which at first seems to belong to the realm of diplomatic exchange, has now become something of a thank offering for Naaman's cure. Politics, power, and statecraft are no longer in view; the world of the prophet, religious ritual, and divine healing are now the focus. Naaman is offering his gift to Elisha for completely different reasons from those of his original plan.

Perhaps it is this change of context that causes Elisha to refuse the gift, though it is not immediately clear why he does so. A variety of explanations have been offered, most of them inferential. But it was not considered untoward at the time for prophets to accept gifts or fees for services rendered. For our purposes, suffice it to say that, given the astonishing nature of this conversion and the status of the person involved, Elisha wants to prevent the slightest misconception of what Naaman has experienced. This is YHWH at work: the conversion of an outsider to Israel's faith, the transformation of an infamous enemy into a friend, the trumping of conventional political and social power by unconventional prophetic power. A gift, no matter how genuinely offered, might have the potential of creating a misunderstanding on the part of the giver, or the receiver, or both.* What Naaman has received from Elisha — from Israel's God — is itself a gift, and Naaman need not offer a gift in return.

At this juncture, a startling scene begins to unfold — startling because it details how Naaman plans to conduct his life as a convert. Usually we are not told much about the life of the outsider once he or she becomes an insider (Ruth, as we shall see, is another exception to this pattern). Typically, most of the emphasis falls on the circumstances whereby the outsider became an insider in the first place.† But this is not true of the Naaman story: Naaman brings up a couple of issues that end up revealing a great deal about the narrator's view of what happens *after* the conversion, especially what happens in the long term.

As soon as Naaman realizes that his gift will not be accepted in spite of his insistence, he requests something of Elisha that sounds strange at best, even bordering on the bizarre: "Might there not be given now to your servant a two donkeys' load of soil?" Naaman quickly provides the rationale for this strange request: "For no longer will your servant offer a burnt offering or sacrifice to other gods except to YHWH" (v. 17). Not only is Naaman sufficiently serious about his newfound faith that he plans to engage in the proper ritual acts; he wants to make sure that he performs those acts, in effect, on Israelite soil. Since he will be nowhere near Israelite land when he returns to Aram, he decides to bring some home with him. We should not see in Naaman's desire a residual superstition or a confused idea about the nature of Israelite religion. Were the latter the case, he probably would have

---

*Elisha may have been able to keep the gift in perspective, but that may have been a more difficult task for his underlings. Of course, as the story soon shows, one of those underlings is so preoccupied with the gift proffered that he loses all sight of the larger issues surrounding Naaman's cure and conversion. It is also instructive to recall Esau's initial refusal of Jacob's gift, which was really a bribe. Only after Jacob realized that Esau had received him as a function of "amazing grace" was he able to prevail on Esau to accept the present (which has become the "blessing"). In both instances, the same word for "insist" is used (*wayyipsar*), except that Esau finally relents, whereas Elisha holds fast (see p. 26) and Gen. 33:11.

†The Esau story, as we saw, does not work along these lines. He is, after all, an insider poised to be the family's bearer of the divine promise, but has to step aside in favor of his younger brother. He performs the outsider's role by finally demonstrating to his brother the nature of the amazing grace that was involved in the divine promise in the first place (see Chapter 1).

asked for a couple containers of "holy water" from the Jordan. Despite the many texts teaching that one can worship or sacrifice to YHWH almost anywhere, there still remains a strong sense of sacred space. Naaman seems to reflect this theological idea, though it is not specified how he came by such a belief. But in a sense it doesn't matter, because characters in biblical stories often "know" more than they could naturally know. In this story, Naaman actually reflects a specific teaching found in Torah: Exodus 20:24 requires that sacrifices be made on an altar of soil (*'ădāmāh*, the same word Naaman has used to refer to "soil"). Wittingly or unwittingly, Naaman is in strict compliance with Israel's covenant with God.

If anything, Naaman's second request is odder still: he asks for nothing less than forgiveness in advance. Apparently, one of his duties back in Aram is to accompany — perhaps even escort — his king to the temple of Rimmon, an Aramean deity. Whether because of age, infirmity, or custom, the king is used to leaning on Naaman's arm during such occasions. What this means is that when the king genuflects in worship, Naaman has to genuflect as well, perhaps to indicate the proper reverence, perhaps to avoid being "above" the king, or perhaps to physically support the king. Regardless of the reason, Naaman is concerned about how this will be interpreted: given the requirements of his job, Naaman has no choice but to be seen in the temple bowing with the king, worshiping Rimmon along with his king and all the other worshipers. The new convert wants to make sure Elisha realizes that, appearances aside, under no circumstances are his actions to be taken as sincere acts of worship, and he wants YHWH to pardon him ahead of time.

Elisha seems to have no difficulty with either request. The first time Naaman left Elisha's presence, he walked off in anger (v. 12: *wayyēlek bᵉḥēmāh*); this time, in response to his two requests, the prophet says, "Go in peace" (v. 19: *lēk lᵉšālôm*). Naaman's conversion is complete, his requests sincerely made, his actions and words implicitly and explicitly blessed. Elisha gives the Aramean no other instructions. The seriousness with which he takes his conversion is amply demonstrated, it's obvious, by his asking for the Israelite dirt and the advance forgiveness. Naaman is free to go — in more ways than one.

Now that we have witnessed Naaman's full conversion and subsequent commitment to live in accordance with his newly adopted beliefs, a few details in the narrative take on a slightly different meaning. One is the use of the Hebrew word *šûb*, which usually means "turn around" or "return." Recall that Elisha's messenger has told Naaman that when he washes in the Jordan, "your flesh will return" (v. 10: *w*ᵉ*yāšōb bᵉśārᵉkā*). Sure enough, that is exactly what happens when Naaman eventually dips himself in the river: "his flesh returned" (v. 14: *wayyāšob bᵉśārô*). After that, Naaman himself "returned" (v. 15: *wayyāšob*) to the man of God, Elisha. At one level, there is little mystery about what *šûb* means in these contexts: the references in which his flesh is the subject of the verb connotes "transformation" or "restoration," while the one in which Naaman is the subject suggests simple movement to a place where one has previously been.

But Hebrew *šûb* is also commonly used in the Old Testament for "turning around" in the sense of repentance or conversion, that is, a moral and religious turning around. Thus Naaman's "turning" in this story has both a literal and a figurative sense. Even *bāśār* ("flesh") may have a dual role. In this episode, its most obvious and literal sense is "skin." But often *bāśār* means something besides the skin specifically: it may refer to one's whole body. More significantly, it sometimes connotes "person" in much the same way *nepeš* ("soul") does not mean an inner part of a human being but a human being in her or his entirety. As the whole account indicates, when Naaman's skin "turns," his whole person is in the process of turning as well. Naaman has gone to Israel to be healed (vv. 3, 6, 7: *'sp*); however, this same verb is never used to describe what actually happens to him. Instead of being simply healed, his skin and his whole person have "turned around" *(šûb)*. Something much greater than healing has taken place.

This also sheds new light on an early reference in the story, namely, that YHWH has given Aram victory *(tᵉšû'āh)* through Naaman's military prowess (2 Kgs. 5:1). In military contexts, *tᵉšû'āh* simply means "victory"; but in some contexts *tᵉšû'āh* means "salvation," that is, moral, religious, or spiritual victory. Of course, 2 Kings 5 is, at first, an obvious military context in that it celebrates Naaman's impressive career in the armed forces. But as the story unfolds, the military context gives way to a very different context. As the military and royal settings recede, the prophetic and religious settings begin to emerge, and in the end they predominate. An initial sense of military *tᵉšû'āh* soon blends into the sense of a different kind of *tᵉšû'āh*. YHWH inexplicably has given Aram, a dreaded enemy of Israel, "victory." But YHWH has a different kind of victory in mind for Aram, a victory that has been played out personally in Naaman but is actually available to all of Aram upon the utterance of a Naaman-like confession of faith.

This brings us back to the issue of Naaman's post-conversion life. Again, we need to keep in mind that biblical outsider narratives usually concentrate on what outsiders demonstrate to insiders (for example, Esau), on what they do wittingly or unwittingly in behalf of the insiders (for example, Tamar), or on the conversion process itself (for example, Rahab). But in this story we get an insight into Naaman's life after he converts. He plans to offer sacrifices to YHWH on borrowed Israelite soil, and he requests forgiveness in advance for when his duty requires him to appear in the temple of Rimmon. Thus he has become an Israelite in terms of belief (v. 15: "There is no God in all the earth except [the One] in Israel") and practice (v. 17: he would offer sacrifices to no deities except YHWH). At the same time, Naaman will retain his Aramean citizenship, so to speak, and apparently continue his military and political career in behalf of Aram. Somehow, this continuing Aramean connection does not in any way undercut his confession or commitment. Naaman has become an Israelite in religious and theological terms, for to believe what he now believes and to act in the way he's planning to act combine to make him part of God's elect people. Nevertheless, in sociopolitical terms, nothing has changed. The issue of what might happen if Aram were ever to advance militarily against Israel again is never broached in the story proper.

In the last scene in which Naaman has a role, the narration does not shy away from indicating that he is a convert to Israel on the one hand but an Aramean officer in good standing on the other. Apparently it is possible to be both without compromising either his faith or his civic responsibilities. It turns out that there are Israelites and there are Israelites. Naaman has become an Israelite in terms of theology and religious devotion; but he is not an Israelite at all in terms of social settings and political arrangements. This dual role as an Israelite convert and an Aramean officer certainly raises a host of questions, but the answers are neither forthcoming nor even hinted at in the immediate narrative. Still, the story is tantalizing in the way it juxtaposes the two "worlds" that Naaman will henceforth inhabit, but not presenting his conversion in a univocal, superficial, or simplistic way. Real converts to Israel in terms of theology and religion but not in terms of social settings or political allegiances would have undoubtedly faced some perplexing difficulties, but the details of these difficulties are not spelled out in this story. The way the Naaman episode proper ends, however, illustrates the fact that such problems existed.

Enter and exit Gehazi

Naaman's departure for Aram does not quite end the story, for he has gone only a short distance (2 Kgs. 5:19) when another character is introduced: Gehazi, Elisha's "boy" (i.e., servant). Gehazi is conceivably the messenger who has spoken to Naaman on his first visit to Elisha's house (v. 10), but we can't be sure of that. In any case, at the very moment he is introduced, we are invited into Gehazi's thought world. What first pops into his head is the fact that Elisha has prevented Naaman from leaving the gift he had intended to give the prophet and his household (v. 20). His perspective on this is scarcely neutral: both grammar and vocabulary suggest at least a bit of disgust on his part. Though the grammar is a little awkward, that in itself may emphasize Gehazi's pique: "Look, my master (that is, Elisha) kept Naaman, this Aramean, from having what he brought accepted." The emphasis clearly falls on Elisha's actions, not Naaman's; the latter obviously would have given a handsome present if Elisha had not intervened. And Gehazi's reference to Naaman as "this Aramean" shows that he thinks Elisha has missed a golden opportunity — literally. After all, if a prophet can't accept something for services rendered from a foreigner, especially one whose wealth may have been enhanced by plundering Israel (note the mention of "raids" in v. 2, one of which led to the abduction of the little Israelite girl), then from whom can one ever accept a present? Clearly, Gehazi is less than pleased with Elisha's declining the gift.

But more than simply rehashing Elisha's handling of the affair, Gehazi follows his displeasure with a counter-action: "As YHWH lives, I'll run after him to get something from him" (v. 20). Here Gehazi takes a position diametrically opposed to Elisha's but uses the same oath formula ("as YHWH lives") that Elisha used to reject Naaman's offer (v. 16) to underscore his own determination to get something tangible from "this Aramean." But a big difference in both language and reality is that, whereas Elisha has said, "As YHWH, before whom I stand, lives . . . ," Gehazi has conspicuously left out the "before whom I stand" part. Gehazi has managed, with a single idea, to position himself as Elisha's opposite.

Both Naaman and Gehazi have "lords" in the story — the king of Aram and the prophet Elisha respectively (see vv. 1, 4, 18, 22, 25). Furthermore, they both distance themselves dramatically from their lords. While Naaman returns to his lord's side and presumably retains his same job, he no longer shares his lord's religious outlook: his being Israelite theologically and religiously will not change even when he has to attend the temple of Rimmon with his lord (v. 18). Naaman's movement away from his lord, therefore, comes across as a highly positive and admirable step. Gehazi also leaves his lord's side — both literally and metaphorically; and when he returns to be with Elisha again (v. 25) and perform his required duties, he also no longer shares his lord's religious outlook, at least not completely. But Gehazi's change is a negative and reprehensible move. Elisha's aide is getting further and further away from Israel theologically and religiously, even though he will continue to live on Israelite soil. In the end, Naaman, who remains Aramean and will live in Aram, is Israelite in the most important sense; but Gehazi, who will remain Israelite after a fashion and still live in Israel, is somewhat less than Israelite in the most important sense.

In the exchange with Naaman, Gehazi does not have to try very hard to procure something valuable. Naaman has already demonstrated how eager he is to leave a present in Elisha's hands (vv. 15-16), even to the point of insisting. Though Gehazi could have gotten the desired result with the simple little lie that Elisha has changed his mind, he uses a much more elaborate and manipulative fabrication. Perhaps this is a function of his eagerness — if not desperation — to get something for himself. Indeed, when he is merely thinking about his course of action, he uses the term "run after him" (*raṣtî 'aḥărāw*); but when he carries it out, he actually "pursued after him" (vv. 20-21: *wayyirdōp . . . 'aḥărê*). Upon assuring a curious Naaman that everything is all right (vv. 21-22), he spins his false tale about two prophets from the prophetic bands in Ephraim who have just come to visit Elisha, prompting his request for a unit of silver and two changes of clothing (v. 22). Considering what Naaman has brought with him from Aram (v. 5), the amount Gehazi fraudulently asks for is extremely modest; it will hardly make a dent in Naaman's holdings. Indeed, Naaman insists that Gehazi take twice the amount of silver he's requested (v. 23). After having his two aides transport the gift close to his house, Gehazi takes it from them and stashes it before reporting to Elisha for duty (vv. 23-25). The deed is done and no one will be the wiser — at least that's the way Gehazi's got it figured. There is irony, once again, in the fact that, while he moves physically closer to Elisha, he has moved religiously far away from the prophet. He now "stood before" Elisha in body only, so to speak (v. 25).

Just as Elisha has known earlier, inexplicably, about what took place when Naaman encountered the Israelite king (v. 8), he again demonstrates a mysterious knowledge of Gehazi's activities. Even so, his manner of questioning still gives Gehazi a chance to come clean. Unfortunately, the latter fails this little test miserably: when asked where he has been, he responds, "Your servant has not gone anywhere in particular" (v. 25). We can't miss the poignancy of Gehazi's referring to himself as "your servant" when he has been behaving as anything but Elisha's servant. And this is the last time he speaks in the story: once he has tried to sidestep Elisha's implicit accusation, there's nothing more to say.

If Elisha's first question to Gehazi allows for the possibility of a positive response, the subsequent questions are tragically rhetorical. Incredibly — and to Gehazi's horror — Elisha's next question indicates that he in effect "saw" what Gehazi has been up to: "Did not my heart go along when a man turned from his chariot to meet you?" (v. 26). With the opportunity for a response now gone, Gehazi can only submit to the force of the rhetorical question's obvious answer. A second question immediately follows: "Is it an occasion for taking silver, for taking garments, olive orchards and vineyards, sheep and cattle, or male and female servants?" Once again, the answer to this question is chillingly apparent: "No, as a matter of fact, it is not such a time." Gehazi's haunting silence shows that he's all too aware of the appropriate answers to these disturbing questions.

Elisha's last words to Gehazi in this episode are not interrogatory but declarative, even prophetic. The same grievous skin disease that had afflicted Naaman is now inflicted on Gehazi and his progeny. This is not just any grievous skin condition; it is the one, tellingly, that "belonged," in effect, to Naaman: "Naaman's grievous skin disease shall cling . . ." (v. 27). When Gehazi left Naaman's presence, he had already been afflicted. The story that began with this disease ends with it, with the difference that its victims have been reversed: the Aramean outsider has become clean, and the Israelite insider has become unclean.

It's important to remember what was most serious about this condition from the point of view of the story. The primary issue was neither the disease's medical implications (whatever those may have been) nor its social stigma (whatever that may have been). The primary issue has to do with access to the divine presence in the temple (see Lev. 13–14). If we are to take Elisha's word literally that this disease will stay with Gehazi and his descendants "for ever" (v. 27: *lᵉʿôlām*), this means that the man is still afflicted when he shows up in a subsequent episode (2 Kgs. 8:4-5). In that instance, he is not shunned by others, nor is there any indication that he is debilitated in some way. That is, his punishment has to do with not having access to the temple, a prohibition that stays in force even though in other ways he functions as he had before, even as Elisha's servant (2 Kgs. 8:4). From an Israelite point of view, no punishment could be worse. As in the story of Rahab and Achan, the account featuring Naaman and Gehazi also deals with an outsider becoming an insider and an insider becoming an outsider, primarily in religious and theological rather than political or sociological terms. Though Rahab is presented as a quintessential Canaanite, she nevertheless ends up in the land that YHWH has promised to Israel. Naaman is not only an outsider religiously and theologically, politically and socially, but spatially as well; he will not live on Israel's land, as Rahab will. Furthermore, Naaman is an outsider whose occupation and standing in Aram make him an enemy of Israel in a concrete rather than an abstract sense. As a military man, he wages war against Israel, even though the aggression may be a simultaneous function of Aramean foreign policy and YHWH's judgment against Israel. And as if those matters are not enough to emphasize his position as an outsider vis-à-vis Israel, Naaman has a disease that would prevent his access to Israel's God even if he were an Israelite insider. Considering all of that, Naaman is no less an outsider in his own way than Rahab has been in hers. In addition, Naaman is able to be adopted into Israel's religious life without giving up his previous social and political life. This puts into bold relief the understanding of grace and openness that underlies this story.

As for Gehazi, we should probably not consider him an insider on a par with Achan, who had as impressive an Israelite pedigree as one could get. Gehazi is given no such résumé. But he is an intimate of Elisha, who is none other than the great Elijah's successor (1 Kgs. 19:15-16, 19-21; 2 Kgs. 2:6-14). As an aide to and disciple of Elisha, Gehazi is part of Israel's inner religious circle. To the extent that the prophets were often representative of Israel at its religious and theological best, Gehazi's status within such an elite group make him a significant insider. And this insider status makes his ultimate fate utterly poignant and tragic. Neither his status as a prophet's aide nor his close acquaintance with Elisha is able to save him. His violation of Israelite faith and theology is as deplorable as Naaman's confession and commitment are commendable. While Gehazi is not physically removed from Israel (2 Kgs. 8:1-6) — being spared the awful fate of Achan and his family — he is afflicted with Naaman's disease into perpetuity. His prohibition from the temple will remain in effect until the requirements of Torah as expressed in Leviticus 13–14 are completed, though these may not apply given the "for ever" nature of Elisha's curse.

Though this story does not provide enough detail to resolve every issue that it raises, it does speak emphatically to the main issue of the nature of Israel's election. Once again we see that ethnicity, geography, social status, prior religious commitment or understanding, and political standing are not the most decisive factors in being part of Israel. Religious commitment and theological comprehension are the primary factors. That is why an outsider such as Naaman can actually become a part of Israel in the most important way, and, conversely, an insider such as Gehazi can find his access to God cut off even though in other ways he remains part of Israel.

CHAPTER 5

Jonah: Prophet Among, To, and Against Outsiders

The biblical story of Jonah is wonderfully strange. The "book" in which he appears is unique among the Latter Prophets in that its primary focus is on the prophet's story rather than his preaching. There is only one oracle in the whole narrative, and it's even a stretch to call it that: it is in prose and uses a scant five words in the Hebrew text.* Never once in this odd, cryptic "sermon" is God so much as mentioned. The one instance where Jonah does wax poetic is in the prayer he offers from the belly of the great fish. Adding to the peculiarity, Jonah is not actually called a prophet in his own book, although he is designated as such in 2 Kings 14:25.† Still, Jonah is clearly a prophet, or at least he functions as one, considering the way God summons him and what God asks him to do. Those who put the Bible together were surely justified in placing the Book of Jonah among the other prophetic books.

Despite its brevity, the book has generated a disproportionate amount of commentary over the centuries — for a number of reasons. One probable reason is the highly unusual positive portrayal of pagans juxtaposed to the negative portrayal of a Hebrew prophet. In addition, Jonah is entirely unconventional: though called by God and supposedly a spokesperson for God, he becomes inconsolably furious when God acts graciously toward those to

---

*Prophetic oracles are typically cast in poetic form.

†Not all scholars have equated the Jonah of Kings and the Jonah of the prophetic book. While it is hardly uncommon for the same name to designate different people, it would be an extraordinary coincidence for there to have been two prophetic figures with the full name Jonah ben Amittai, since that would have meant that they, as well as their fathers, had the same names.

whom Jonah has spoken. Still, despite his petulance and bizarre behavior, we cannot dismiss him as a false prophet. After all, God does not summon false prophets; they speak on their own. Another reason for the extraordinary interest in this book is its stunning report that an entire pagan city turns to Jonah's God upon hearing his one puny pronouncement (Jonah 3). Plus, this was not just any nondescript pagan city; this was Nineveh, the capital city of Assyria, one of Israel's most feared and vilified enemies, and the nation that actually caused the destruction of the Northern Kingdom of Israel (2 Kings 18:9-12). And then there's the "whale" — the incredible role of the "great fish" that swallowed Jonah at God's behest, holding him in its belly for three days and three nights, and finally regurgitating him up unceremoniously onto dry land, once more at God's urging (Jonah 2). No wonder people have been fascinated by the Book of Jonah for some time.

Though the Book of Jonah raises a number of tantalizing issues, our task is to concentrate on the insider-outsider motif: when we do, we are struck right away by the different perspective this story has on that theme. Of the several accounts of outsiders we are examining in this book, the Book of Jonah alone features outsiders collectively: the totality of a ship's crew and a large city's entire population. In every other narrative discussed here, the outsider is an individual and, with the exception of the "woman at the well" in the Gospel of John (see Chapter 7), a named individual: Esau, Tamar, Rahab, Naaman, Ruth.* Conversely, the prophet of the Book of Jonah, the sole insider, is the only character with a name. In both scenes where he interacts with other people — on board the ship and in Nineveh — he is surrounded by outsiders with no names, whether they are pagan sailors or the city's citizens and royalty. Not even the captain of the ship or the king of Nineveh is given a name, even though they have eminent status and crucial roles in this story. These and other features are suggestive of the intriguing way in which the Book of Jonah approaches the outsider theme.

God's call — Jonah's flight

As the story gets under way, outsiders are immediately in view. The episode begins with a standard formula that signals a pending command

---

*Rahab is something of an exception to this pattern in that her entire family is also preserved along with her. Still, Rahab is the only outsider in the episode who acts or speaks; her family is offstage, so to speak.

from God (Jonah 1:1). However, though the formula is a common one, it has a twist. Jonah is hardly the only Israelite prophet whom God instructs to announce judgment on foreigners, but he is virtually the only one ever told to deliver such a message to them on their home territory. Being told to denounce Nineveh or any other outsiders because "their evil has come up before me" (1:2) was more or less typical fare for YHWH's prophets. That explains the presence of many "oracles against the nations" in the prophetic materials. What was extraordinary in Jonah's case was God's added insistence that he go to the outsiders' home to deliver the message: "Rise, go to Nineveh. . . ." Considering this divine directive, the reader has every expectation that a most interesting and potentially volatile scenario is about to unfold. Even when Israelite prophets spoke under God's orders against other Israelites, they were far from welcome; on the contrary, they were often reviled and rejected — or worse, as is well documented.* How much more of a hostile reaction would an Israelite prophet provoke by having the effrontery to rail against foreigners on their own turf? Presumably, Jonah is about to find out; and, as readers, we can't help but anticipate the sparks that will almost certainly fly.

But it is one thing for God to expand Jonah's prophetic vocation by ordering him to speak out against a foreign city while in that city; it is another thing entirely when the city happens to be Nineveh. At the first mention of the target for Jonah's oracle(s), YHWH refers to Nineveh as "the great city" (1:2). It is not quite clear what God has in mind with that description. Nonetheless, one does not have to speculate much about what "Nineveh, the great city" would have meant to the average Israelite. As I've mentioned, Nineveh was the capital city of Assyria, a country that was a perpetual enemy of Israel, the cause of the desolation of its Northern Kingdom, and once the terrifying besiegers of Judah and its capital, Jerusalem (2 Kgs. 18:13-37). Considering how Assyria is loathed and feared by Israel, it is not surprising that the entire prophetic Book of Nahum is devoted to a vilification of that foreign country. Any Israelite prophet worth his or her salt would have readily thundered against Nineveh at the slightest divine prompt. But doing so in the middle of Nineveh would surely

---

*One famous example of the disdain with which Israelite prophets were met in their own homeland is found in Amos 7:10-17. In that instance, Amos perhaps encountered more intense opprobrium since he was a prophet from Judah speaking out against the Northern Kingdom of Israel. Still, even "hometown" prophets were resisted mightily (see 1 Kings 22:13-28).

have been considered tantamount to suicide. Yet that is precisely what YHWH orders Jonah to do.

When God tells Jonah to go to Nineveh and cry against it for its evil, God does not enumerate the city's specific sins. YHWH apparently sees no reason to provide Jonah with those details; the divine summons itself is presumably enough. Nor does YHWH bother to tell him what to say. Evidently, a generalized oracle of judgment will suffice: God wants Jonah to "cry out against" Nineveh, but the exact wording of the oracle will, we gather, be up to him. It turns out that Jonah's mission, despite its inherent danger, is actually quite simple. Nineveh has been guilty of something that leads God to send a prophet its way with a generic word of condemnation. Jonah must call on his own prophetic experience and his own homiletic imagination for the appropriate content. It's a tough assignment, to be sure, but in a way rather straightforward.

But Jonah's response to God's clear directive complicates matters in a hurry. Jonah gets ready to leave, just as he has been told, but not for Nineveh. Instead, he flees the divine presence. Why does Jonah react in this way? Is he afraid of Nineveh's predictable negative reaction? Is he willing to preach judgment against Nineveh, but only from within the friendly confines of Israel, or at least from a more neutral venue? Does he intuit some hidden agenda, as though this were a sneaky way for YHWH to put him at risk? And, if so, why would YHWH have it in for him anyway?

We get nothing but silence from the text on these questions. We know that Jonah is being disobedient, but the reasons elude us. Given the popular conception that biblical prophets were more or less eager to proclaim "gloom and doom," one might have thought that Jonah would have jumped at this opportunity. But this particular prophet, on this particular occasion, wants nothing to do with "crying against" Nineveh. We are not given the reason, only the result: he arises to flee to Tarshish, away from the presence of the Lord.

As an Israelite prophet — apparently one for whom it is not unusual to receive direct orders from God — Jonah obviously has impeccable insider credentials.* If an ordinary Israelite was an insider by virtue of being part of the "chosen people," how much more of an insider would a prophet be, given the prophetic role as one who speaks for and acts on behalf of the

---

*Jonah never questions the source of his call. He comes off in the story as experienced in receiving a divine summons (compare the call of Moses in Exodus 3:1–4:17).

very God who elected Israel in the first place? Yet, insider status or not, once Jonah hears God's call to go to Nineveh and preach, he moves abruptly and resolutely toward the "outside" — literally and figuratively. He does this in two ways. First, by refusing to do what God has asked him to do, Jonah is in effect behaving as though it makes no difference that YHWH is his people's deity or that he is a prophet in YHWH's employ. Jonah acts as though he is an "independent contractor" who has the luxury of accepting or rejecting YHWH's retainer. But that's not the way it's supposed to work for Israelite prophets; the expected prophetic response is: "Here am I, send me" (see Isa. 6:8). Second, Jonah not only takes a giant step toward becoming an outsider by disobeying God outright, he also goes so far as to leave Israel and in the process tries to move out of God's presence and beyond the divine reach (Jonah 1:3). In one precipitous move Jonah attempts to position himself not only outside Israel but outside the putative jurisdiction of Israel's (and his) God.

Jonah's departure for Tarshish gives us our best clue about what he's thinking. In terms of the geography reflected in this story, Tarshish is as far away from Nineveh and Israel as one can physically get. Isaiah 66:19 says that Tarshish is a place where God has never been known. Of course, there is another implication to the reluctant prophet's escape route. Not only does Jonah wish to distance himself completely from Nineveh, but he also needs to put as much distance as he can between himself and the deity who has saddled him with such an onerous task. Perhaps he knows of Tarshish's reputation as one of the remote places where YHWH is not known. Whether he does or doesn't, the fact remains that, by booking passage on a ship bound for Tarshish, he knows that he will not only avoid Nineveh but will stay away from Israel, where things might get dicey for a fugitive prophet trying to stay out of God's clutches. Granted, we cannot actually know what is going through Jonah's head when he makes his audacious break, but there is nothing to prohibit us from drawing inferences based on his actions.

The "perfect storm"

If Jonah thinks that the sea he has to traverse to get to Tarshish will keep him out of God's range, he's in for a rude awakening. The ship is barely under way when YHWH "hurl[s] a great wind at the sea" (Jonah 1:4). This generates a "great storm," so powerful that the ship "thought" to break up. Whatever Jonah figures might have befallen him had he gone to Nineveh with his bleak message, could it have been any worse than what currently threatens him? His attempt to find sanctuary on the sea and leave God back in Israel or standing helplessly on the dock at Joppa suddenly appears ludicrous. The ship he has imagined as his means of escape is about to become his casket, at least if it cannot negotiate the high seas.

But Jonah is not the only one in jeopardy. The ship's crew, not to mention any fellow passengers, are also in grave danger. As might be expected with this turn of events, the sailors now come to center stage. Though they are professionals, they become terrified when the storm hits (1:5). Perhaps it is precisely because they are professionals that they get so scared: who would better know the likely outcome of a severe storm on the sea in a vulnerable vessel? Still, as natural as their fear is, it certainly does not paralyze them. As soon as the storm comes up, they all cry out to their respective gods. Everyone in the ancient world was religious, and these mariners are no exception. In fact, considering their hazardous occupation, they may be more devout than most. These good polytheists immediately appeal to any gods who might be willing to help. Since most gods in the ancient world were "specialists," who knew which ones might have brought about this terrible circumstance or which ones might alleviate it?*

Compared to Jonah, the ship's crew consists of outsiders; yet, though they are non-Israelites, they are not atheists. They are willing and able to perform whatever religious activity is necessary to get themselves and their ship out of this horrible situation, including calling on gods. The sailors' religious fervor is underscored by the fact that, before they engage in a single naval maneuver, they pray. No matter how strong their instincts as mariners are, before they trim any sail, batten down a single hatch, or grab the helm, they invoke their gods. Only after that do they conduct themselves as seamen, throwing gear and baggage overboard to lighten the load and make it easier for the ship to stay afloat. A plight as desperate as this one requires desperate responses — both religious and

---

*When I say that most gods were "specialists," I am referring to the ancient belief that various gods were in charge of or exercised control over certain areas of life. Thus, the sun, moon, and other heavenly bodies were deified; likewise, a river, mountain, sea, or any number of animals might be considered gods. Part of biblical monotheism was the view that there was not only one God but that this deity was sovereign over all the other "specialties" supposedly covered by other gods.

practical ones. The crew is up to the task, but whether their efforts will succeed remains to be seen.

Remarkably, while all the sea's fury and the sailors' frenzied activity are going on, Jonah is utterly oblivious: he has gone down into the hold of the ship and has fallen asleep (1:5). It seems likely that Jonah has gone down there prior to the storm, though the grammar is such that it is conceivable that he has gone into the hold in response to the storm. More plausibly, we can picture Jonah, soon after boarding the ship or just after it gets underway, going down to the hold in order to relax and take his mind off his recent unpleasant encounter with God. But it would be only slightly less astounding for him to fall asleep just as he sees the storm come up. For whatever reason, Jonah so far is completely unfazed by the threat that is swirling around him.

Curiously, when the captain confronts Jonah, he moves quickly past his astonishment that Jonah can sleep in the chaos that has engulfed the ship. More significantly, he barks specific orders: "Get up, call on your God" (1:6). Here is an echo of God's initial command, for both the deity and the captain order Jonah to "arise/get up" and "call."* Again, it is most interesting that the captain asks Jonah to pray rather than help the crew. Wouldn't every able-bodied person have been enlisted to do whatever physical job needed to be done? But this good polytheist wants all the religious bases covered first. In a setting where one has no idea which god or gods might have brought about the storm — for such things were scarcely considered accidental — it would be prudent to appeal to every deity in the pantheon. This sleeper's deity might be just the one who could get them out of this mess. The captain says as much: "Maybe your deity will give us a thought so that we do not perish."

It should not be lost on us how religious the sailors are portrayed in this scene; not only that, the portrayal of them is quite sympathetic. Given their theology, they are conducting themselves in a most appropriate way. They believe some god or gods have put them in an awful bind, so they are doing whatever it takes to get the god(s) responsible to reverse themselves. Or, if only one god is the cause of their being on the brink of disaster, then the sailors have no choice but to find out which god that is. That's why they also compel Jonah to pray. This is no time for religious reticence. Of

---

*The difference is that YHWH has told Jonah to "cry *against*" (qārā' 'al), whereas the captain instructs him to "call *on*" (qārā' 'el).

course, from an Israelite point of view, the theology of the sailors is dead wrong. And we readers have known since Jonah 1:4 that only one deity is responsible for what has been going on: YHWH. The sailors' prayers could not be more futile. They don't know that of course; they are simply acting on their own religious impulses. Their theology may be fatally flawed, but there is nothing wrong with their faith. The narrator acknowledges that credit must be given where credit is due.

Jonah represents the opposite end of the spectrum. As we shall soon learn, his theology is completely orthodox, yet his faith is deficient. He may believe correctly, but his credo is belied by his actions. This comes to the surface when the sailors, frustrated that their prayers are doing them no good, decide to cast lots to reveal the person among them who is responsible for their terrifying dilemma. And we are not the least bit surprised when the drawing of lots points to Jonah (1:7). Naturally, once this has singled Jonah out, the sailors pepper him with probing questions (1:8), the most incisive of which has to do with whether Jonah is to blame for the calamitous storm. Sidestepping a number of the questions, Jonah gets to the heart of the matter. His short answer vaguely hints that he is responsible, though he removes any lingering doubt when he elaborates on his remarks.

"I am a Hebrew" is all he says at first (1:9).* But what he says next must have been as stunning as it was chilling to the sailors: "YHWH, the God of the heavens, who made the sea and the dry land, I reverence." Jonah's statement seems innocuous to us today; he seems merely to be identifying his own religious preference. But we must view his statement within the ancient Near East culture: the deities of the ancient world all specialized in some activity or were dominant in some sphere. "Sea," "dry land," and even "heavens" were either the realms of the gods over which certain ones exercised control — or were gods themselves. Jonah's comprehensive and uncompromising affirmation that his God is the God of the heavens and the creator of all the other realms is an unmistakably monotheistic apologetic: there is only one God around — namely, his God — and this deity is sovereign over everything. After all, a deity whose territory is the heavens, sea,

---

*The Israelites often used "Hebrew" rather than "Israelite" when in the presence of foreigners. Sometimes Israelites used the term about themselves; at other times foreigners referred to Israelites with this terminology (see Genesis 39:14, 17; 41:12; Exodus 1:16, 19; 2:6-7; 1 Samuel 4:9).

and dry land by virtue of having sovereign control over it all, not to mention having created it all in the first place, effectively eliminates any and all rival deities. By making this announcement, Jonah joins the voice of the narrator, who has informed us all along that it is in fact YHWH who has hurled the wind and caused the storm that got the present sequence of events rolling. No wind god or storm god or heaven-sky god has done that. YHWH alone is sovereign. Indeed, YHWH is alone, period.

It is important for us to keep in mind that Jonah has already informed the crew of his reason for taking this voyage: he is running away from his God (1:10). But that information would not have been necessarily alarming to the sailors because, for all they knew, YHWH was the sort of deity they knew about — restricted either in terms of power or geography. In that light, it would not have seemed unusual to have a passenger embarking on a journey to escape a local deity. But given Jonah's claims about YHWH, his efforts to escape suddenly appear foolhardy. Not only that, the sailors now realize that, as unwitting accomplices in Jonah's imprudent decision to go AWOL after his God has summoned him, their lives may also be at stake. If YHWH is truly as Jonah describes, this is not the kind of deity with whom one can trifle.

Jonah's response to the sailors about himself and his God sets in bold relief the sharp disjunction between his beliefs and his actions. If Jonah were sincerely convinced of the truth of his affirmations about YHWH, then his actions after getting God's instructions make no sense at all. How can one get away from such a deity? Isn't it absurd to think that any body of water or tract of land, no matter how remote, could have provided a hiding place from this kind of God? Weren't there Israelite traditions familiar to Jonah emphasizing that YHWH is everywhere, that there is no adequate place to conceal oneself (for example, Psalm 139)? As a prophet, wasn't Jonah intimately aware of YHWH's impressive attributes and abilities, the very ones that would have formed part of the foundation for his prophetic preaching? Considering that Jonah must have been fully aware of what YHWH was capable of, his plan to make himself invisible in Tarshish is quite laughable. What possible good is his theological orthodoxy in light of a faith so impoverished? It would have been better for him to have been a good honest skeptic. With insiders like the prophet Jonah, who needs outsiders!

Jonah looks even worse when we compare him to the pagan sailors. As I have noted, their theology leaves everything to be desired: they are wrong about almost everything they believe. Yet they comport themselves most admirably; in fact, their religious fervor is enviable. There is not the slightest gap between what they believe and how they act. When trouble comes, their first instincts are to pray. Not only that, at least one of them — the captain — is "evangelistic" in getting one of his sleeping passengers (perhaps his only passenger) to pray. Plus, the captain apparently is not at all defensive about the gods to whom he or any of the other mariners are praying. If Jonah's deity ends up being the one to calm the storm, so be it. This is no place for religious one-upmanship.

Actually, the sailors seem to realize the stark implications of Jonah's explanation more than Jonah himself does. If he has spoken truthfully, isn't their "great fear" totally justifiable (1:10)? A deity as powerful as the one claimed by Jonah can only evoke fear, if not outright panic. Also, we need to remember that this discussion is not taking place in a coffeehouse or pub. These people are fighting for their very lives in a raging storm. Thus, their follow-up question to Jonah underscores their sense of dread and helplessness: "What is this you've done?" The point of their accusation suggests not only their frustration but their incredulity. What would possess anyone to try to escape a deity of this power? At this point the sailors reveal that they already know Jonah is fleeing YHWH's presence. Again, that was not necessarily remarkable at the time he told them, for there were many deities in the ancient world that could be avoided or deceived, their power neutralized if one simply got outside their "sphere of influence."* But Jonah has testified that YHWH is no such deity: this God has made everything and is, therefore, sovereign everywhere. There's simply no rational explanation for Jonah's attempt to get away from YHWH, and that's why the sailors are petrified.

Since Jonah's God is behind this — or so he maintains — it follows that he may know how to pacify his God, hence the sailors' next question: "What shall we do to you to get the sea to desist from us?" (1:11) Though it means certain death to him, Jonah does not shrink from a truthful answer: "Lift me up and throw me into the sea, then the sea will desist from you. For I know that it is because of me that this great storm is upon you" (1:12). Once again, Jonah's theology comes off as impeccable, and everything he

---

*For example, in the famous Epic of Gilgamesh, the deity (En-Lil) who sends a great flood on the earth with the intention of destroying humanity has his diabolical plans thwarted by other deities, who provide a way of escape for Ut-Napishtim and his wife.

knows theologically turns out to be true. But once again, the disconnect between his beliefs and his actions could not be more pronounced. Why would someone who knows such things comport himself in such a self-destructive manner? However, no matter how critical we may be of Jonah's actions up to this point, we cannot accuse him of dishonesty. He may have been stupid to become a fugitive in the first place, but when cornered he does not dissemble.

Even more remarkable than Jonah's willingness to be forthcoming, with no regard for the likely personal consequences, is the selfless professionalism and integrity of the sailors. With the storm about to do in the ship, one might conclude that the sailors would take Jonah at his word and toss him overboard without hesitation. The death of one passenger would be tragic, to be sure, but not nearly as tragic as the drowning of everyone aboard. Might there be some operative maritime principle involving the sacrifice of one to save the many in such an awful circumstance? Did the sailors have any realistic option?

Yet, despite apparently having no choice but to take Jonah up on his offer, the crew will have none of it. Paying no attention to what Jonah has told them, they row toward shore (1:13). From the perspective of sailing strategy, this is evidently an ill-advised maneuver, though it shows the sailors' behavior to be even more noble. Rowing toward shore in such bad weather makes little navigational sense, but they are determined to save the one passenger whose presence on the ship is the cause of all their woes. Their integrity and honor as mariners trumps their wisdom about the best nautical procedures under the circumstances. These are most impressive pagans.

The amazing crew

We have seen Jonah, right from the beginning of the story, moving rapidly and steadily to get outside the Israelite community, physically and religiously, despite his clear insider status. His Israelite theology is never suspect, but it is rendered moot in light of his questionable actions. His faith simply does not match his theology. Conversely, the sailors, as a group and from the beginning of the storm, also move in a certain direction — away from their obvious outsider position. By the time the episode comes to the point where the sailors run out of viable options for dealing with the storm, we observe them moving inexorably toward the inside. In effect, Jonah and the sailors pass each other as they head in the opposite direction from where they began.

To show how much the sailors take Jonah's assertions about YHWH to heart, they stop at nothing to try to save this God's reluctant prophet. That's why they row foolishly toward shore when all they have to do is throw Jonah into the sea. As they get closer to Jonah in terms of theological outlook, their actions are much more commensurate with what they are coming to believe. Unlike Jonah, these mariners have a connection between their theology and their actions — both in terms of their pagan perspective and in terms of their incipient Israelite perspective.

There is no need to speculate about this because the sailors are forthcoming in their thought processes. Having heard from Jonah what YHWH is like and having tried unsuccessfully to row to shore, they then do a little theologizing of their own. They realize that the storm is too strong to overcome, and this means they no longer have a choice: they apparently will have to take Jonah up on his recommendation and throw him into the sea. But if they do that, won't Jonah's God become angrier at them than at him? Once more, in desperation, they resort to prayer, this time not to their gods but to YHWH. Their prayer consists of a plaintive plea and a theological assertion: first, they plead with YHWH not to allow them to perish on account of "this man" (having finally concluded that they will all perish if Jonah stays with the ship); as a corollary, they implore God not to punish them should they end up throwing Jonah overboard, which would constitute a charge of "innocent blood" against them (1:14). From YHWH's standpoint, of course, Jonah is hardly innocent. But the sailors don't have anything against him: this difficulty is between Jonah and YHWH. They want to avoid being caught in the middle of what amounts to a domestic spat between Jonah and his God.

This forlorn prayer emphasizes the extreme ethical sensitivity of the crew, not to mention their willingness to act on a theological insight into YHWH that they have only recently acquired. The final part of their prayer is actually an assertion about the sovereignty of YHWH: "For you are YHWH, you do whatever you will." This statement is noteworthy on two levels. First, though we are well aware that the sailors have invoked any number of gods earlier in the story (1:5), this is the first deity they refer to by name. So far Jonah has spoken about his God only in the third person; but the pagan sailors have now spoken to God by uttering the divine name twice. Second, it is clear that the sailors have taken Jonah's claims about YHWH with utmost seriousness. Seeing the reality of the God of the heavens, the Creator of the sea and dry land, the One who has caused the storm in an effort to quash Jonah's rebellion and reverse his flight, the sailors have come to acknowledge that this is a deity they can ignore only at their peril. From the first, their (pagan) faith was in line with their (pagan) theology; now they are beginning to manifest an inkling of Israelite faith in line with their fledgling Israelite theology.

What happens next confirms this. Left with no options, the sailors finally do the only thing Jonah has said will work: they throw him overboard into the roiling waters. And they find that Jonah was correct in telling them that this is their only hope: the storm immediately stops (1:15), and the calamity of a sinking ship is averted. This has to be a big reinforcement of what the sailors have just recently come to believe about Jonah's God. It also indicates once again that Jonah's theology throughout this episode has been on the mark: every single thing he has insisted about his deity has proved to be true, in spite of the fact that he was unwilling to conduct himself in accordance with his belief system. But Jonah's anemic faith does not deter the sailors.

For the second time, we learn that the mariners have a "great fear" of YHWH, this time more directly (Jonah 1:16; see 1:10).* "Fear" in this usage has the nuance of respect, reverence, and awe as well as its more usual connotation. Having heard Jonah's confession and having seen YHWH's actions firsthand, the sailors assume the appropriate religious posture: in this final scene the sailors offer sacrifices and make vows to YHWH. These religious gestures are hardly remarkable in themselves; sacrifices and vows to the gods were part of the warp and woof of ancient Near Eastern religion, Israelite or other. What is different in this case is that YHWH is the object of the sailors' devotion. And we should not lose sight of the fact that, at the close of this segment of Jonah's story, the sailors are engaged in acts of worship directed toward Jonah's God at the very moment that the prophet is offstage, struggling in the sea precisely because his response to his God has been flight rather than "fear" and honor.

It is not necessary to construe the sailors' praying, vowing, and sacrificing to YHWH as a full-scale conversion. Strictly speaking, the narration

---

*The first time, the sailors' fear is a function of what Jonah declared about YHWH; the second time, YHWH is more explicitly the object of their fear or reverence.

does not inform us one way or the other on that question. The narrator, while ambiguous, is content to say that, just before the mariners fade from the scene, they are acting as good Israelites would act. They may have simply added YHWH to their pantheon, perhaps even according this new deity pride of place — at least from their vantage point. At the same time, the story portrays the mariners as taking what Jonah has said about YHWH extremely seriously. Since every word Jonah uttered about his deity has been unwaveringly orthodox, he has provided the pagan crew with a brief Israelite catechism, a first-rate religious education, as it were. In light of Israelite theology, it is impossible to recognize YHWH as merely one god among the other gods; nor is it an improvement to regard this deity as first among equals, or even as one god superior to all the other gods. As far as believers in YHWH are concerned, there are no other gods. Thus, to the extent that the sailors are depicted as offering prayers, making vows, and presenting sacrifices to YHWH, it does not strain credulity to see them comporting themselves as properly orthodox and devout Israelites. If that is the case, then it is perfectly plausible to view them as converts in the strict sense. Perhaps these outsiders have become insiders. At the very least, their *actions* have become indistinguishable from those of insiders. Had Jonah exercised even a fraction of the faith the sailors manifested, there would never have been a storm in the first place.

The great fish

When Jonah is deposited unceremoniously into the raging sea, for the briefest moment it appears that his story has come to an inglorious end. The rapid succession of concluding events looks for all the world like a denouement: the sailors throw Jonah overboard, the storm breaks, and the sailors worship YHWH (Jonah 1:15-16). But the action continues — only the scene changes. Before Jonah has time to thrash wildly in the sea, gasp for air, or contemplate his certain demise and eventual descent to a watery grave, YHWH once again puts events into motion. Jonah's God does what might be expected of a deity who is "God of Heaven . . . who created the sea and the dry land" (1:9). YHWH "appoints" a great fish to swallow the now helpless prophet (1:17[Heb. 2:1]).

Ironically, whereas Jonah has not spent a single night on board the ship, he ends up staying in the great fish's belly three full days and three full nights. Also, in contrast to his time on the threatened vessel, this time he prays to his God without having to be prompted by a pagan sailor (Jonah 2:1[Heb. 2]). The irony is deepened when we recall that, though Jonah had been urged to pray on the ship, he never actually did so. This fits with his failure to display any act of piety whatsoever, in spite of his orthodox stance. Although Jonah's prayer from the confines of his new intestinal surroundings is interesting in itself, we need to ask whether it pertains to the insider-outsider motif. After all, Jonah is completely by himself at this point; the only outsiders we've encountered are now far away. It remains to be seen whether another set will appear on the horizon.

It turns out that several things Jonah says in his prayer do speak to the insider-outsider issue. At first blush, the most surprising aspect of Jonah's prayer is that it is a model of Israelite piety. One wonders what has happened to the old Jonah, who was as impious as he was orthodox. Having refused to offer even a "foxhole" prayer in the belly of a ship about to sink and even after being urged explicitly to join everyone else in prayer, he now calls on YHWH in the midst of his distress and further expresses supreme confidence in YHWH's willingness to hear him (2:2[Heb. 3]). Nor is he deterred by his own comparison of the fish's innards with Sheol, the realm of the dead. He knows that God is listening nonetheless. Jonah goes on to describe his hopeless situation, which he ascribes completely to divine actions, evidently seeing the sailors as little more than YHWH's instruments (2:3-4[Heb. 4-5]). Again, however, Jonah's newly discovered piety rises to the top: he worries that he has been driven from God's sight and further that he may never gaze on God's holy temple again. This is a man who just a short time earlier had done everything in his power to escape God's gaze and avoid at all costs the holy temple where he might run into God.

After further elaborating on his impossible plight, he once again focuses on God: he actually praises God for saving him from death (2:5-7[Heb. 6-8]). Clearly, Jonah sees the fish's role as an act of rescue rather than judgment. This makes sense, for Jonah would certainly have drowned but for the fish. However unpleasant and frightening his sojourn in this gruesome setting for three days and nights is, it is infinitely better than death. Again, his use of pious language is remarkable: Jonah acknowledges that his prayer comes before God in the holy temple. What greater symbol of piety was there for a sincerely religious Israelite?

The final lines of the poetic prayer are most revealing. Not only do we get a better glimpse into Jonah's psyche, but we discover that the piety reflected in his prayer is a function not of heartfelt religion but of distortion and arrogance. Jonah probably feels that he is being sincere and transparent, but his words betray him. As the prayer comes to a close, Jonah criticizes "those who attend to vain idols," thus "forsaking their welfare" (2:8[Heb. 9]); in contrast, Jonah insists, he not only sacrifices to the deity with "loud thanksgiving" but indeed follows through on what he vows (2:9[Heb. 10]). Though there's no doubt that this is a swipe at pagans and that Jonah is trying to show his own religious behavior in the best possible light, his claims are the complete opposite of what has actually happened with the only pagans in this story, those on the ship. As we saw in Jonah 1, they did not forsake but embraced YHWH at the expense of their own deities — "vain idols," as Jonah dubs them. Besides, only the pagan mariners (who may now even be converted) offered sacrifices and vows to Jonah's God. Furthermore, all the bad things that have happened in this story so far have come about for no reason other than Jonah's shabby religious performance: he is a fugitive from God and his own prophetic vocation. This might have been a great prayer had it been offered by someone other than Jonah, a man who is having a very difficult time distinguishing reality from fantasy.

Jonah's final statement in this prayer is a grand affirmation: "Salvation belongs to YHWH" (2:9[Heb. 10]). Once again he speaks the truth, despite the vast distance between his belief and his former behavior or present understanding. Not only is this statement true in general — indeed, wasn't this a major tenet of Israelite faith? — but so far in the story God has already saved the mariners and even Jonah. While he is theologically correct, Jonah seems to have no existential insight into what he is saying. And as though to react with an exclamation point to Jonah's whole prayer, including the final sentiment, the Lord has the fish vomit the pitiful prophet onto dry ground. This is not the usual way to conclude a prayer. But in the case of this particular prayer by this particular prophet, it seems to be just the right touch — a great fish's regurgitation supplanting the more customary "amen!"

Nineveh's reversal

After the fish incident, the story goes back to its original formula (Jonah 1:1). In spite of the prophet's previous stubbornness, YHWH still wants him to go to Nineveh, and this second command is virtually a verbatim repetition of the first one (3:2), except that this time YHWH specifies that Jonah is to say "what I say to you." Unlike his first response, when he "rose" to "flee," now Jonah arises to "go" (3:3). There is no way to determine whether Jonah obeys because he is chastened by what has happened to him, so that his piety now more closely matches his theology, or merely because he does not want to try YHWH's patience again. In any case, he does go straight to Nineveh.

At this point in the story we also get a better idea of why Nineveh is designated as "the great city": it takes three days to walk through it. But Jonah is ready to deliver his oracle after only one day's journey into the city, as though he cannot wait to unburden himself of what he has to say (Jonah 3:4). Does this suggest that Jonah is still somewhat reluctant? Or does Jonah simply want to declaim from a more central location than the city's periphery? The answer has to await further developments.

When Jonah at last does what a prophet is supposed to do, that is, deliver an oracle, it could not be more brief and cryptic. Indeed, his utterance abounds in "unstable properties": that is, one can translate the oracle either as "In yet forty days Nineveh will be destroyed" or as "In yet forty days Nineveh will be turned around [that is, delivered]." Put simply, it is impossible to tell whether Jonah has predicted judgment or deliverance. Even the "yet" is ambiguous, for it leaves open the timing: does this mean within forty days or at the end of forty days? Or might the "forty days" suggest an indefinite period? Then again, does the oracle announce what *will* happen or what *may* happen? Furthermore, are the Ninevites to understand that Jonah's God — whom Jonah does not mention — is the agent who will be finally responsible for Nineveh's either being "destroyed" or "delivered"? It is curious that Jonah's statement is ambiguous at all, since YHWH's plain assertion at the beginning is that "their evil has come before me" (1:2). Why isn't the oracle categorically negative? Finally, does the issue turn on Nineveh's response? In other words, will the people themselves determine whether the "destroyed/delivered" verb is to be applied negatively or positively?

Apparently, this last condition is what is meant. Despite the brevity and cryptic nature of Jonah's announcement, the people of Nineveh believe in God upon hearing it (3:5). But what do they believe? Do they conclude that Jonah's God — whom Jonah has yet to mention — is capable of either destroying or delivering them? On what basis do they believe that? And what about counter-arguments? Why is this one prophetic announcement by a foreigner taken so seriously? Why isn't it laughed off or taken as an impertinence? None of these questions gets an ounce of consideration. Rather, the story ignores these and any other potential questions and makes the astonishing declaration that the people have come to believe.

Moreover, this amazing display of belief is not at all superficial. The Assyrians accompany their immediate assertion of belief with the act of donning sackcloth, which clearly symbolized contrition. These people are deadly serious. In addition, the whole city participates in this astonishingly positive response: everyone dresses in mourning clothes, "from the great to the small." Nothing short of a religious revival seems to have gotten under way in downtown Nineveh. The depth and extent of the Ninevites' response to Jonah's oracle are amply illustrated by what takes place when word reaches the king. He might well have been expected to scoff at his subjects' inexplicable behavior and upbraid them for acting like something other than red-blooded Assyrians. But his behavior is equally perplexing. He rises from his throne, takes off his regal garments, and dresses himself in sackcloth. To punctuate the depth of his contrition, he sits on an ash heap. Furthermore, not content to allow these events to unfold spontaneously, he and his royal cabinet make an official proclamation that a fast is to be observed (3:6-7). Even more astounding is the proclamation that this observance is not only to be kept by all Ninevites but is to be applied to their animals as well — including sheep and cattle. The king wants nothing left to chance and no living creature excluded.

The specifics of the royal decree exemplify not only how sincere this move toward (Jonah's) God is, but also the theological rationale behind it. The king's orders make clear that all people and all beasts are to be outfitted in clothes befitting repentance (3:8). It doesn't seem to bother the king or his nobles in the least that this decree is somewhat redundant, since the Ninevites, "from the great to the small" (Jonah 3:5), have been dressed in sackcloth from the very first time they heard Jonah speak. But being appropriately dressed is only part of the requirement. The decree goes on to urge the people to "call on (Jonah's) God with intensity" (3:8). Finally, the king's decree implores the people to turn away from their evil ways, including any violence of which they are guilty.* This revival is to include mind and heart.

Finally, the actions toward which the king urges his subjects are based on a plain theological assumption, namely, that God will relent from the

---

*The operative word is *šûb*, the main Old Testament word for repenting.

judgment that is pending, according to the prophet: "Who knows whether God might turn and repent; he may turn from his anger so that we do not perish" (Jonah 3:9). We are not told how the Assyrians came to believe that Jonah's God was capable of such a change of mind; all we know is that they are putting the ball in God's court. Having heard the message, which they take as a dire judgment but which nonetheless also affords an opportunity, they respond as appropriately as one could imagine: they show remorse, dress in garments of penitence, mend their ways, pray fervently, and trust that God's mercy will trump God's justice. Is there anything else anyone could have asked of them?

As amazing as the sailors' response to Jonah's God was, at least that could be explained in part as a function of good old-fashioned fear in the face of almost certain death. People might be tempted, under those circumstances, to try all manner of religious innovations. But all the Ninevites have to go on is Jonah's ambiguous and truncated five-word oracle, something they could just as easily have been inclined cavalierly to dismiss. Who even knew what it meant? Yet the Ninevite response epitomizes sincerity. Has any Israelite city ever responded to a prophetic utterance so immediately, so thoroughly, and so admirably? Nineveh has just become a model for how to respond to the prophetic words of the Israelite prophets.

Whether or not we are impressed with Nineveh's response to Jonah, YHWH certainly is. When YHWH sees their actions and the fact that they have repented of their evil ways, YHWH responds in kind. In a remarkable quid pro quo, when Nineveh has repented of its evil, YHWH repents of his anger, rescinding the judgment the Ninevites would have faced had they reacted inappropriately (3:10). It turns out that Jonah has never had a thing to worry about. In fact, he will go down in history as preaching a sermon in which the positive response was in inverse proportion to its length (perhaps a secondary lesson for all preachers). This prophet will henceforth be known as having been the impetus for one of the most successful revivals found in Israelite tradition. Would any prophet have a better reason to be proud of what his eventual obedience, however initially reluctant, had wrought?

No matter what our expectations of Jonah's response are, he is not only not proud of his role in Nineveh's turnaround, he is downright disappointed (4:1). For the second time in the story he prays, in this instance not to extol or petition, but to inform (4:2). Jonah's prayer reveals his innermost feelings, which finally explain why he first ran away from YHWH:

"O Lord, was this not my word while still in my land, so that I anticipated fleeing to Tarshish? For I knew that you were a compassionate and gracious God, mildly tempered and given to mercy, even
one who repents of evil. Now, O YHWH, take my life from me this
minute, for my death is better than my life" (4:2-3).

Once again Jonah reveals his thoroughly orthodox outlook, but that is
precisely the source of his displeasure. Rather than rejoicing over serving a
deity with such a wonderful nature, Jonah is disgusted by these traits. We
now come face to face with the unpalatable and disturbing fact that Jonah
has fled his God not because he was worried about Nineveh's likely negative reaction to his preaching but because of its potential positive reaction
to YHWH, which might induce the deity to withdraw punishment. To Jonah, apparently, this divine response has the effect of undercutting the ir-
revocable judgment that he had wanted to deliver, despite the ambiguous
nature of the vocabulary he ultimately chose. Perhaps he could have coun-
tenanced the ambiguous term — which, remember, could be taken as either "destroy" or "deliver" — had the Ninevites reacted negatively, which a
betting person would probably have taken odds on. But their response,
which is not only positive but exemplary, has radically altered the equation: a word of judgment is transformed into a word of hope. Phyllis Trible
summarizes the effect of the whole scene:

> From the Ninevites' perspective the prophecy offers the hope,
> though not the guarantee, of repentance human and divine. From
> God's perspective their repentance overturns divine evil to bring
> deliverance. From Jonah's perspective, the divine deliverance over-
> turns his prophecy to discredit it.

It is not clear whether Jonah would have been less angry had he
preached a similar message to Israelites, leading them to repent in such a
way that God would withdraw potential punishment. Perhaps he would
not have minded Israelites being treated graciously by YHWH. But he is
without question greatly troubled in this outsider context. Jonah seems to
reflect the view that when Israelite prophets speak of or to outsiders, judgment and only judgment is the proper content of their message. A gracious
and forgiving God is presumably fine for insiders, but anathema for outsiders. At the same time, by his own admission, Jonah is well aware that

God's propensity toward graciousness is easily extended toward outsiders also. After all, that's why he ran away in the first place (4:2-3). In fact, it is this thorough and consistent orthodoxy that likely compelled Jonah to use terminology in his oracle that could be taken negatively or positively in the first place. Jonah seems incapable of being anything other than orthodox, but he doesn't have to like it!

Jonah does not allow his accurate understanding of God's character to calm his agitated state. Rather than answering directly when God quizzes him about justifying his petulance, Jonah stomps off in a huff to the city's outskirts (4:4-5). This is, to be sure, a less extreme reaction than his flight to Tarshish, but the difference is quantitative, not qualitative. He cannot mask his abject aversion to the character of the God he serves. He just can't stand the divine relenting of judgment on Nineveh; YHWH's behavior makes him one miserable prophet.

As the story comes to a close, Jonah does not budge an inch from his breath-holding tantrum. If anything, his attitude is shown to be even more petty. When he stalks out of the city to station himself east of it, he erects a lean-to for shade. From that vantage point he'll watch to see what might transpire in the city under judgment (4:5). Does he think there's a chance God will pull off a double reverse and destroy the city in spite of its repentance and the initial stay of execution? If that's what Jonah is thinking, his hopes are soon dashed. Nineveh's sentence has been commuted, and YHWH is no longer dealing with the city, period. Rather, YHWH has a prophet to deal with. In the story so far, the outsiders are doing just fine, thank you, but there is much to accomplish with this one ungracious insider.

YHWH tries to teach Jonah the necessary lesson with a series of almost comical actions. First, God appoints a plant to grow up over Jonah to give him relief from sun-induced distress (4:6).* It is not obvious why Jonah's lean-to is insufficient for blocking the blistering sun's rays. Maybe the plant offers a double layer of insulation; or perhaps it envelopes both the booth and Jonah. Regardless, the prophet is grateful for the plant — in fact, nothing short of ecstatic about it (4:6). Jonah's mood swings are pa-

---

*The same word (*wayᵉman*) is used of the big fish (Jonah 2:1). It is also used of the worm God "appointed" to devour the plant and the east wind God "appointed" to wither Jonah (Jonah 4:7-8). God did not, however, "appoint" the wind that caused the storm on the sea; God "hurled" that wind (Jonah 1:4). Still, all these verbs underscore YHWH's sovereignty throughout the narrative. This includes when YHWH "spoke" to the great fish when it was time to vomit Jonah up on the shore (Jonah 2:11).

thetic in this situation. Just a moment earlier, he has been seething because an entire city has found itself in God's good graces. But then he exudes unbridled joy because God sees to it that he has a shady spot. It's all about Jonah! His momentary comfort is so much more important than Nineveh's beneficial and potentially long-term relationship with God.

However, since YHWH is attempting to instruct Jonah rather than comfort him, the deity next enlists a worm to attack the plant the following morning at dawn, causing the plant to wither (4:7). Adding insult to injury, YHWH sees to it that a scorching east wind bears down on Jonah's head to the point of his swooning (4:8). The one time in the whole story that Jonah is in a decent mood turns out to last barely a single night, and now this wind turns into a nightmare. From Jonah's perspective, the only solution to his sorry situation is death, for which he begs shamelessly (4:9). We should not lose sight of the fact that his death-wishing distress is all because he has lost his source of shade. That's why YHWH asks Jonah straight up whether the plant's withering and dying lies behind his desperation. The prophet does not give an inch, remaining adamant in his feelings about the plant: for him the situation is so deplorable that death is the only possible relief.

The episode ends with YHWH asking Jonah a rhetorical question, which exposes how truly shallow the man is. God has elected Israel as the community through which the whole world will eventually be blessed (Gen. 12:1-3). Prophets, including Jonah, have a strategic role to play in this divine plan; but Jonah apparently likes only the part of the plan that involves his people, Israel. Though his preaching in Nineveh has been successful beyond anyone's wildest imagination, this does not please him at all. Quite the contrary, he is pleased only when a plant offers him a little shade. YHWH wants to know how it is that Jonah can generate such positive feelings toward an ephemeral plant, which he neither planted nor nurtured, yet begrudge YHWH's caring for Nineveh (4:10-11), a city that boasts a population of 120,000, not to mention its animals. Without God, the Ninevites did not know their left hand from their right; but their response to God's grace would change that. Shouldn't that have caused great rejoicing in Israel? If Jonah's reaction is typical, evidently not.

The Book of Jonah leaves us with some spectacle. In two amazing and disparate scene locations, two different sets of outsiders elicit our admiration. First, the sailors act in a way in which their pagan piety and theology perfectly coincide. Then, as they move toward Jonah's God, they freely offer prayers, vows, and sacrifices to that deity. We never learn the actual extent of their "conversion," but the glimpse we get of it remains quite impressive. It is considerably more impressive than Jonah's religious expression.

Then the Ninevites enter the scene. This is a people under God's judgment, one to whom God has dispatched a prophet with a presumed word of judgment. But the prophet's word is of necessity double-edged (given God's character, according to Jonah's confession): it may connote judgment, or it may connote deliverance. The Ninevites take it as the latter, and God relents of the judgment. Jonah, orthodox to the end, still does not like the implications for Israelite orthodoxy. For him, insiders are insiders and outsiders are outsiders. Though he never once deviates from an orthodox point of view, his impoverished faith and pitiful behavior after the Nineveh episode illustrate that he has never been able to embrace fully the radical nature of a gracious God, a God who has constituted insider Israel precisely for outsiders such as those in Nineveh. Jonah is orthodox, but he never quite gets to the place where he realizes what that orthodoxy suggests: in the end, God wants insiders and outsiders to be part of the same divinely constituted community.

CHAPTER 6

Ruth: The Moabite Connection

The Book of Ruth has long enjoyed a reputation among Jews and Christians as a delightful and uplifting, even idyllic, narrative. Though the story has some obvious conflict (what story does not?), it is resolved peaceably, according to proper legal procedures and cultural standards, and with a satisfying conclusion for everyone concerned. Compared to so many Old Testament stories that are replete with gross human failure, extreme familial dysfunction, personal or mass violence, perfidy and treachery — not to mention considerable divine judgment — the Book of Ruth is a veritable "island of tranquility." It is a wonderful read, safe (mostly) even for the children.

However, even without denying the story's charms, we may come to realize on closer examination that it does contain elements of tension, risk, and moral compromise. In fact, reading the story from the perspective of the insider-outsider motif brings just such elements to the fore. This is especially true when we investigate the book's placement in the biblical canon. Were we to read Ruth as an isolated story, it would be difficult to fully appreciate its importance, poignancy, and irony. But when we recall Eric Auerbach's famous dictum that biblical narratives are "fraught with background," and when we consider this narrative in the light of its allusions to other canonical ideas, events, and people, the Ruth episode takes on an entirely different flavor.

For openers, the introduction places the account squarely in a period of enormous turmoil: "In the days when the judges ruled" (Ruth 1:1).* The

---

*I use the conventional translation of "judge" in spite of the fact that it conveys a more

era of the judges, as recounted in the Book of Judges, is the polar opposite of the era preceding it, in which Israel is presented (in the Book of Joshua) as an obedient people. The Joshua 7 story of Achan (see Chapter 3) is an exception to that rule and a negative object lesson for the people (Josh. 24:31). Conversely, the Book of Judges portrays Israel as a community that not only continuously violates its covenant with God but whose leaders, the judges themselves, are each more morally deficient than the one before. None other than the great Gideon, for instance, is guilty of idolatry (Judg. 8:24-27). By the time one gets to Abimelech, Jephthah, and Samson, significant moral failure is the rule (Judges 9–16). This wicked era concludes with the abduction of a priest (Judges 17–18) and a civil war in Israel triggered by the rape of a Levite's concubine (Judges 19–21). A refrain in the last five chapters accents how corrupt and chaotic this period had become: "In those days there was no king in Israel; everyone did what was right in his own eyes" (Judg. 17:6; 18:1; 19:1; 21:25).* In Auerbach's terms, these sordid deeds are part of the "background" with which the Book of Ruth is "fraught."

Adding to the complexities of the setting in the time of Israel's judges is a famine that has endangered the land (Ruth 1:1).† Famines are serious enough in their own right, for obvious reasons; but in terms of the overall biblical story, they involve more than the failure of crops and the resulting scarcity. Famines had severely threatened the future of God's people more than once before; in fact, the medieval rabbis who annotated the Hebrew text of the Bible marked the phrase "there was a famine in the land" as hav-

---

judicial nuance in today's English. The "judges" in the Book of Judges did not preside over courts of law or engage generally in jurisprudence (the one exception is perhaps Deborah [Judg. 4:5]). Instead, they commonly engaged in military activity; whatever political functions they fulfilled have receded almost completely into the background. For this reason Norman Gottwald refers to them as "military virtuosi"; the Jewish Publication Society translation offers "chieftains." Presumably, the word "judge" was used in earlier English to convey the idea of executing the sovereignty of the state or community, in this case Israel.

*The complete formula appears twice, in Judges 17:6 and 21:25.

†In Greek and Latin versions of the Old Testament — the Septuagint and Vulgate respectively — the Book of Ruth follows Judges and precedes 1 Samuel. In that arrangement, the story is set in the period of the judges not only by virtue of its initial statement but also by its actual placement. However, in the arrangement of the shorter canon of the Hebrew Bible, the Book of Ruth is part of the final section — the Writings. Nonetheless, the signal struck by the first four words is sufficient to fix the story in the period of the judges, regardless of its order in the Hebrew canon.

ing occurred in this exact wording two other times — in Genesis 12:10 and Genesis 26:1. In both these instances Israel's ancestors responded to famines in ways that exposed the divinely chosen family to extreme danger and potential forfeiture.

Abraham and Sarah fled to Egypt when confronted with famine. On the way, Abraham convinced his beautiful wife to introduce herself as his sister, fearing that the Egyptians would kill him to get her. When she agreed to this dubious strategem, she was immediately whisked off to be part of Pharaoh's harem. Only God's swift and decisive action rescued Sarah from her predicament and prevented the disaster that would have followed (Gen. 12:10-20).

During another famine, Isaac and Rebekah, whom God had this time around forbidden to seek refuge in Egypt, sought sanctuary in Gerar, which was controlled by the Philistines and their king, Abimelech. But like Abraham, Isaac was afraid his life was in jeopardy, and he also presented his wife as his sister. Once again, the family of promise was saved at the last moment, this time because the king was honorable and therefore amenable to YHWH's suasion (Gen. 26:1-11). Both of these stories introduce famine not as a mere happenstance of nature or an ordinary economic downturn but as an event in which the chosen people's ancestors came close to losing a grip on their future. And though we are not aware of it at first, this is precisely the situation that comes into focus as we read the story of Ruth.

The ancestral family was threatened by famine yet a third time, in the Jacob narrative, though there the precise phrase used in Ruth and the Genesis narratives does not appear. Jacob's family would have been subjected to the ravages of seven years of famine had not his second-youngest son, Joseph, been strategically positioned in Egypt, which was once again thought of as a safe haven. This time around, however, the family went to Egypt only to buy supplies, not to stay for an extended period. Joseph, who had long since been sold as a slave to an Egyptian officer but had miraculously come to occupy an enormously influential office, was crucial to the family's rescue. Otherwise, God's agenda to bless the whole world (Gen. 12:1-3) through this family would have come to naught (Gen. 41–45; see especially 41:53-57; 42:1-5; 43:1-2; 45:7). All this shows that the role of famine in Israel's metastory cannot be considered incidental: famines threatened Israel's future and therefore God's agenda. Consequently, the story of Ruth is squarely located in an era of double jeopardy, the time when judges ruled and a famine menaced.

In this particular story, one Israelite family responds to famine by heading from Bethlehem for Moab (Ruth 1:1) instead of Egypt or Philistia.* Moab is not simply another nondescript geographical location on a Near Eastern map. According to the biblical story, few countries had a more repulsive origin than Moab, as recorded in Genesis in an incident involving Lot and his daughters. It was immediately after YHWH had destroyed Sodom, Gomorrah, and the cities of the plain that Lot found himself alone with his two daughters in a cave; his wife and sons-in-law had already perished (Gen. 19:14, 26, 28-30). Thinking that they had lost all opportunity for future marriage, Lot's daughters conspired to get him drunk and become pregnant by him. They succeeded in their depraved plot: each conceived and had a child by her father, Moab and Ammon respectively (Gen. 19:31-38). Moab was a country, therefore, whose very existence was a result of the most shameful behavior.

If it's possible to make matters worse, Lot was, of course, a nephew of Abraham and thus related to the family through whom God planned to bless the world (Gen. 11:31; 12:1-3). But despite Lot's kinship to Abraham, he was probably not supposed to accompany the patriarch when the latter heeded the divine call. God had told Abraham to go from "your land," "your place of birth," and "your father's house" (Gen. 12:1). Almost certainly, "your father's house" refers to Abraham's extended family. But when Abraham set out per God's instructions, the text explicitly says, "and Lot went with him" (Gen. 12:4). Any ambiguity about whether this constituted Abraham's first act of disobedience seems informed by the fact that every single incident involving Lot turned out negative, threatening the family of promise in one way or another.†

---

*There is perhaps a hint of irony in the family's trek from Bethlehem of Judah to the fields of Moab. This is because "Bethlehem" in Hebrew means "house of bread/food"; and as it turns out in this story, Bethlehem's connection with necessary resources of food existed in name only.

†In Genesis 13, due to a dispute between their respective shepherds, Abraham offered Lot the first choice of land, opening up the possibility that his nephew might select the very land God had promised to the patriarch. Later, Lot managed to get himself captured by a coalition that had attacked Sodom, which was in the territory Lot had chosen in that dispute. Naturally, this obligated his uncle to rescue him, thus endangering Abraham's life and therefore his divine mission (Gen. 14). Finally, Lot still lived in Sodom when God decided that it was time to destroy the wicked city, which explains Abraham's attempt to talk God out of that divine plan (Gen. 18:16-33). In the end, God did rescue Lot, not because of Abraham's argument, but simply because of his relationship to the patriarch (Gen. 19:29). Unfortu-

The eventual impact of the incest of Lot and his daughters is set in bold relief in three separate biblical narratives. First, during the wilderness trek on the way to the land of promise, Israel encamped in the plains of Moab (Num. 22:1). While they were there, King Balak of Moab, acting on behalf of his people — who were deathly afraid of Israel's numbers and prior military success — arranged to have Israel cursed by a professional prophet, one Balaam (Num. 22:2-6). But YHWH did not permit Balaam to curse the Israelites; in fact, the prophet ended up actually blessing Israel while cursing Moab and others (Num. 22:7-41; 23; 24). In a second scenario, right after the Balaam episode, Israelite men cavorted with Moabite women and took part in Moabite religious practices, which led to a devastating divine judgment (Num. 25:1-9). Finally, during the judges era, Moab oppressed Israel for eighteen years, which was God's judgment on Israel's wickedness (Judg. 3:12-14). Considering Moab's scandalous beginnings and its subsequent negative relationship with Israel, it is hardly surprising that Mosaic legislation expressly forbade Moabites (and Ammonites) from ever entering the assembly of YHWH (Deut. 23:3). Moreover, Israel was never to promote Moab's (or Ammon's) welfare or prosperity (Deut. 23:6). Putting the matter bluntly, Moab and Ammon were anathema to Israel.

Thus, when this Israelite family, identified as Elimelech (the father), Naomi (the mother), and the sons Mahlon and Chilion (Ruth 1:2), travel to the fields of Moab to escape a famine ravaging Israel, it is difficult to exaggerate what a radical and potentially foolish step this is in light of the biblical epic. Moab is just about the last place one would expect any self-respecting Israelite to regard as a sanctuary. And considering the past relationship, could any Israelite reasonably anticipate anything but the most villainous behavior from Moabites? Yet this threatened Israelite family heads for Moab as though that were the most natural course of action to take. Indeed, in fleeing the deprivation of famine-afflicted Israel for the hope of food in Moab, this family clearly opts for life over death, regardless of any drawbacks that might result from their temporary residence there. As bad as Moab's past has been, and as questionable as its present might conceivably be, the fact of Israel's famine makes Moab preferable. At this juncture the contrast between Moab and Israel is one of hope versus hopelessness.

---

nately, God's sparing of Lot, along with his daughters, afforded the latter the opportunity to seduce their father and give birth to Moab and Ammon. In the later Levitical legislation, incest was expressly forbidden (Lev. 18:6).

Promise and tragedy in Moab

Before we find out whether this small family enjoys so much as a single meal in the country of its sojourn, it suffers a significant reversal: Elimelech dies (Ruth 1:3). So instead of life, the family immediately confronts death. As a depressing reminder of this new, crushing circumstance, the boys go from being *his* sons (that is, Elimelech's) to *hers* (that is, Naomi's). It is hardly a stretch to assume that an intact Israelite family would struggle to survive under the best of circumstances in a foreign setting, to say nothing of a specifically Moabite venue. Surely a truncated family would find it that much more difficult, especially since they had lost their breadwinner. In all likelihood, a widow with two sons would experience hardship even in Israel. Aren't the prospects infinitely poorer in Moab?

It turns out that the immediate answer to this question is somewhat surprising. For even though Moab is initially a place of death for this visiting family, in the compact narrative of the Book of Ruth it becomes a place of life again: Naomi's two sons end up marrying Moabite wives — Orpah and Ruth (1:4). As though to underscore that this newly constituted family has actually done quite well, the narrator notes that they have lived in Moab for ten years. Though it is still portrayed as a sojourn, it is a long one. Despite losing Elimelech, the family has managed to survive, if not thrive, in Moab. Marriages put the accent on the future, because children and their promise of new life typically follow marriage stories. But the biblical narrative does not tell us that either Orpah or Ruth ever becomes pregnant during the ten years of the stay in Moab. The potential for future life has not been fully realized just yet. Yet, in welcoming Moabite wives into its midst, this family also flirts with moral disaster. After all, the infamous incident at Beth Baal-Peor (Num. 25) began when Israelites had carnal relations with Moabite women. Marriage is not mentioned in that context, but marrying outside the Israelite family could often be problematic. Marrying Moabites would have been especially difficult in that the latter were denied entrance to the sacred assembly (Deut. 23:3-6 [Hebrew: 23:4-7]). The biblical text mentions no censure of Mahlon and Chilion; but we can't help wondering about the prudence of their marrying Moabite women, even though on one level it offers the luckless family a new lease on life.

So far it is unclear whether we are to see Moab in this story in positive or negative terms. A positive cast is suggested by the fact that it has food when Israel does not, especially since a common biblical theme is that bounty is a function of divine blessing and dearth of divine curse. When Elimelech dies, the negative aspect prevails: premature death raises the specter of divine displeasure. But there is an upturn when the males in the family marry, even though their wives are foreigners. Unfortunately, just when we are about to see Moab's role as more positive than negative (two positives: food and wives; one negative: Elimelech's death), there is yet another horrible reversal: Mahlon and Chilion die (1:5). From Naomi's perspective, things could hardly be worse: not only does she not have a husband to provide and care for her and her family, but she is bereft of her sons as well. The emotional loss is compounded by the social and economic implications: all Naomi has left in the world are her two Moabite daughters-in-law, now both widows. Widows were always vulnerable, even in Israel; they were probably no less vulnerable in Moab. If Naomi had experienced any sense of hopefulness when she first traveled with her family to Moab, her hopes have now been dashed.

Now, having run out of options, Naomi decides to return to Israel. This is not a function of either whim or desperation; it is a sensible decision because she has learned right there in Moab's fields that Israel's God YHWH has visited the land and given the people food (1:6). But she will still go back home a widow, and she will have the difficulties that go along with that status. So far Israel has been something less than a source of blessing in Naomi's life: initially, it has threatened her family with death by starvation; later it offers some hope of physical sustenance but not without her paying dearly for it. Without husband or sons to rely on, she will have to make her way in the Israelite economy on her own. She can perhaps count on her two daughters-in-law, but they are Moabite women and will have their own struggles with widowhood. Besides, won't they simply remain in Moab, leaving Naomi to go back to Israel by herself? Naomi's economic and social prognosis appears pretty grim even in her motherland of Israel, which she was forced to abandon and to which she now returns.

The return home

When Naomi begins the return trip to Judah, the two daughters-in-law tag along. But it is not clear whether they plan to go all the way with Naomi and take up residence in her country or simply want to walk with her a short distance before saying a final farewell (Ruth 1:7). Regardless of their plans, Naomi has plans of her own, which don't actually include keeping her daughters-in-law with her. Evidently, she wants to make a complete break with her previous life in Moab. And who can blame her? After all, while she has survived in Moab for at least a decade, she has also suffered numbing losses. So she orders her daughters-in-law to return to their respective mothers' homes. Her imperative comes with an appropriate blessing: she asks that YHWH deal with them as graciously as they have dealt with her deceased husband and sons and with her. Naomi also hopes that God will grant each of the women security in the homes of future husbands. Clearly, Naomi believes that her daughters-in-law still have a chance at marriage in their own country. Wouldn't that be their best opportunity for the future? So she kisses them and they have a good cry together (1:8-9). From Naomi's perspective, this pending separation is as painful as it is necessary.

At this point we might expect Orpah and Ruth to do exactly as Naomi has urged. There are currently no desperate circumstances, such as those when Naomi's family first traveled to Moab from Israel, that would prompt the daughters-in-law to follow that course in reverse. In fact, as Naomi has pointed out, their prospects are much better in Moab. Though Israel no longer has famine, there is no suggestion that Moab's resources are insufficient, and there's simply no practical motivation for the women to follow Naomi back to Israel. But that is exactly what they propose to do (1:10). Furthermore, they seem quite well aware of the implications of such a move, for they acknowledge that returning with their mother-in-law means taking up with "your people." But Naomi again discourages them from coming with her. Perhaps sensing that they are being more emotional than rational, she reminds them that she has no other sons for them to marry, and considering her age, her chances of remarrying are all but nonexistent. Even assuming that she were to remarry the instant she got back home, would the daughters-in-law wait around until new sons, were she even able to bear them, grew to manhood (1:11-13)? The idea is preposterous!

From Naomi's point of view, there is a still more compelling reason for the women to forego their sweet but foolish wish to stay with their mother-in-law. She is not a woman who can point with any confidence to YHWH's blessings in her life. On the contrary, Naomi accuses YHWH of having turned against her, thus leading her to a bitter end. If God had not waited so long to give Israel food, the family would never have had to flee to Moab; perhaps Elimelech, Mahlon, and Chilion would still be alive; and likely the family would have enjoyed a satisfactory if not prosperous life in its own land. But the famine changed all that. For all the kindness that the daughters-in-law have shown in her family — which Naomi freely admits — her life has mainly turned out poorly, which she blames on God. And for this reason it is irrational for Orpah and Ruth to cling to her.

Orpah finally takes Naomi's point. After a second bout of crying, she kisses Naomi, thereby signaling that she will heed her advice. But Ruth will have none of it; she will not leave Naomi's side. Indeed, she refuses to budge even when Naomi points to her sister-in-law's eminently reasonable behavior: "Look, your sister-in-law has returned to her people and her gods" (Ruth 1:15).* Naomi doesn't try to proselytize her daughter-in-law in any way; she even appears to realize what is at stake not only socially ("your people") but religiously ("your gods"). What stronger evidence could she give Ruth for heeding her directive? But Naomi's arguments are unconvincing to Ruth in the end.

For the first time in the narrative, Ruth emerges as more than just one of Naomi's two daughters-in-law. She now takes center stage. In a mini-speech to her mother-in-law, she lets her know precisely where she stands. Indeed, this speech is the first time one of the daughters-in-law speaks individually rather than in tandem (see 1:10). First she asks Naomi to stop attempting to persuade her to remain in Moab; then she insists that she will go wherever Naomi goes and lodge wherever she lodges. Furthermore, to show that her commitment transcends personal attachment to her mother-in-law, Ruth goes on to "adopt" Naomi's people and deity: "Your people [shall be] my people, your God [shall be] my God" (1:16). After she goes on to declare that where Naomi dies and is buried, she will likewise die and be buried — that is, in the land of Israel — Ruth actually invokes the personal name of Israel's God: "Thus may YHWH do to me, and much more, if death should separate me and you" (1:17). After hearing this extraordinary sentiment reflecting such a determined posture, Naomi accepts the inevitable: Ruth will become a permanent member of her household back in Israel (1:18). Whatever fate awaits Naomi in Israel, she will confront it together with her persistent and loyal daughter-in-law.

---

*It is impossible to know from the spelling whether Naomi meant to say "god" or "gods," for the forms are exactly the same. Since she is referring to a Moabite, and therefore polytheistic, context, we should probably understand her to be saying "gods."

With virtually no elapsed time in the narrative, the unlikely duo arrives back in Bethlehem, creating a bit of a stir (1:19). We don't know what Naomi expects when she walks into Bethlehem, but the women of the town are excited, thinking they recognize her right off: "Is this Naomi?" However, rather than being cheered by this immediate and warm reception, Naomi expresses herself in a lugubrious outburst. She laments her shabby treatment at God's hands and says that her name, which connotes delight, is no longer apt; considering everything she's gone through, Naomi tells them that a much more appropriate name for her would be Mara, which means "bitter." The new name would be appropriate, she says, because she left Israel "full"(having a husband and two sons) but has returned "empty" — with only a single daughter-in-law whom she did not even want to remain with her. She figures that all this misery is God's doing (1:20-21).

Before the curtain falls on this act, the narrator reminds readers of two important facts. One is Ruth's continuing Moabite connection: despite her adoption of Naomi's God and her people (1:16-17), the narrator keeps Ruth's Moabite identification before the reader — in fact, underscores it with a redundancy: "So Naomi returned together with Ruth the Moabite, her daughter-in-law, who came back with her from the country of Moab" (1:22). The narrator doesn't want us to forget Ruth's foreign identity for a second. How Ruth will affect Naomi's return home and her attempt to start all over again remains to be seen. She plays no part in the reunion scene, but her being a Moabite remains in the foreground. The second fact is a simple but important one. The two women arrive in Bethlehem at the beginning of the barley harvest, which confirms that the famine referred to in the first verse of Ruth 1 is truly a thing of the past. Harvest suggests resources, possibility, life, and future. Whether the embittered widow Naomi and her still Moabite daughter-in-law Ruth are able to take advantage of that harvest will become clear in the ensuing chapters. The story began ironically when its subject family was forced to vacate Bethlehem — which means "house of bread" — because it was producing no bread; now, on their return to the town, the meaning of its name may once again become appropriate.

The rich relative

As Naomi and Ruth begin their new lives back in Bethlehem, we are immediately caught off guard. First off, we learn that Naomi has a prominent and well-to-do relative on her husband's side of the family (Ruth 2:1).* What strikes us as most curious about this new information is that Naomi's situation would appear to be rather more promising than her previous lament would imply (1:21). If she has a wealthy relative in these parts, why does she consider her circumstance so hopeless? It's true that this man, Boaz, was kin to Elimelech, who is now deceased; but surely an in-law would be at least a possible means of some support. In any case, up to this point Naomi has not thought of Boaz as a potential resource. In light of the complaint she has expressed on arriving back in Bethlehem, she transparently thinks of herself as a woman completely on her own and with no recourse to anyone else, let alone a rich relative.

The second thing we discover is equally surprising. Ruth (whom the narrator once again reminds us is a Moabite, as though worried we might forget) suggests that she be allowed to glean in the fields of someone who might respond favorably to her (2:2). That Ruth knew about gleaning is not that remarkable, for the custom was sufficiently well known to be included in legislative material (Lev. 19:9-10; 23:22; Deut. 24:19-22). In fact, gleaning rights in the Levitical law were extended specifically to the poor and to the resident alien — both of which apply to Ruth.† Naomi qualifies for only one of the criteria: she is poor. Perhaps the custom of gleaning was practiced in other cultures as well, so that Ruth knew about this in Moab. In any case, what appears unusual is that Ruth takes the initiative in an Israelite setting. So far only Naomi has expressed bitterness over her poverty. Why, then, isn't she the one to put into motion plans to alleviate the financial distress she and her daughter-in-law are suffering? For that matter, why doesn't she remember her well-to-do kinsman Boaz? All she does in response to her dilemma is to assent to Ruth's request: "Go, my daughter."

---

*This relative, Boaz, is described in Hebrew as a *gibbôr ḥayīl*, a "man of substance." Typically, the phrase connotes social or political importance and financial means beyond what is ordinary. The financial aspect usually is indicated only by context, as is certainly the case in the Book of Ruth.

†In Deuteronomy those who are to have access to harvested fields are, in addition to the resident alien *(gēr)*, the widow and the orphan; the poor are not mentioned specifically. Again, Ruth would qualify as a resident alien and a widow; Naomi qualified only as a widow.

Presumably, if Ruth were not to have sprung into action, Naomi would have been willing to wallow in her desperation. The Moabite widow decides to take matters into her own hands; the Israelite widow sits on her hands.

It is not memorable that Ruth makes good on her plans to glean because this is what poor widows did in that culture. It is thus noted almost off-handedly that Ruth was among other gleaners (2:8, 22-23).* However, the field where she begins to glean makes us sit up and take notice: it just "happens" to belong to Boaz, Elimelech's relative (2:3). This is an astounding stroke of good luck, so much so that it is difficult to shake the impression that this turn of events is to be thought of as a "providential accident." Of all the fields where she might have ended up gleaning, how is it that Ruth finds herself in the one belonging to Naomi's relative?

Furthermore, Boaz's reaction when he learns Ruth's identity has the effect of foreshadowing a reversal of fortune for Ruth and her mother-in-law. Perhaps Boaz knows all the other gleaners, because he asks only about Ruth (2:5). The servant whom he asks responds in a way that again emphasizes Ruth's foreignness: "She is the Moabite who came back with Naomi from the country of Moab" (2:6). It is instructive that he doesn't even mention her poverty, only her position as a resident alien. Presumably the other women gleaning are unremarkable in that they are merely poor Israelites. On hearing of Ruth's Moabite status, the request she has made of the chief harvester (2:7), and the fact that she has worked all day without a break, Boaz responds in an extremely positive manner, the reason for which is not immediately mentioned. Are we to assume that he is simply an extraordinarily kind and considerate man? Is he somehow impressed by Ruth's arduous labor? Is he drawn to her because of her looks — though there is no mention of them in the text? No answers to these questions are forthcoming right away. But we may recall that when Ruth first asked Naomi for permission to glean, she said that she would go to a field "behind someone in whose sight I might find favor" (2:2). Again, the coincidence of coming on Boaz's field appears providential, because what she hoped for has certainly come true: she has found favor with Boaz.

---

*Gleaners apparently represented a variety of socioeconomic strata. The women with whom Ruth gleaned are referred to as "belonging to" Boaz. This seems to mean that they had some familial or economic relationship to his household or his business operations. They may have been on the "payroll," so to speak, but still were relegated to gleaning to make ends meet. Ruth initially was in a different situation in that she gleaned as a complete stranger.

It's hard to imagine Boaz's reacting more favorably to any woman, let alone a Moabite. He urges her to continue gleaning in his field while staying close to "my young women." He also assures Ruth that he has warned the young men not to bother her. Finally, she should not hesitate to slake her thirst by drinking water that these same young men have drawn from his well (2:8-9).* It is when Ruth expresses her gratitude for Boaz's helpfulness that we finally learn what has motivated his exemplary kindness. Word has come to him about how well Ruth has treated Naomi since the death of her father-in-law and her husband; her caring for her mother-in-law has gone beyond the call of duty in that she has left her native land and taken up residence with a foreign people (2:11; see also 1:8). Boaz has seen in Ruth's behavior a religious and theological twist; and he hopes that she is rewarded fully by YHWH, under whose wings she has sought refuge (2:12). Ruth is overwhelmed by this response, noting that Boaz has treated her as a trusted servant even though she isn't in his employ (2:13).

Considering Boaz's gracious gesture toward Ruth, it is perplexing that Naomi has remained so passive. Is she unaware of Boaz's character? Is her grief so great that she can't even think straight about how to improve the social and economic situation of herself and Ruth? When Ruth mentions that she has decided to glean, why doesn't Naomi bring up the fact that Boaz owns fields that are being harvested? Is she in the dark about this? But no matter how passive Naomi is, the fact remains that Ruth "happens" on the right field at the right time.

As if Boaz has not done enough for Ruth already, at lunchtime he shares his meal with her (2:14-15). After that he sees to it that her gleaning will be more successful than normal when he arranges for his young harvesters to allow her to glean in the most advantageous spots, and also in-

---

*From what Boaz says, it's possible to infer some details about gleaning as a regular practice. Suggesting that Ruth stay in his fields indicates that gleaners might move from field to field, either to find better pickings or not to wear out their welcome by staying in one place. The warning to the young men seems to indicate that female gleaners were especially vulnerable. By and large, they would not have been gleaning in the first place if they were under the protection of males in their family, whether husbands, fathers, or brothers. The fact that they did not have such male protectors made them easy targets for reapers who were up to mischief or sexual harassment. Even the remark that she could drink water drawn by the young men may mean that gleaners could not automatically count on daily provisions of food or water being supplied by the harvesting team. Ruth was getting special treatment.

structs them to let some extra grain fall from the gathered bundles so that there will be more for Ruth to glean (2:16). Boaz thus makes sure that none of Ruth's gleaning is left to chance; indeed, she will have almost as much success as the primary harvesters. This Moabite woman will be able to do as well as any Israelite gleaners and better than most, all because of Boaz.

After Ruth returns to Naomi, she has no conversation with her mother-in-law until after they have eaten. Only then does Naomi become a little curious, perhaps because Ruth's take has been so impressive (2:18). Still showing no knowledge whatsoever of how and why Ruth has done so well, she asks innocent questions: "Where did you glean today? Where did you work?" She is inclined to ask a blessing on the person who has treated Ruth so well, but she still does not realize that it is her relative Boaz (2:19abc). When Ruth finally cites Boaz as the source of her good fortune, Naomi reveals that she sees the day's events in completely providential terms: "Blessed be he by YHWH, whose kindness has not forsaken the living or the dead" (2:19d-20). She now sees YHWH's loyalty and Boaz's kindness in tandem, and, suddenly seeing the light, identifies Boaz as one of "our nearest kinfolk, even one who could redeem us" (2:20). Not only has Naomi's previously befuddled memory cleared up, she now self-consciously makes Ruth an integral part of the family. It somehow doesn't matter anymore why Naomi ignored Boaz previously; everything has changed now that Ruth has come under Boaz's protection and blessing. After Ruth tells of how Boaz insisted on her staying close to the servants until the end of harvest, Naomi reinforces the arrangement by encouraging her daughter-in-law to do as Boaz has instructed. This wonderfully productive arrangement is to last throughout the entire harvest (2:21-23). We are still reminded that Ruth is "the Moabite" (2:21), but that does not alter the fact that she is in a better gleaning position than the average Israelite woman and that she and her mother-in-law find themselves being well taken care of, at least for the time being.

The plot thickens

Though it was Ruth's initiative that led her to Boaz's field in the first place, it is now Naomi's plan that is designed to secure a more permanent resolution. At this point Naomi is thinking only of Ruth's benefit (3:1); at the same time, the two of them constitute a family (recall the use of "our" and "us" in Ruth 2:20), so that any benefits accruing to Ruth should accrue to Naomi as well. What Naomi has in mind for Ruth does not require any radical departure; indeed, all she has to do is continue her gleaning with the other women in Boaz's field (3:2). But Naomi does intend for Ruth to up the ante, so to speak, by positioning herself in such a way that Boaz may realize that this Moabite woman has more potential for him than merely being a gleaner in his field. Naomi tells Ruth to wash, perfume herself, put on her best outfit, and then go to the threshing floor where Boaz will be. Her instructions are to leave Boaz alone until he has finished his meal, after which she is to "uncover his feet" and wait for orders from him (3:3-4).

Overcoming her earlier passivity, Naomi's new strategy is by all means bold, perhaps to the extent of being dangerous: an unmarried, foreign woman who has already captured Boaz's eye to some degree is to present herself to him in a manner in which the offer of a sexual favor is hardly subtle. Add to this the fact that Boaz will have just finished eating and drinking, and that this is during the harvest season (perhaps suggesting more revelry than usual), and the makings of potential disaster are present. Whereas Boaz earlier went out of his way to prevent his reapers from making any sexual moves toward Ruth, he might not be able to resist so overt and compelling an offer himself. But even with these obvious risks, Ruth readily accepts her mother-in-law's directives (3:5). Curiously, though she could not have been more stubborn the first time Naomi gave her orders (about staying in Moab: 1:8-18), this time she could not be more compliant. On the other hand, Naomi is as proactive in this scene as she was passive in the previous ones.

For all of her cleverness, Naomi gets one thing wrong. She tells Ruth to wait for Boaz to tell her what steps to take (3:4); but Ruth is the one who tells Boaz what to do once he discovers her lying beside him in this suggestive position. When he awakens startled and asks who she is — is he still half asleep, or is it too dark, or is he a little inebriated? — Ruth not only identifies herself but tells him to spread his cloak over her because, after all, she is a close relative. Her daring sexual posturing is matched by her audacious appeal to Boaz. Has she just crossed the threshold from bold to foolish? Will Boaz take her actions and words as effrontery? Has Naomi miscalculated and in the process put her daughter-in-law in harm's way? Is the carefully constructed plan about to unravel?

Boaz's response puts Ruth and the reader at ease: he is completely taken by her. He blesses her by YHWH, noting that this last act of her loyalty has superseded the first one: that is, he is smitten by the fact that she has not even entertained the idea of seducing any of the younger men, regardless of their financial means, but is content to make herself available to him, presumably an older man and therefore less attractive or "vigorous." Without the slightest demurral, Boaz assures Ruth that he will make good on her request, which will be made easier by the fact that his people are well aware that Ruth is a substantial woman (3:10-11). At Boaz's mention that Ruth is a substantial woman, one cannot miss that this is the same way *he* was first introduced in the story (2:1). Ruth, a Moabite woman, has somehow managed to attain the same status as that of a well-respected and prominent man of Bethlehem. As both Naomi and Boaz have pointed out, this is something of a reward for the past loyalty she has shown to an Israelite family and for the present loyalty she is demonstrating toward Boaz. A plan that might have blown up in both Naomi's and Ruth's faces turns out to offer them more hope than they have had since the menfolk in the family died. Considering Naomi's bitter lament on returning to Bethlehem, things have turned out rosy indeed: plain good fortune and providential circumstance seem to have combined to give Naomi and Ruth a brand new start.

But there is a potential glitch. We are almost unnerved to learn, for the first time in the story, that there is another relative in the picture; in fact, he happens to be a closer relative to Elimelech than is Boaz. This means that he has what we might call the right of first refusal. Does this mean that Naomi's plan and Ruth's execution of it have taken a cruel turn? Does this mean that Boaz, who so far has responded so marvelously, will fade from view? What is this other kinsman like? Will he end up ruining a story that has appeared to be moving toward such a happy ending? Regardless of how these questions will be answered, and in spite of the possibility that Boaz may have to relinquish his central role, he continues to do all he can for Ruth. He arises early to help Ruth sneak away unnoticed, perhaps wishing to avoid a scandal (3:14); but before she goes and before he heads for the city gate, he gives her an extra portion of grain (3:15). Once Ruth returns and reports on the night's events, Naomi seems to know that there is nothing to do now but wait (3:16); however, she seems confident that Boaz will try to get the whole matter settled with dispatch. Unfortunately, no matter how quickly the business at hand is transacted, there is no way to know whether Boaz or the newly mentioned kinsman will end up playing the role of redeemer for Ruth and, by extension, Naomi.

Investing in the future

Just as Naomi has predicted, Boaz wastes absolutely no time getting to the town gate, where business is normally conducted (Ruth 4:1). Once he gets there, the business at hand is accompanied by another marvelous juxtaposition of sheer randomness and tacit providence: no sooner has Boaz taken a seat than the very relative in question appears. Though this kinsman, according to Boaz's own admission, has the prior right to redeem Elimelech's property, the story seems reluctant to give the man too much "narrative privilege." Thus, instead of revealing his name, Boaz calls him, incongruously, "Mr. So-and-so." Though he is more closely related to Elimelech — and thus to Naomi — than Boaz is, neither Boaz nor the narrator offers the courtesy of a name. This closest of relatives remains anonymous.

However, if we think that "Mr. So-and-so," because he is so nondescript, will exit stage left without further ado, we have another think coming. Surrounded by city elders who are witnessing the transaction about to take place, Boaz informs his relative of Naomi's interest in selling Elimelech's parcel. Boaz mentions that he will redeem the land should "Mr. So-and-so" decline, but he is certainly making the offer in good faith at this point — at least on the surface (4:2-4). Considering Boaz's prominence so far in this drama, compared to the late-appearing and curiously nameless next-of-kin, we might expect a cursory "thanks, but no thanks." The exchange itself would heighten the drama a little by delaying Boaz's purchase of the plot; but once the little interlude would be over, Boaz would step forward to exercise his right as redeemer of Elimelech's property, along with the obligation of taking care of Naomi and Ruth in whatever manner was appropriate. (For Ruth, surely marriage was in the offing, given the scene at the threshing floor.) For this reason, we can't help but be flabbergasted that this literal nobody, who comes out of nowhere to interrupt the flow of the narrative, now readily accepts Boaz's offer ("I will redeem it") without so much as asking a single question.

Yet, almost before we can even grasp this strange turn of events, Boaz plays what amounts to his trump card. So far Boaz has not referred to Ruth at all; he has mentioned only Elimelech and Naomi (4:3). He does remind the kinsman of the journey to and from Moab, but he remains silent about Ruth's present position in the family. But now he finds it necessary to bring her up. Upon hearing that the kinsman is interested in redeeming the land, Boaz introduces Ruth into the equation (4:5). Unfortunately, the Hebrew text is somewhat unclear at this point: taken one way, the text says that Boaz informs "Mr. So-and-so" that he must acquire Ruth the Moabite along with Elimelech's land; taken another way, it shows Boaz offering the land but not Ruth. In either case, acquiring Ruth along with the land has important implications for maintaining her deceased husband's name in the future. What is clear is that, as soon as Boaz brings Ruth up, the kinsman bows out of the transaction altogether (4:6).

What are we to make of this? If Boaz is offering the land but not the Moabite woman, are we to understand that the kinsman is disappointed Ruth is not part of the deal? On the other hand, if Boaz is saying that the land and Ruth are part of the same package, does the kinsman's backing out of his initial positive response indicate that he wants nothing to do with a foreign woman? Another possibility is that the need to ensure the family's future through Ruth was not appealing to him because their offspring, though his biologically, would not perpetuate his own name. This would parallel Onan's refusal to impregnate Tamar (Gen. 38:9; see Chapter 2). However we construe this, it is clear that once Ruth is added to the mix, Mr. So-and-so decides that his own interests will not be served by his redeeming the property in question. Whether or not he has made a sound decision, with him out of the way Boaz now occupies the position toward which he and Ruth were moving at the end of the previous chapter.

Once the deal is closed before the assembled town fathers with the strange gesture of removing a shoe, Boaz announces unambiguously that he has legitimately purchased the land belonging to Elimelech and his two sons, Chilion and Mahlon. Just as important, he emphasizes that he will take the Moabite Ruth as his wife, thereby ensuring the continuity of Mahlon's name in the future. Once again, Ruth's Moabite connection is in the foreground of the text (4:7-10). There is not the slightest doubt that Mahlon's name will be kept alive by a union of the Israelite Boaz and the Moabite Ruth; and despite her Moabite background, there is not a peep of protest from any of those witnessing Boaz's declarations. On the contrary, their witness segues into an expression of hope and a confession that has the effect of placing this Moabite in the category of some of the most prominent and significant women of Israel's history (4:11-12).

What they say about Ruth at this moment is nothing short of incredible. The group witnessing this amazing turn of events — "all the people" and the "elders" — concentrate more on Ruth than they do on their own prominent citizen, Boaz. They proclaim (in the grammar of a wish) that

YHWH will make her like Rachel and Leah, both of whom were largely responsible for building up the house of Israel. Aware of the mysterious ways of YHWH's sovereignty and providence, they also invoke (vv. 11-12) the name of another outsider woman: Tamar (Genesis 38; see Chapter 2). With this last reference comes an interesting coincidence: Boaz is a descendant of the house of Perez, one of the twins born of Judah's union with Tamar. Not only has Boaz expressed his wish to marry Ruth the Moabite to carry on the name of her Israelite husband; it turns out that his own future was once secured by the actions of another outsider woman. That's why the witnesses don't have the slightest reluctance to include outsiders like Tamar and Ruth with insiders such as Leah and Rachel: these outsider women and these insider women contribute equally to Israel's future. Perhaps even more engaging is our realization that Boaz's very life depended on having an outsider woman in his ancestral past (Tamar), just as his future life will be the result of having an outsider woman as part of his genealogical legacy (Ruth).

As the story moves toward its conclusion, the narrator allows no doubt to linger about God's role in the marriage of Ruth and Boaz. Just as YHWH has so many times in the past been instrumental in bringing about a strategic pregnancy (Gen. 21:1-2; 25:21; 29:31; 30:17, 22; see also 1 Sam. 1:19-20), once more there is divine intervention that results in conception (4:13). When the baby is born, the Bethlehem women pronounce a blessing on Grandmother Naomi, a blessing that pertains to Naomi's family not fading from existence; indeed, this child will be a restorer and nurturer of Naomi's life. At the same time, Ruth's extraordinary contributions — to Israel's life in general and Naomi's in particular—do not escape anyone's attention. Once more the women bring up Ruth's unstinting love for her mother-in-law, a daughter-in-law's devotion that is, incredibly, more than that of seven sons (4:14-15). With this gratifying result, it is hardly surprising that Naomi takes care of this special child as if it were her own. Indeed, when the women name the child — the prominence of women as a collective body in this story cannot be ignored — they declare that "a son has been born to Naomi." That underscores both Naomi's resurrected life in Israel and this child's role in Israel's future. The child has a Moabite mother, but his contribution to Israel's future cannot be exaggerated (4:17).

Without the loyalty and love of the Moabite Ruth for Naomi, her willingness to go to the fields on her own, her blithe confidence in her mother-in-law's risky plan, and her plucky character and courage, the child, Obed, would never have been born. Without Obed there would have been no Jesse; and most important, without Jesse there would have been no David (4:17). Like Tamar before her, Ruth the outsider has acted to save her own future, Naomi's future, Boaz's future, and Israel's future. And from the point of view of the Christian story, Israel's future and the world's future go hand in hand (Gen. 12:1-3). David and the Son of David were instrumental in that awesome divine task (Matt. 1:1, 3, 5-6), and once again an outsider makes it possible.

The story of Ruth ends with that most dreaded of biblical literary forms, the genealogy (4:18-22). Yet, considering the drama in which this Moabite woman has played such an astonishing and central part, nothing could be more appropriate. Israel's metastory features a divine plan for blessing the whole world. As Israel's history evolves through time, there are any number of births without which the outcome would have been singularly different and the divine plan compromised. Almost every single time an essential birth takes place, one observes an inexplicable combination of providence and human choices. Even more remarkable, outsiders keep showing up to invade the narrative space and promote Israel's future and therefore God's agenda.

CHAPTER 7

The Woman at the Well

In this final chapter I wish to show that the outsider theme that is so prominent in the Old Testament appears in the New Testament as well. Furthermore, just as the examples we selected from the Old Testament are found in every canonical section, one encounters the outsider theme throughout the New Testament narrative traditions.* This should come as no surprise, because the biblical witness, from start to finish, emphasizes that God chose one people, an insider faith community, with the express purpose of eventually including all the world's peoples in a single community oriented toward one God, the only One who actually exists. As I have tried to show in earlier chapters, YHWH's *exclusive* election of Israel's ancestors had an *inclusive* purpose: the blessing of all the families of the earth (Gen. 12:1-3). However, to say that the New Testament has its own version of the outsider motif does not go far enough, for the very essence of New Testament thought is rooted in the conviction that God's designs for Israel have come to fruition in what God did in and through Jesus, Israel's *messiah/Christ*.† Thus the outsider theme is not incidental in the New Testament but at the core of its central message.

We can readily see this by briefly surveying the New Testament's nar-

---

*Torah/Law: Esau and Tamar; Former Prophets: Rahab and Namaan; Latter Prophets: Jonah; Writings: Ruth.

†The Greek term "Christ" means "anointed" and thus is the semantic equivalent of the Hebrew term "messiah" *(māšîaḥ)*, which also means "anointed." The Fourth Gospel is the only one to equate Greek "Christ" with the transliterated Hebrew term "messiah."

ratives.* For example, at the beginning of Matthew's Gospel, three of the female outsiders whose stories are prominent in the Old Testament are cited in Jesus' genealogy: Tamar, Rahab, and Ruth (Matt. 1:2-3, 5). Furthermore, at the very beginning of his ministry, John the Baptist warns certain Pharisees and Sadducees not to presume special insider status by appealing to Abrahamic parentage, since God is able "from stones" to raise up children to Abraham as long as they bear fruit indicative of a penitent attitude (Matt. 3:7-10; see also Luke 3:8). Later, Jesus himself makes the astonishing claim that he has observed more faith in a certain Roman soldier than in anyone in Israel (Matt. 8:5-13, especially v. 10; see also Luke 7:1-10). This is all the more remarkable given Jesus' admonition that his disciples are to concentrate *exclusively* on "the lost sheep of the house of Israel" (Matt. 10:5-6). Jesus even goes so far as to tell the disciples to avoid Gentiles altogether (that is, non-Israelites/Jews) and Samaritans (non-"mainstream" Jews).

A slight variation on this theme occurs when Jesus reproaches two Israelite towns, Chorazin and Bethsaida. Jesus' rebuke includes the accusation that, had similar works been accomplished in the foreign (outsider) cities of Tyre and Sidon, those cities would have long since repented (Matt. 11:20-24; see also Luke 10:13). Making a stronger case still, Jesus predicts that the time will come when Ninevites and the "queen of the South" will condemn "this [insider] generation" at the final judgment. Why? Because the former repented when they heard Jonah's preaching and the latter listened attentively to Solomon's wisdom (Matt. 12:41-42). Finally, there is a scene where Jesus adamantly refuses the pleas of a Canaanite woman from the area of Tyre and Sidon who is desperate to have a demon exorcised from her daughter. Jesus' reluctance to help is a function of his insistence that his ministry is reserved for Israelites. When the woman persists, Jesus dismissively declares that it is inappropriate to give food fit for children to dogs. Clearly, the "children" are Jews/Israelites, the "dogs" virtually everyone else. But the woman remains unfazed by Jesus' harsh posture and demeaning rhetoric, replying that even dogs eat the crumbs that fall from the table. Hearing this response, Jesus is greatly moved by the outsider's faith and accedes to her request (Matt. 15:21-28; see also Mark 7:24-30).

---

*Of course, the outsider motif also is present in non-narrative sections of the New Testament (see, e.g., Rom. 1:5, 13, 16). But an investigation of those sections goes beyond the immediate designs of this book.

There are two important outsider scenes in Mark's Gospel. In addition to the incident paralleled in Matthew (15:21-28), the healing of the Syro-Phoenician woman's daughter (Mark 7:24-30), there is the amazing scene at Jesus' crucifixion. One of the Roman soldiers there exclaims at the moment Jesus takes his last breath, "Truly this man was God's son" (Mark 15:39). Though Mark, among the Gospel writers, makes least use of the outsider motif, the military man's confession at the foot of the cross almost makes up in quality for what Mark lacks in quantity. Here the only confession made about Jesus at the time of his death is not only offered by an outsider, but by a Roman soldier at that. Poignantly and ironically, this man was part of the political machinery that was responsible for Jesus' horrible and unjustified death in the first place.

As for Luke's Gospel, in addition to the examples for which there are parallels in Matthew (noted in the parentheses above), there are other instances of the outsider motif. On one occasion, Jesus appeals to two outsider stories in the Jewish Scriptures to make a point.* He cites the fact that of all the widows in Israel during the time of Elijah, that great prophet was sent to a widow *outside* Israel to get help during a great famine (1 Kings 17:8-24). Jesus also calls attention to the fact that, of all the lepers in Israel during the time of the prophet Elisha, the latter healed Naaman alone (2 Kings 5; see Chapter 4).

Still, just as in Matthew's Gospel, Jesus takes pains in Luke to emphasize that his ministry is restricted to Israel. Indeed, in a complete reversal of the positive Samaritan response we will observe in John 4, in Luke a whole Samaritan village rejects Jesus outright, prompting James and John to propose calling down fire from heaven as punishment (Luke 9:52-56). The explicit reason offered for the Samaritan attitude is that Jesus had his

---

*In Jesus' day the Scriptures did not yet constitute a "book" or "Bible," as would later become the case. There were a number of writings that functioned authoritatively in the various expressions of emerging Judaism. It would take years for these to be transformed into *the Bible*, that is, Judaism's Holy Scriptures. By the time Christianity became an entity completely separate from Judaism, its Scriptures were made up of the Jewish Bible and, eventually, the materials we now refer to as the New Testament. Of course, the non–New Testament Scriptures the Christians called the "Old Testament" (a designation that made sense only after there was a "New Testament"). Thus, whenever someone says that Jesus referred to stories or statements in the Old Testament, it is only for the sake of convenience. In truth, to use the designation "Old Testament" (which is distinctively Christian nomenclature) for the time of Jesus is a complete anachronism.

"face set toward Jerusalem" (Luke 9:53), a phrase that underscores the singular Israelite context of Jesus' ministry as well as his inexorable journey toward death.

Nevertheless, even though Jesus has a pronounced commitment to the insider group Israel, he warns that even reprobate outsiders such as the inhabitants of Sodom, whose reputation was famously nefarious (see Gen. 19:1-29), would fare better on judgment day than those who reject the seventy he sends in pairs to minister to locales in Israel (Luke 10:1-12). Also, in spite of the highly negative portrayal of the Samaritans in Luke 9:52-56, Jesus makes a Samaritan traveler one of his most prominent heroes (Luke 10:25-37). In fact, this "good Samaritan" is the moral superior of a priest and a Levite, two quintessential Israelite insiders (vv. 31-32). Finally, when Jesus heals ten lepers, the only one who bothers to thank him just happens to be a Samaritan, leading Jesus to express disappointment at the ungrateful insiders while praising the sole grateful outsider (Luke 17:11-19; esp. v. 18).

Aside from the Synoptic Gospels and John, whose principal contribution to the outsider motif is the subject of this chapter, the only other sustained narrative in the New Testament is the Acts of the Apostles.* It, too, has its own version of the outsider motif. Yet, just as with the Synoptics, the main insider contingent is "Israel," or "the Jews," who are identified with varied terminology.† At the same time, an important subset of the Is-

---

*The first three Gospels are referred to as "synoptic" because they have so much material in common. For example, virtually all of the Gospel of Mark appears in both Matthew and Luke. In addition, some scholars have hypothesized that the authors of the Synoptics had another source at their disposal, which has been conventionally referred to as Q. Scholars convinced of the validity of the Q source believe that there are materials in the Synoptics that do not belong in Mark, for example, but are too similar not to derive from a common source.

†The actual term "the Jews" is used rather sparingly in the first three Gospels: about five times in Matthew and Luke, about six times in Mark. But other terms often refer in one way or another to "Jews" generally or sub-sets of that larger, amorphous community: Pharisees, Sadducees, the "crowd," scribes, priests, lawyers, etc. In the Acts of the Apostles, "the Jews" appears over seventy times; and it appears upwards of seventy times in John's Gospel as well. The reason I use the adjective "amorphous" to describe this community is that in the first century of the common era there were numerous groups insisting that their traditions, interpretations, and practices were constitutive of being "true Israel" or "Judaism" (a later term). Those Jews who accepted the claims made by or about Jesus were among these groups.

raelite insiders are the followers of Jesus: they see themselves not only as inheritors of Israelite traditions and faithful practitioners of its religion, but also, more importantly, as followers of Israel's true messiah, Jesus, the very one who finally accomplished what God had intended for the elect community from the beginning. Thus, those Jews who believed in what Jesus taught and did and those who did not were together part of the same insider group — albeit as rival factions. As the drama unfolds in the Book of Acts, many of the Jews who have not yet accepted Jesus begin to respond positively to the apostolic preaching (for example, Acts 2:37-42, 47; 4:4; 5:14); in this way the "Jesus sect" of the insider group continues to grow. Nonetheless, as the story progresses, the two "branches" of the same insider group — Jews who accept Jesus or claims made about him and Jews who do not — start to take on the characteristics of distinctly separate communities. Furthermore, given the understanding of those first followers of Jesus as depicted in Acts, the good news is not to be confined to the insider group, Israel, indefinitely. After all, Jesus himself provided the "outline" that the Book of Acts would follow when he announced at his ascension that his disciples would be witnesses not only in Jerusalem and Judea, which was insider territory, but also in Samaria and to the ends of the earth — clearly outsider spheres (Acts 1:8).

Thus it is hardly startling that throughout the Book of Acts outsiders are continually added to the ranks of the Jews who already believe in and proclaim the gospel of Christ. This certainly does not happen without a struggle, which is at the center of the Book of Acts, beginning more or less with the conversion of Cornelius (Acts 10) and concluding more or less with the Jerusalem Council (Acts 15). Nevertheless, in spite of this epic struggle, Acts leaves no doubt that God's insider group, Israel, is fundamentally designed to include any and all who confess Jesus as the Christ. In a radical and dramatic conclusion, when the Apostle Paul arrives in Rome, symbolically perhaps suggestive of the "ends of the earth," he bears witness to the original insider group. Granted, he has had a measure of success in convincing his fellow Jews that the law of Moses and the prophets speak of Jesus. But the resistance he also encounters leads him to quote a section of Scripture that in his mind prophesies the in-group's recalcitrance. The Apostle's final words have the effect of reversing Jesus' own previous determination to minister exclusively to the "lost sheep of the house of Israel"; for Paul, the main target of ministry would henceforth be the Gentiles, the ultimate outsider group (Acts 28:16-31; esp. vv. 24-25, 28).

Outsiders in the Gospel of John

In the story of the woman at the well, John's Gospel arguably contains the longest and most elaborate narrative in the entire New Testament on the outsider theme. Naturally, that's why I have chosen the episode for this final chapter. But it is also true that John's "take" on the outsider motif is somewhat different from that in the first three Gospels and Acts. Thus, before dealing with the story of Jesus and the woman at the well in detail, it is instructive to set the episode in the larger context of John's narrative as it pertains particularly to the outsider motif.

Admittedly, many have regarded the healing of the royal official's son in John as a more or less straightforward outsider story (John 4:46-54). Without question, if the man is not to be understood as Jewish, then this is clearly an outsider episode. But nowhere is the official *(basilikos)* explicitly identified as an outsider. He might have been Roman, but he could just as likely have been a Jewish administrative officer. Given the ambiguity, there is no warrant for seeing this as an outsider story pure and simple. Another possible reference to outsiders may occur in John 10:16, where Jesus notes that he wants to bring into "this fold" the "other sheep" who do not currently belong. Yet here it is not transparently clear that Israelites/Jews are "this fold," whereas the "other sheep" are not. It is equally probable that "this fold" denotes Jews who have accepted Jesus' claims and messiahship, while the "other sheep" are those Jews who have not. About the only other conceivable reference to outsiders may be seen in John 12:20-22, where certain "Greeks" ask for an audience with Jesus. Though there is no question that these people are outsiders in the sense that they are not Jews of any stripe, there is no particular development of the motif in the accompanying dialogue (John 12:23ff.).

Despite these few ostensibly Synoptic-like parallels to the outsider theme in John, it seems that, as I've suggested above, the insider-outsider antithesis plays somewhat differently in the Fourth Gospel. In John, rather consistently, the true insiders are Jesus, his disciples, and those Jews who embrace Jesus' message. This is why Jesus and his disciples are presented throughout as thoroughly Jewish. It is also why the *other* Jews are depicted variously. It is surely true that "the Jews" are generally portrayed negatively in John's Gospel. But the negative slant is religious in character: that is, the Jews are portrayed as largely resistant to Jesus and what he proclaims. This is unquestionably why a great deal of the discussion about the alleged anti-

Semitism of the New Testament centers on the Fourth Gospel. But while admitting this negative bias in John, we should recognize that that Gospel does not present "the Jews" monolithically or stereotypically; further, as I have noted, we must keep in mind the strictly religious character of the portrayal. The Jews are not vilified for being *ethnically* Jewish; instead, they are castigated for refusing to see what God was obviously doing in and through Jesus the Christ.

In light of this *religious* orientation, it is not the least bit unusual that the Fourth Gospel throughout presents Jews who respond sometimes neutrally, sometimes openly, and sometimes very positively to Jesus and his teaching. More than once, Jews are said to have believed in Jesus either because of the signs he performs or for some other reason (John 2:23; 7:31; 8:30-31; 10:41-42; 11:45; 12:9-11, 42).* Nicodemus, a leader of the Jews, though he is never described as having become a convert per se, acknowledges that Jesus' signs indicate he comes from God (John 3:1-10). Then again, Jesus baptizes Jews as disciples (John 3:22; 4:1-2). A few times Jews are reported to have said that Jesus is a prophet (John 6:14; 7:40; 9:17). When Jesus speaks about "true bread," some Jews ask to receive it (John 6:34). And on a number of occasions the Jews are characterized as divided between a negative and positive response to Jesus (John 6:52; 7:12-13, 43, 47-52; 9:16; 10:19).

In this light, even if one has to admit that the overall picture of the Jews is negative in the Fourth Gospel, one should not lose sight of the many neutral, conflicted, or positive responses.† This need not — indeed

---

*The words "signs" *(sēmeia)* and "believe" *(pisteuō)* are extremely important in John's Gospel. "Signs" are more than miracles, though the miraculous element is often present. Generally, the signs are symbolic of the ultimate "work" the Father has given Jesus to do (see Raymond Brown, *The Gospel According to John I–XII* [Garden City, N.Y.: Doubleday, 1966], pp. 525-32). The importance of "believe" may be seen in the fact that it is used many more times in the Fourth Gospel than in the three Synoptics combined: in Matthew, Mark, and Luke the verb appears 34 times altogether; in John alone it is used 98 times. Not only do we discover over and over that people respond to Jesus by either "believing" or "not believing" in him, the purpose of writing the Gospel in the first place was to induce belief. Indeed, promoting belief lies behind the narration of the many signs (John 20:30-31). Places where signs and believing are explicitly combined are: 2:11, 23; 4:48; 6:30; 7:31; 10:41-42; 11:47-48; 12:37; 20:30-31.

†Perhaps the most difficult thing for modern readers to keep in mind is that at the time when the New Testament was written, there was no such thing as a fully formed, hermetically sealed, and monolithic *Judaism* or *Christianity*. Add to this the fact that in the first cen-

should not — blunt the Gospel writer's disappointment, so to speak, at the largely negative response to Jesus on the part of the broader Jewish community. Plus, any proper evaluation of this negative response must also take into account the fact that belief in Jesus was sometimes difficult even for his disciples (John 6:60, 64, 66; 20:25-29) or his own brothers (John 7:5). It turns out that the author of the Fourth Gospel is an "equal opportunity" critic of those who rejected, did not fully embrace, or did not entirely understand Jesus, his claims, or claims made about him. But now it is time to get a fuller picture of this Gospel's understanding of insiders and outsiders by investigating the story that better than any other in John — or the New Testament, for that matter — speaks to this crucial topic: the woman at the well (John 4:1-42).

Traveling through Samaria

Curiously, in the opening scene of a story that is well enough known to have acquired a sort of unofficial title, there is neither a woman nor a well anywhere in sight. For that matter, Jesus is nowhere close to where this famous scene takes place. All we know at the outset is that it is necessary for him to leave Judea in the south and head for Galilee in the north. The change of venue becomes necessary when Jesus hears that certain Pharisees have learned that he has been making and baptizing more disciples than has John the Baptist. Evidently, Jesus' activities run the risk of engendering hostility among this group (John 4:1-3). Now, in John's Gospel, Jesus has already been in Galilee (1:43); indeed, that was where he performed his first "sign" (2:1-11). So, because of this newly perceived pressure, it is natural for him to head back to a territory that is presumably more welcoming.

But as Jesus travels north, we are informed that it is necessary for him to go through Samaria (4:4). At first, it seems that this fact is provided for utterly mundane reasons, either because the route through Samaria is shorter or more convenient. One should certainly not ignore the plain

---

tury of the common era those Jews who rejected the messianic claims made by or about Jesus far outnumbered those who accepted such claims. When one factors in the demonizing vocabulary that was employed in the religious altercations of that era, one has no trouble anticipating that polemical religious literature, which certainly describes what much of the New Testament is at least in some sense, will contain language that grates harshly on modern ears.

meaning of the phrase "it was necessary" (actually a single word in Greek, *edei*); but, as is often the case in an artful narrative, words may play a dual role. So it's conceivable that the "necessity" for Jesus to go through Samaria involves not only geography but some more significant purpose as well. Might providence also be the impetus for the route Jesus takes? Granted, it's difficult to see anything transparently providential right away; yet, by the end of the story, that dimension must surely be considered. Supporting this claim, this same Greek word elsewhere in John's Gospel underscores a number of "necessities" that are anything but ordinary (see John 3:7, 14, 30; 4:20, 24; 9:4; 10:16; 12:34; 20:9). They involve God's important work.

In the initial exchange between the two main characters of the story, Jesus and the Samaritan woman, we immediately are made aware of a serious rift between Jews and Samaritans every bit as intense as what existed between Jesus and the Pharisees in Judea. Indeed, the conversation has hardly begun when it becomes ever so clear that Jesus' having to go through Samaria on the way to Galilee is tantamount to his jumping from a "Jewish frying pan" into a "Samaritan fire." Nonetheless, before the characters in this drama make that point explicit, we have to realize that the earliest readers of this Gospel would have perked up their ears at the very first mention of a Jewish entourage traversing Samaria. The reason for this is simple: regardless of the impressive "denominational" variety that was part of Jewish religious expression in the period when the Gospels were written, the Samaritan community would have been considered by a majority of these same Jews to be completely beyond its religious boundaries. Pharisees, Sadducees, and any number of other such factions might quarrel over a dizzying array of doctrinal or practical issues; but at the end of the day they would have seen themselves as arguing essentially from within the confines of *mainstream* Israelite/Jewish religious tradition. That would not be the case with Samaritans. Debating with Samaritans would not have been considered an intramural activity, because they belonged to the "other" — outsiders par excellence.* No wonder that, later in the Gospel of John, certain Jews viciously accuse Jesus of being a Samaritan *and* having a demon, underscoring their slanderous contention that such "characteristics" were mutually inclusive of the same despicable condition (John 8:48).

---

*The outsider status of Samaritans is what makes their appearance elsewhere in the Gospels so radical, as in the story of the "Good Samaritan" or the "grateful" Samaritan leper (Luke 10:25-37; 17:11-19).

Whether or not one is aware of the hostility between Jews of almost any sect and Samaritans, the opening conversation between Jesus and the woman immediately evokes this long-standing tension between the two communities. Jesus is alone at the well when the woman arrives at noon to draw water (John 4:6). The disciples have left for town to buy lunch, while Jesus sits at the well to rest. Adding to the drama about to unfold, the narrator makes sure we know that this pending conversation takes place on not just any piece of turf and not just at any old well. The patriarch Jacob had given this particular plot to his son Joseph (4:5-6). This detail is scarcely extraneous; rather, it informs us that the events that follow occur in a place fairly oozing with religious tradition of the most consequential kind. After all, Jacob was one of the most important bearers of God's promise and the very man whose name God changed to become the name of the whole community: Israel (Gen. 32:27-28; 35:9-10). Equally, without Joseph the family of promise would have perished in a great famine (Gen. 37–50). The narrator does not seem to want us to forget for a minute how "holy" the ground is where Jesus and the woman have their famous tête à tête. As we shall see, the singular import of this sacred ground will soon be a crucial factor in the dialogue.

When the woman gets to the well, we are prodded to keep in mind her status as a Samaritan. She is not merely a "certain" random woman, but a woman "of Samaria." What Jesus thinks of this datum is ignored. He simply asks a small favor when she appears: "Give me a drink" (4:7). Curiously, it is at this point that the narration uses an aside to remind us that Jesus is alone because his disciples have gone to purchase food in town (4:8). Are we to gather that, had they been there, he would have depended on them to draw water for him? Is he so tired (4:6) from the journey that he is helpless? Is Jesus sitting there waiting for someone — anyone — to show up so that he can get his thirst quenched, or does her arrival prompt him to realize that he, come to think of it, is thirsty? None of these questions is answered, though the juxtaposition of his request with the note about the disciples' absence is tantalizing. Still, perhaps nothing more significant is happening than that a woman has shown up, allowing Jesus to seize on the opportunity for a cool drink.

But as soon as Jesus asks for water, the woman counters with her own question, one that seems designed to transform his apparently off-the-cuff request into a full-scale conversation. Her spontaneous reaction to Jesus' request immediately shows us that this encounter is going to involve more than a matter of Samaritan hospitality. Keeping in mind the woman's outsider status (relative to Jesus) when she is introduced as a "woman from Samaria," we may be puzzled at first at the redundancy. Since Jesus is traveling through Samaria, why does it need to be said that there he encounters a Samaritan person — whether female or male? Wouldn't one expect to find Samaritans in Samaria? Yet, in the woman's rejoinder, not only does the narrator mention her Samaritan connection a second time, but she herself broaches the identity issue: "How do you, being a Jew, ask me, being a Samaritan woman, for a drink?" (4:9) Then, just in case we have not yet gotten the point, the narrator adds a parenthetical statement to underscore the pronounced insider-outsider flavor of this exchange, leaving no doubt whatsoever about what is transpiring before our eyes. Indeed, considering what is declared, one might wonder how this conversation ever gets off the ground in the first place. If, in fact, "the Jews have no dealings with Samaritans," as the parenthetical phrase declares, why does Jesus say anything to the woman at all? He appears to be completely ignorant of the local customs at best, or deliberately provocative at worst. The woman, on the other hand, seems to reflect a much more socially sensitive posture.

As a matter of fact, whether Jesus is in the process of committing a slight social faux pas or a much more serious violation depends on what we determine to be the precise nuance of the phrase "have no dealings with." It may mean something as relatively innocuous as "do not associate on friendly terms with"; or it may suggest "avoiding contact so as not to be ritually defiled." In either case, from the woman's perspective, Jesus is clearly out of line. For her, there is a gender issue as well as a religious issue involved in his boldly asking her for a drink from the well. Without question, this heightens the outsider issue: she is in a sense doubly distant from Jesus; he is male, she is female. Her being taken aback by Jesus' request suggests that public exchanges between men and women were highly regulated by custom. Evidently, an unaccompanied man was not to speak to an unaccompanied woman. And even beyond the strict gender issue, Jesus is not just any man — he is a Jewish man speaking to a Samaritan woman. They would likely have avoided contact had they both been of the *same* sex; their being of opposite sexes accentuates the social tension. This is an insider-outsider interaction of a most jarring kind. Jesus is either unaware of this or doesn't care; the woman is acutely aware of it and immediately addresses the matter.

A woman's nerve

For the briefest moment, the Samaritan woman has the upper hand. She, in effect, chides Jesus for his audacious violation of reigning social and religious customs. Actually, her response to his initial question appears to be rhetorical. It is as though a literal comeback to her question would be something on the order of the following: "I, a Jewish man, am asking a drink from you, a Samaritan woman, because I am either ignorant of or insensitive to local mores." At this point, anyone overhearing the exchange would plausibly conclude that the woman knows what Samaritan-Israelite protocol demands, whereas this Jewish stranger is clueless. Regardless of Jesus' role in the Gospel of John, for a second he appears incongruously to have put himself in a position where he needs to be instructed — and by a Samaritan woman, of all people. Nor does she shrink from the assignment, Jewish man or no Jewish man. And whether he's thirsty or not, she can't quite fathom his social clumsiness in requesting water from her.

At this point, Jesus seems to sidestep the woman's startled question with a not-so-subtle rebuke. Without any attempt to justify his actions, Jesus deflects her criticism by noting that she would be the one asking him for water if she knew either the "gift of God" or the identity of the one whom she is addressing (4:10). Had she done the asking, Jesus would have provided her with "living water." Regardless of the precise meaning of "gift of God" or "living water," both clearly refer to something that transcends ordinary water. Put in another way, just as ordinary water is necessary to sustain biological life, there is another kind of water essential to another kind of life.

All but forgetting the way she responded to Jesus' initial request, she now reacts to this business of living water. She takes Jesus quite literally, and thus wonders how he can supply living water — or any other kind, for that matter — since he lacks the proper vessel for drawing water from a deep well (4:11). Her follow-up question presumes that Jesus will have to do something extraordinary or perhaps miraculous if he is going to make good on his offer. With no jar, and a deep well, Jesus will have to prove himself superior to the great ancestor Jacob, whose well is the scene of this odd conversation (4:12). Again, the woman's question sounds rhetorical, as though the answer expected is on the order of: "No, of course, I am not greater than Jacob." By now, the matter of gender, ethnic identity, and religious affiliation have faded into the background. The conversation has gone in a completely different direction.

Jesus continues the dialogue by elaborating on the nature of the water to which he refers. Drinking the water from Jacob's well, as good as that may be under normal circumstances, will slake one's thirst only temporarily, he says (4:13). Indeed, that's the nature of ordinary water, regardless of how pure, cool, or sweet it might otherwise be. But the water Jesus has in mind is another kind altogether: it takes care of thirst for good ("for the age" or "eternally": *eis tōn aiōna*); furthermore, this water has the property of being perpetually replenished, leading to eternal life (4:14). At the beginning of this encounter, the woman is depicted as all but shocked that Jesus, a Jewish man, speaks to her. Now her shock must surely rise to a new level: his offer of living water that takes care of thirst once and for all and also leads to life eternal has a shock value of a different kind. Previous issues of gender and religious orientation suddenly fade into insignificance.

We are now deep into a conversation that should never have started, according to the woman's own assessment of proper social conduct based on the proscriptions of gender and religious differences. Even a cursory interaction would have been proscribed, let alone this increasingly involved one. But Jesus has begun the exchange, while she, despite her protestations, has allowed herself to be engaged. And though she could have walked off in a huff at any point, or even have slipped away demurely, she does neither. To the contrary, she not only remains involved, she reveals a genuine curiosity. Now she asks for some of that living water that Jesus has referred to. Her continuing literal understanding leads her to believe that Jesus' living water will mean not only an end to physical thirst but an end to the arduous task of constantly having to draw water. Nonetheless, she demonstrates a remarkable openness to what Jesus has said (4:15). In an interesting twist, a conversation that began with Jesus announcing his thirst has come to a point where the woman acknowledges her own.

What makes this all the more remarkable is that the person expressing this transparent eagerness to acquire living water from Jesus is a Samaritan woman who is ever so aware that her dialogue partner is a Jew. Even were she able to overcome the matter of their gender differences, how could any self-respecting Samaritan so willingly succumb to a Jew's ministrations? Indeed, as an indication of how difficult her positive response is for a Samaritan, regardless of gender, one need only compare it to the reluctance of one of Jesus' well-positioned Jewish conversation partners, Nicodemus (John 3:1-15). Even though Nicodemus was a "ruler of the Jews" and therefore more or less on Jesus' same religious wavelength, he never quite manages to "get" what Jesus is saying about being born from above (3:3ff.). He says to Jesus, almost in exasperation, "How can these things be?" (3:9). Jesus answers that question with one of his own: "Are you a teacher in Israel, and yet you do not understand these things?" (3:10). The reluctance and obtuseness of Nicodemus, who is a prominent member of the very insider group to which Jesus himself belongs, are sharply contrasted to the blithe openness of the Samaritan woman, whose pronounced outsider status proves to be no impediment whatsoever to her willing posture before Jesus. This Jewish man has access to living water that deals with thirst as a recurring condition. She wants that, her Samaritanism notwithstanding. Who can blame her? How important is one's Jewish or Samaritan identity when one is faced with the prospect of acquiring water of the kind this man is describing? The woman may be an outsider, but she is no fool.

Salvation is of the Jews

At this moment the conversation between Jesus and the woman has reached a decisive point. Jesus has offered "special" water, and the woman has signaled her desire for it. Isn't this an opportune moment for Jesus to "close the sale"? But this does not happen. Instead, Jesus appears to direct the conversation not only in a brand-new direction, but one that seems completely irrelevant to the one previously taken. He tells the woman to fetch her husband and return with him in tow (John 4:16). Curiously, rather than saying that Jesus' request makes no sense, and is utterly off topic to boot, the woman volunteers that, in point of fact, she has no husband to fetch. This seems to be her attempt to skirt Jesus' strange request and get him back on the subject at hand. But if this is her purpose, it doesn't work. Jesus accepts her statement as true, but then goes on to reveal that he is fully aware of her past. The fact is, he reminds her, she has had five husbands, and the man she is now living with is not actually her husband (4:18).

Many interpreters over the years have seized on the woman's having had multiple husbands and a current "living arrangement" as a clear signal of a sordid past and an unsavory present. But is that a fair analysis? First of all, the woman's five spouses may have died, a circumstance reflected in Mark 12:18-23, where some Sadducees try to prove to Jesus that there is no resurrection. Second, if the woman has been divorced multiple times, it is highly unlikely that she would have triggered the procedures. Initiating divorce was for the most part a male prerogative. Third, a woman in the ancient Near East would have had little choice but to remarry after divorce or the death of her spouse, for she would be economically dependent on a husband. This is why so many Old Testament laws call for supporting the vulnerable — among whom are mainly orphans and widows. To be sure, the fact that this woman is currently with someone who is not actually her husband does not speak well of her. At the same time, one must ask whether this arrangement is as much a function of economic necessity as of sexual promiscuity. Granted, Jesus seems to go out of his way to bring her current situation to light; yet, at the same time, he refrains from anything more than a fairly mild and largely implicit criticism. We are thus led to wonder what Jesus had in mind when he introduced this topic.

Perhaps the answer lies in the woman's response: "Sir, I see that you are a prophet" (4:19). That is, the second Jesus reveals his clairvoyant knowledge about her domestic situation, she intuits that he is more than just some passerby requesting a drink. In her mind, apparently, only someone with prophetic abilities could possess such information about her. If that's the case, then it's likely that we are to infer that Jesus brought up the subject of the woman's husband and current "arrangement" in the first place to demonstrate his prowess as a prophet. Far from denying Jesus' charge, she confirms it, and she also draws the logical conclusion as to what led him to it.

But perceiving Jesus' prophetic status is not enough for her. She moves the dialogue to another plane by embarking on a high-level theological discussion. After all, it's not every day one finds oneself chatting alone with a prophet. Since this one is, in addition, a Jewish prophet, by her own calculation, she is afforded an excellent opportunity to bring up some salient issues, especially ones having to do with the long-standing Jewish-Samaritan schism. No longer worrying in the slightest about the impropriety of her speaking with the "Jewish man at the well," she launches into the topic of the preferred location for worship (4:20).

When the woman raises the topic of worship, a slight shift occurs: she begins to speak collectively, as though she has been mysteriously appointed to represent the Samaritan perspective. Similarly, her language demonstrates that she sees Jesus as embodying the typical Jewish stance. "*Our* fathers," she declares, "worshiped on this mountain, but *you* say [plural: *legete*] that in Jerusalem is the place where it is necessary to worship" (4:20). This dispute over the proper place of worship was, of course, a main bone of contention between Jews and Samaritans. Furthermore, in the context of this dialogue, the turn of conversation serves to highlight not only the stark differences between the Samaritan woman and the Jewish Jesus, but it keeps in the foreground the woman's outsider status vis-à-vis Jesus (from the perspective of the Gospel). By broaching this particular subject, the woman certainly draws no closer to Jesus in terms of the religious beliefs they hold in common; indeed, she becomes even more of an outsider as she articulates a significant area of theological disagreement.

But Jesus, instead of dealing with this controversy by arguing on behalf of the Jewish position, says something that in effect relativizes both points of view. Jesus declares that, before long, debates about which mountain is the best site for valid worship of the divine Father will be entirely moot (4:21). Curiously, this statement seems to indicate that both Jews and Samaritans take positions on the matter that are, in a word, irrelevant; if it doesn't matter where worship takes place, then neither Samaritans nor Jews are barking up the right theological tree. But, having said that, Jesus leaves no doubt that he finds the Jewish tradition correct: "You [i.e., Samaritans — plural] worship what you [plural] do not know. We [Jews] worship what we know, because salvation is from the Jews" (4:22). That is an astounding assertion in the Gospel of John, which does not hesitate to sharply criticize the negative response of the majority of Jews toward Jesus. Still, "the Jews" are the legitimate insiders, even though the steadfast perspective of the Fourth Gospel is that such insiders should find Jesus' signs and messianic claims persuasive.

Jesus elaborates on the point about the true location for divine worship by referring to God's essential nature ("spirit") and the time ("hour") being at hand when God beckons true worshipers to worship in "spirit and truth" (4:23-24). When the woman hears this explanation, she neither reacts to its implications for her own Samaritan theological framework nor for Jesus' somewhat off-center Jewish stance. Rather, out of the blue, she puts forward her belief that when Messiah comes, he will reveal everything "to us." (Does she mean Samaritans? Samaritans and Jews? Everyone?) A question that comes to mind is this: Why does she mention Messiah at this juncture? Are we to conclude that she has construed Jesus' words as so theologically incisive that thoughts of the Messiah have sprung spontaneously into her head? Or, was she being sarcastic, that is, was she belittling Jesus' remarks by saying, more or less, that he would be straightened out when Messiah arrived to settle such squabbles once and for all? Before answering, Jesus alters the whole tenor of the conversation with a most radical statement. Without bothering to sort out her belief about the Messiah compared to his, as a Jewish prophet might have been expected to do, he instead announces something that would have been equally astonishing and provocative to Samaritan or Jew: "I am he [i.e., Messiah], the very one speaking to you."

This claim is far beyond one more theological datum or a point scored in a doctrinal debate. Suddenly, in saying that he is none other than Messiah, Jesus' person is more in the spotlight than is his argument. Initially, the woman addressed Jesus with the polite "Sir" (4:11; *kyrios*); later in the episode, she perceived that he was a prophet (4:19). Now she finds herself having to decide whether to believe that he is the Messiah. It's true that she has readily confessed her belief that "Messiah is coming" (4:25); but to be told by a Jewish stranger who is sitting at the well and engaging her in theological dialogue that he is, in fact, Messiah is as radical as it gets. What does one say when presented with startling information like that? Will she scoff and walk off rolling her eyes? Will she think that this man's contact with reality is somewhat tenuous — as some prophets were occasionally viewed? Will she conclude that, as she has undoubtedly often heard, the bankruptcy of the Jewish understanding of reality goes far beyond a flawed theology or faulty interpretive methods? Or perhaps worse, has this man's unquenched thirst driven him to pitiful delusions of grandeur? Finally, if she is still intent on remaining open to what this fascinating if odd Jewish man has to say, will she simply probe his stupendous claim further? Regardless of how one answers these questions, one thing is certain: in light of Jesus' claims about himself, the woman's previous query about whether he was greater than the ancestor Jacob (4:12) is no longer rhetorical. It's as though Jesus is giving a delayed yet resounding answer to that question: "Yes, now that you mention it, I am."

This is a moment of high drama in the dialogue; we can hardly wait to observe the woman's response. But the dramatic tension is allowed to build even further because, as she is presumably poised to react, Jesus' disciples return from their lunch-buying errand (4:27). Caught up in what has become a most riveting conversation, we have forgotten all about them. Indeed, they haven't been mentioned since before the woman arrived at the well (4:8). What an inopportune time for them to come back and interrupt the narrative! No doubt they'll soon be busily discussing what they bought, who gets what order, and what Jesus might want for lunch. And although the fussing around to get everyone a bite to eat is a relatively high priority for a group of hungry travelers, it isn't for us readers; we're much more eager to find out what the woman will say in response to Jesus' identifying himself as the Messiah. Granted, we won't have to wait that long, considering the story's telescoped temporal framework. Yet there's no question the disciples' return has interrupted the flow of the conversation and certainly retarded the action — and all just for a small matter like lunch!

Evangelism and Samaritan conversion

As we wait for the main action to resume, the returning disciples figuratively nudge the woman to the side. She is still there, but she now falls uncharacteristically mute. There is no question that the disciples are quite aware of her presence; in fact, they are amazed that Jesus is speaking to a woman. But nothing about her religious affiliation seems to disturb them. Apparently, it is enough that Jesus has engaged a lone woman in conversation. Also, in glaring contrast to the woman's easy and prolonged conversation with Jesus, the disciples are conspicuously silent. They don't bother to ask her what she wants, and they refrain from questioning Jesus as to why he would speak with her (4:27). It is most curious that Jesus the Jew and the woman of Samaria are in the middle of an intriguing exchange whereas the disciples incongruously hold their tongues in front of both of them. This insider and outsider somehow converse more freely, at least at this moment, than do Jesus and his closest fellow insiders. In fact, it now dawns on us that Jesus and his disciples have not exchanged a single word since the chapter began.

But if we are waiting for the woman to break the silence of this moment, we can't help but be disappointed. She says nothing. In fact, she exits the scene, and it turns out that she has spoken her last word to Jesus. She still has a few lines left in this narrative, but her audience is no longer Jesus but her fellow townspeople — a whole village full of outsiders. At the same time, though her conversation with Jesus is completed, the effects of that conversation remain. And those effects are remarkable,

This is indicated in two ways. First, when she walks away from the well, we are provided with an odd detail: she leaves behind her jug (4:28). This is a wonderfully ambiguous action on her part. Is she simply being forgetful? Or, in what would be a delightful combination of symbolism and literalism, does she figure that, since she now presumably has access to the "living water" Jesus offers, there is no reason for her to hold on to a jug? If one will never thirst again, of what use is a water jug? Again, is the woman so excited that she has possibly been in the presence of the Messiah that something as mundane as remembering a jug no longer has any importance at all? However we answer these questions, we must bear in mind that virtually no details in artful biblical narratives are incidental. Also, parallel to her leaving her jug behind, we have to remember that this woman who came to the well precisely to draw water never managed to get so much as a single sip. Her ordinary yet important task has been overwhelmed by her encounter with Jesus.

Second, when she dashes off to her village, we discover that the issue of messiahship is uppermost in her mind. Not for a second has she forgotten Jesus' last words to her, in spite of the interruption of the returning disciples. As soon as she is within earshot of her town, she blurts out: "Come, see a man who told me all that I ever did. Might this not be the Messiah?"(4:29). With this phrasing, the woman combines her perception of Jesus' prophetic acumen with his claims about being the Messiah. Though she said nothing at the actual moment Jesus made his stunning claim, what she now thinks about it could hardly be more transparent.

In addition, the particular group she speaks to in town is instructive, especially considering the gender issue she herself raised at the beginning of the story, plus what seemed to be the sole source of the disciples' astonishment, if not pique, when they returned to the well. An inclusive translation, such as that of the New Revised Standard Version, has the woman giving her testimony to "the people" (4:28). This is certainly possible; after all, the collective inhabitants of any town would obviously include people of both genders. Still, in the Greek text we are told that the woman spoke *tois anthrōpois*. Depending on context, this phrase can mean "to the men," not in the generic sense but in the specific sense of "males." In this setting, it is impossible to determine. Nonetheless, the narrator may intend a delicious irony here: that a woman who formerly opined how inappropriate it was for her to speak to a lone man, and vice versa, now speaks brazenly to an entire contingent of the men of the town.

The composition of the group the woman addresses doesn't ultimately matter; what is important is that they take what she has to say with utmost seriousness. Her words prompt immediate action: her listeners head straight for the man she has spoken of without hesitation or even questioning. However, just as we get geared up to watch a most interesting encounter between the townsfolk and Jesus, once again there is a narrative interruption that slows the action — this time in the form of a monologue that Jesus delivers to his disciples.

Jesus embarks on this monologue when the disciples urge him to eat (4:31). Brushing aside their invitation, he responds with a remark reminiscent of what he has said to the woman; only this time he claims to have special *food* rather than special water: "I myself have food to eat of which you are unaware" (4:32). In a response that parallels the woman's response, the disciples take this remark literally, asking among themselves whether anyone has already slipped Jesus some food (4:33). It remains true that the only time they have actually spoken to Jesus is when encouraging him to eat. Pointedly, the narrative lets us know that their question about whether anyone has already offered Jesus a bite is among themselves only: "So the disciples said *to one another . . .*" (4:33). Once again, it is impossible to miss the contrast between the Samaritan woman and the Jewish disciples in their relationships to Jesus. The outsider has talked openly, freely, and meaningfully with Jesus; the insiders have said only one thing to Jesus ("Rabbi, eat") and one very mundane thing about him ("Has any one brought him food?").

It is difficult to miss the implication that the Samaritan woman, the quintessential outsider in this particular episode, is on the verge of becoming an insider, while the natural insiders, none other than Jesus' own disciples, are depicted as awkward and puzzled. They are still insiders, of course, but a true understanding of the really important matters raised in the previous conversation seems to have eluded them completely. The Samaritan woman has hurried back to her town without paying the slightest attention to her (or her household's) need for water. Ordinary thirst no longer seems to matter; for her, another thirst is about to be slaked. In contrast, the disciples have been concentrating only on the rumble in their stomachs. Their perplexity at the sight of Jesus talking with this woman does not deter them from fulfilling the only mission they have in the whole episode: "Rabbi, eat."

That is perhaps why Jesus' monologue almost has the appearance of a condescending lecture. What he now says to his disciples underscores most emphatically the nature of what has just transpired. He sees the significance of his conversation with the woman in terms of his most basic mission: "My food is to do the will of him who sent me, and to accomplish his work" (4:34). That work involves harvesting, and harvesting presupposes planting. In this missional arrangement, it doesn't particularly matter who does the planting and who does the reaping. What is crucial is that the "fruits" of the appropriate labors be gathered (4:35-37). And here Jesus emphasizes the strategic role that has been played in this story not only by him but by the woman as well.

At one level, we have watched her on her way to becoming a convert to Jesus as the conversation has unfolded. Each new point made by Jesus has had the effect of drawing her closer to belief in his claims. But this has been much more than winning her over in an argument: this is about eternal life (4:14). As she has become convinced that Jesus is more than a prophet (4:19) and quite possibly the Messiah (4:29), it means that Jesus is in a position to give her the special life-giving water that she has so blithely requested (4:15). Throughout the narrative of John's Gospel, it is one thing for Jesus to make any number of Jewish converts, for he concentrates on Jewish audiences; it is quite another thing to make a *Samaritan* convert. Indeed, one might find it easier to convert Gentiles over Samaritans, given the way the latter had twisted Jewish teaching and traditions (from a Jewish perspective). Yet Jesus has done just that: the woman is at least on the verge of conversion given what she has said to her fellow townspeople (and how they eventually respond).

We have seen this before with "outsider" stories: the most unlikely of people come to a profound insiders' faith, for example, Rahab, Naaman, Ruth, and the sailors and Ninevites in the Jonah story. In the Gospel of John, no outsider would have been any more unlikely than this Samaritan woman. Here is a woman who first thought it imprudent even to speak with Jesus (4:9), then questioned his ability to acquire ordinary water (4:11), but became intrigued with his offer of extraordinary water (4:15), and ended up not only thinking he was a prophet but quite possibly the Messiah as well (4:19, 29). This outsider, with whom Jews were not supposed to have any dealings at all, is about to become, in effect, a Jew herself — religiously speaking. In John's Gospel, when Jews come to believe in Jesus' signs and works, and therefore in what God is doing in and through him, conversion of the most profound sort takes place (for example, John 9:35-38; 11:45). But it is an even higher order of conversion, if that is possible, when a non-Jew comes to faith. As we noted at the beginning of this chapter, there are no unambiguous accounts in John of Gentiles coming to faith in Jesus (which contrasts sharply with the Synoptics). But there is this story of a Samaritan woman coming to faith, a person who was part of an outsider group that the insiders had no trouble demonizing (John 8:48). She is the only outsider in John to become an insider, and she was the most quintessential of outsiders at that.

But there is another, perhaps more fascinating, aspect to the movement of this remarkable woman from the outside to the inside. She is not content to believe in Jesus and let it go at that. She also acts in such a way as to become virtually one of Jesus' disciples. We have already seen how she bolts from Jesus and his disciples, running into the village and leaving her water jug behind (John 4:28-29). It turns out that her witness is most effective, for many other Samaritans believe in Jesus because of her testimony (4:39); apparently, it is this group of new believers that is headed out to see Jesus while he is talking to his disciples about sowing and reaping (4:30, 31-36). Not only that, the woman's initial testimony concerning Jesus leads to more converts still. This is a result of the newly converted Samaritans inviting Jesus to stay with them, which leads to his spending two days with them. As a result of this visit and Jesus' own teaching ("word") in this Samaritan town, many more come to believe (4:40-41). The Samaritans go so far as to say to the woman that, after Jesus' stay, their belief is not only a function of what she has testified but is related to Jesus' own words. What the Samaritan converts conclude from all this reflects a conversion of the most thorough kind, namely, their conviction that Jesus is the savior of the world, a "world" that obviously includes them (4:42).

Finally, Jesus' own remarks to the disciples about sowing and reaping put into boldest relief the woman's amazing evangelistic role. Toward the end of his statement, Jesus cites an adage: "One sows and another reaps" (4:37). Apparently, the basic point of this saying is that any harvest depends equally on those who plant and those who gather the results of such planting. All other things being equal, it doesn't seem to make one bit of difference what part of the planting-reaping process one participates in. But in this instance it turns out that perhaps not all other things are, in fact, equal. When it comes to Jesus and his disciples, one would think that the latter would have planting as a primary duty and high priority. Isn't this why Jesus has called the disciples in the first place? Jesus and his disciples have already been baptizing and making new disciples (John 3:22; 4:1-2); but in Samaria the pattern is altered. The woman at the well does the planting (4:29, 39). This means that the disciples may surely rejoice that converts are being added to the company, for sowers and reapers are to celebrate together (4:36). But their rejoicing will be as reapers who are gathering in what another has planted (4:38). The "other" who did the planting in this situation, of course, is the Samaritan woman. The disciples may by all means gladly enter into her labor, but the fact remains that she has done the initial work. In almost every other instance, it would be a matter of insignificance whether one planted or harvested. But when the planter turns out to be an outsider such as here represented by this remarkable Samaritan woman, and the reapers turn out to be disciples of Jesus himself, one cannot help but be impressed. Typically, insiders do the planting, hoping to transform outsiders into insiders. But that process has been reversed in this instance. A Samaritan woman takes on the role of one of Jesus' best Jewish disciples and performs not only admirably, but spectacularly. She is the crown jewel outsider of John's Gospel.

Notes

Notes to Chapter 1

I published the contents of this chapter in a more technical form in Spina, "The 'Face of God': Esau in Canonical Context," in *The Quest for Context and Meaning: Studies in Biblical Intertextuality in Honor of James A. Sanders,* ed. Craig A. Evans and Shemaryahu Talmon [Biblical Interpretation Series, 28] (Leiden, New York, Cologne: Brill, 1977), pp. 3-25.

15 On the subject of Edom, Bruce C. Cresson says that "it is scarcely hyperbolic to say that never a kind word is spoken about Edom in the Old Testament"; see Cresson, "The Condemnation of Edom in Postexilic Judaism," in *The Use of the Old Testament in the New and Other Essays: Studies in Honor of William Franklin Stinespring;* ed. James M. Efird (Durham, NC: Duke University Press, 1972), p. 125. Bert Dicou contends that Edom assumes the position of the representative of foreign nations deserving of divine judgment; see Dicou, *Edom, Israel's Brother and Antagonist: The Role of Edom in Biblical Prophecy and Story* [JSOTSup, 169] (Sheffield, UK: Sheffield Academic Press, 1994), p. 26. Of the texts treating Edom or Esau, Syrén classifies only Deut. 2:4-6; 23:7-8 as positive; as neutral he cites Num. 21:4; 33:37; 34:3; Josh. 15:1; 1 Kgs. 9:26; 2 Kgs. 3:9; Jer. 40:11; Dan. 11:41; see Roger Syrén, *The Forsaken First-Born: A Study of a Recurrent Motif in the Patriarchal Narratives* [JSOTSup 133] (Sheffield, UK: JSOT Press, 1993), pp. 114-115.

16 On Rebekah's failure to conceive, the Masoretes note that the verb used in this instance *(wayye'tar)* is found three other times; in each case God is implored and immediately responds (see Ex. 8:26 [Eng. 8:30]; cf. vv. 24-25 [Eng. vv. 28-29]; Ex. 10:18; cf. v. 17; Judg. 13:8). Isaac's intercession *('tr)* and Rebekah's seeking *(drš)* divine assistance may have cultic associations; see Ronald S. Hendel, *The Epic of the Patriarch:*

Notes

The Jacob Cycle and the Narrative Traditions of Canaan and Israel [HSM, 42] (Atlanta: Scholars Press, 1987), p. 39. See also J. P. Fokkelman, *Narrative Art in Genesis: Specimens of Stylistic and Structural Analysis* [The Biblical Seminar, 12; 2nd ed.] (Sheffield, UK: JSOT Press, 1991 [1975 Van Gorcum & Comp. B. V.]), p. 88, fn. 4.

On the question of firstborn privilege, see Syrén, *The Forsaken First-Born*, p. 81; Fokkelman, *Narrative Art*, p. 88; M. Malul, "'AQEB 'Heel' and 'AQAB 'To Supplant' and the Concept of Succession in the Jacob-Esau Narratives," *VT* XLVI/2 (1996): 196. On Esau's crudeness, see E. A. Speiser, *Genesis* [AB, 1] (Garden City, NY: Doubleday, 1964), p. 196; see also Malul, "'AQEB and 'AQAB," pp. 206-207.

The phrase "inarticulate appetite" is Robert Alter's. In addition, he suggests that the word *l't*, which is found only once in the Bible, usually is used for the feeding of animals. BDB (p. 542) cites a meaning, "to stuff cattle with food," in "late Hebrew" (see Alter, *The Art of Biblical Narrative* (New York: Basic Books, 1981), p. 44.

16 Of the verbs in Gen. 25:34, Speiser refers to the "drumbeat effect" of these verbs, five in all. The fifth is: "he despised [the birthright]" (see *Genesis*, p. 196). On the "crude hunter," see R. P. P. Warmoes, "Jacob ravit la bénédiction d'Isaac (Gen 27:6-40)," *Assemblées du Seigneur* 29 (1966): 23 (the phrase in French is "le rude
17 chasseur"). The Hebrew for "so Esau despised the birthright is *wayyibez 'ēśāw 'et-habb'kōrāh.* "Despise" is the RSV rendering; JPS translates it "spurn." In Prov. 19:16, *bāzāh* is opposite of *šāmar*, "to regard, pay attention to, be careful about, guard," etc. "Disregard" may be acceptable in this Genesis passage, though perhaps too anemic. The contextual idea seems to be "wantonly disregard" or "cavalierly dismiss." Malul presents an elaborate argument that *bāzāh* in this instance should be seen in the light of ancient Near Eastern legal procedures having to do with relinquishing property rights (see "'AQEB and 'AQAB," pp. 205-6). Curiously, the one time Esau refers to the birthright (Gen. 25:32) he uses no personal pronoun intimating his rightful ownership. Only Jacob (v. 31) and the narrator (v. 33) ever acknowledge that the birthright indeed belonged initially to Esau. Not only in the story, but grammatically, Esau's hold on the birthright was tenuous. Compare these instances with those in Gen. 27:36 where Esau mentions "my birthright" and "my blessing," perhaps indicating a heightened sense of possession but at a point in the story where such awareness is too late.

17 On Jacob's extortionary nature, see Alter, *Art*, pp. 45-46; Fokkelman, *Narrative Art*, p. 97.

17 On Esau's portrayal as an outdoorsman, if a cultural contrast between the "desert and the sown" was once indicated by this juxtaposition, it has been largely subordinated in the present context; see the discussion of Martin Noth's understanding of the antithesis between the huntsman and the herdsman in J. R. Bartlett, "The

Brotherhood of Edom," *JSOT* 4 (1977): 16. Malul's suggestion that Esau became an outlaw dwelling in the steppes after losing his legal rights is not cogent in that Esau is already a "man of the field" before any dealings with Jacob (see "'AQEB and 'AQAB," p. 206).

17-18 On Jacob's nature as *tām*, the RSV has "quiet"; JPS: "mild." See Hendel, who has "mild" (*Epic*, p. 112; cf. fn. 35); Speiser, who has "retiring" (*Genesis*, p. 193); and Warmoes, who has "homme tranquille" ("Jacob ravit," p. 18). These renderings, though, seem inconsistent with the general characterization of Jacob, whose reputation is summarized with the statement that he had "striven with God and men and had prevailed" (Gen. 32:28). Source critics have identified Gen. 25:27-28 and 32:22-32 as Yahwistic, so that these differing characterizations — if one accepts that *tām* means "mild" or the like — could not be explained as belonging to separate sources. See M. Noth, *A History of Pentateuchal Traditions*, trans. B. W. Anderson (Englewood Cliffs, NJ: Prentice-Hall, 1972), pp. 264-65. Fokkelman translates it "bent on one purpose," which has the connotation of "single-mindedness," but not necessarily in the sense of "upright" (see *Narrative Art*, p. 91). See also S. D. Walters, "Jacob Narrative" [ABD, 3] (New York, London: Doubleday, 1992), p. 600; Alter, *Art*, p. 43.

18-19 On Rebekah's actions, Christine Garside Allen argues that Rebekah should be viewed positively in this story since she makes it possible for God's will to be accomplished. She notes that Jewish exegetical sources are generally more positive about Rebekah than are Christian ones. While it is true that God's will is facilitated by Rebekah's actions, one need not construe those actions as necessarily positive or moral. This would not be the only time that a biblical character "meant it for evil while God meant it for good" (e.g., Gen. 45:5-8; 50:20). See "On Me Be the Curse, My Son!" in *Encounter with the Text: Form and History in the Hebrew Bible* [Semeia Sup., 8], M. Buss, ed. (Philadelphia: Fortress Press; Missoula: Scholars Press, 1979), pp. 163-171.

After Jacob's lie to Isaac, curiously, the next time Jacob offers his name, it serves as a confession (Gen. 32:27). Note that he does not name himself explicitly when he encounters his mother's family (Gen. 29:12). Walters suggests that Jacob's providing his name to the mysterious "man" with whom he wrestled functions as the confession that is missing from Jacob's prayer in Gen. 32:9-12 (see Walters, "Jacob Narrative," p. 605). See also Warmoes, "Jacob ravit," p. 22: "Pour se tirer d'embarras et rendre le mensonge plus efficace, il va jusqu'à faire appel à Yahvé lui-même!" Compare verbal and nominal forms of *ḥlq* in Isa. 30:10; Ezek. 12:24; Pss. 5:10; 12:3-5; Prov. 2:16; 5:3; 7:5; 26:28; 28:23; 29:5; Dan. 11:32. See Walters, "Jacob Narrative," p. 603. For the way the Genesis narrator uses other voices as "displaced personae" to confirm the narrative's perspective see Michael Fishbane, *Biblical Interpretation in Ancient Israel* (Oxford: Clarendon Press, 1985), p. 377; compare Gen. 29:25-26.

20 That Isaac's two blessings are antithetical appears in the RSV and NRSV (but note the qualification in the footnote). See John R. Bartlett, "Edom in the Nonprophetical Corpus," in *You Shall Not Abhor an Edomite for He Is Your Brother: Edom and Seir in History and Tradition* [Archaeology and Biblical Studies, 3], ed. Diana Vikander Edelman (Atlanta: Scholars Press, 1995), p. 17; Dicou, *Edom,* p. 119; Fokkelman, *Narrative Art,* pp. 101, 111; Syrén, *Forsaken,* p. 99; Claus Westermann, *Genesis 12–36,* trans. John Scullion (Minneapolis: Augsburg, 1985), p. 27. Westermann rejects the view, however, that Isaac's words regarding Esau are "virtually a curse." On both brothers being promised prosperous futures, see also Walters, "Jacob Narrative," pp. 601-602; I. Willi-Plein, "Genesis 27 als Rebekkageschichte. Zu einem historiographischen Kunstgriff der biblischen Vätergeschichten," *Theologische Zeitschrift* 45 (1989): 320-22 ("vom Fetten der Erde her wird dein Wohnsitz sein und vom Tau des Himmels von oben").

For the relationship of the last line of the blessing to Gen. 12:3 and Num. 24:9b, see Westermann, *Genesis,* p. 441. On taking *tārîd* from *rwd,* see Fokkelman, *Narrative Art,* p. 112, fn. 37. Boecker takes Isaac's remarks to Esau as a full-fledged curse, though he grants that the technical language typical of a curse is missing; see Hans Jochen Boecker, *1. Moses 25,12–37,1 Isaak und Jakob,* ed. H. H. Schmid [Zürcher Bibelkommentar] (Zürich: Theologischer Verlag, 1992), p. 50. On Esau's prospects for the future, see Walters, "Jacob Narrative," p. 602.

20-21 On the primary and secondary blessing, Fokkelman makes the point that the "second blessing" (i.e., Esau's) shows that the story is equally concerned with Esau. See *Narrative Art,* p. 100.

22 On Esau's third wife, see Syrén, *Forsaken Firstborn,* p. 121. Hendel notes that when Esau marries Ishmael's daughter, he takes a "proper wife" (see *Epic,* p. 148).

22 On the impending meeting with Esau, there may be some "tease" in the vocabulary in that *liqrā't* is often used in the context of military confrontation (see Judg. 7:24; 20:25, 31; 1 Sam. 4:1; 1 Kgs. 20:27, etc.). Still, there is nothing explicit in the text that suggests that Esau's men are, in fact, armed retainers. One might speak of "re-establishing" a fraternal relationship; but, strictly speaking, Jacob and Esau never had one. They are never portrayed as having a single amicable encounter. Walter Brueggemann comments incisively on this passage: "There is no hint of remorse on his [i.e., Jacob's] part" (see *Genesis* [Atlanta: John Knox, 1982], p. 262). Coats correctly sees that Jacob prepares the gift "as a means for buying off the anger of his brother" (see "Strife Without Reconciliation," p. 103).

23 On Jacob's prayer's failure to acknowledge wrongdoing, see Walters, "Jacob Narrative," p. 605. Fokkelman, on the other hand, regards the prayer as "impressive" and faithfully expressed (see *Narrative Art,* p. 204). In my judgment, Fokkelman's contention is weakened by Jacob's attempts at bribery that precede *and* follow the

prayer. The verb *qāṭōntî* suggests not only his unworthiness, but also the fact that Jacob is the younger (*qāṭôn;* see Gen. 27:15, 42); see Brueggemann, *Genesis,* p. 264. Procksch notes that *kpr pnym* always connotes guilt (cited by Westermann, *Genesis 12–36,* p. 510); compare Prov. 16:14.

24 On Jacob wrestling with God, see Walters, "Jacob Narrative," p. 605. On the Jacob-Esau reversal, see Fokkelman, *Narrative Art,* p. 200.

24-25 The sequence of verbs in Gen. 33:4 reminds us of the succession in the birthright episode (Gen. 25:34); but this time the verbs are suggestive of positive rather than negative behavior (see Hendel, *Epic,* p. 130). Note a similar succession in the scene where Laban meets Jacob for the first time, with the exception of falling on his neck (Gen. 29:13). Boecker remarks on this reunion scene: "An keiner Stelle des Alten Testaments aber steht das alles, wie hier, beieinander, wird von einer so herzlichen und intensiven Begrüßung erzählt wie von dieser" (see *1. Moses 25,12–37,1,* p. 107).

Jacob accepts that Esau is sincere, but sees his behavior not as a function of moral character but of radical mood swings attributable to a wild man given to rash anger or extreme passion. But he does opine that Esau's refusal of the present is insincere; see Benno Jacob, *The First Book of the Bible: Genesis* (New York: Ktav, 1974), pp. 645-66. In this instance, Jacob's psychological "take" on Esau is, at best, a hunch completely unsupported by anything in the narrative itself. Fredrick Holmgren acknowledges that Christian readers of this story tend to sympathize with Esau and criticize Jacob, but this is moralistic, in his view. For Holmgren, a Jewish perspective is more on the mark: "Jacob is the sincere participant in this meeting, and Esau is the manipulative, crafty one who covers up his vengeful desires with insincere words and acts of love"; see Holmgren, "Holding Your Own Against God! Genesis 32:22-32 (in the Context of Genesis 31–33)," *Interpretation 44/* 1 (1990): 14. Again, this interpretation requires us to ignore the rather plain meaning of the text.

Plaut plays down Esau's initial refusal of the present by suggesting that it was an old custom to preface the acceptance of a large gift by first politely refusing it. Equally, he sees no significance in Jacob's saying that he saw in Esau the "face of God," dismissing this statement as "extreme flattery"; see W. G. Plaut, "Genesis," in *Torah: A Modern Commentary* (New York: Union of American Hebrew Congregations, 1981), p. 219.

24-25 On "seeing the face of God," see Walters, "Jacob Narrative," p. 605; Coats, "Strife without Reconciliation: A Narrative Theme in the Jacob Traditions," in *Werden und Wirken des Alten Testaments,* Claus Westermann Festschrift, ed. R. Albertz, H.-P. Müller, Hans Walter Wolff, W. Zimmerli (Göttingen: Vandenhoeck & Ruprecht; Neukirchen-Vluyn: Neukirchener Verlag, 1980), p. 101 (see fns. 40-41).

25 On the land being unable to support both brothers and their holdings, see Gen. 36:6-8. Note the similarity of the language with that used in the separation of Abraham and Lot, obviously for the same reasons (Gen. 13:5-7).

26 On Jacob offering his blessing, see Fokkelman, *Narrative Art,* p. 234.

27 In other contexts, having the yoke on one's neck broken is a figure for liberation. See Bob Becking, "'I will break his yoke from off your neck': Remarks on Jeremiah xxx 4-11," in *New Avenues in the Study of the Old Testament: A Collection of Old Testament Studies Published on the Occasion of the Fiftieth Anniversary of the Oudtestamentish Werkgezelschap and the Retirement of Prof. M. J. Mulder* (Oudtestamentische Studiën, XXV; A. S. Van der Woude, ed.; Leiden: E. J. Brill, 1989): 63-76. Thompson suggests that the text reflects a socio-political situation that has been retrojected into the Jacob-Esau fictional tale. See Thomas L. Thompson, "Conflict Themes in the Jacob Narratives," *Semeia* 15 (1979): 17. On the meaning of *tārîd* in Gen. 27:40 (cf. Jer. 2:31; Ps. 55:3) see Fokkelman, *Narrative Art,* p. 112.

27 On the question of a conciliatory gesture, see Walters, "Jacob Narrative," p. 605; see also Coats, "Strife Without Reconciliation," p. 103.

On Jacob as the sole bearer of covenant promise, see Walters, "Jacob Narrative," p. 599. For a comparison of Ishmael and Esau, see Dicou, *Edom,* pp. 132-35. In regard to Ishmael, see Gen. 16:7-15; 21:14-21; 25:12-18. Ironically, Ishmaelites, who were descended from Abraham and the Egyptian Hagar, were the ones who sold Joseph to the Egyptians (Gen. 16; 37:25-28).

Gen. 36 also emphasizes Esau's wealth; in fact, this chapter gives as the reason for Esau's move to Seir the fact that Canaan is not able to accommodate his and his brother Jacob's vast holdings (Gen. 36:6-8). Language used in Gen. 36 is reminiscent of Gen. 13:5ff., when Abraham's and Lot's possessions were too great for the land to sustain. That circumstance led to a parting of the ways, with Abraham staying in the land of promise and Lot moving outside of it (Gen. 13:9-13). See also Fishbane, *Biblical Interpretation,* p. 46; Westermann, *Genesis,* p. 562.

29-30 On the parallel between Israel's and Edom's conquests, similar language occurs in Deut. 2:21-22. Note that the descendants of Lot receive similar benefits, presumably by virtue of their relationship to Abraham (Deut. 2:9-11). On the later condemnations of Edom, G. J. Botterweck, for example, is insistent that the harsh passage in Mal. 1:2-3 is related to actual historical events, but concedes there is no way to determine which ones are in view (see "Jakob habe Ich lieb — Esau hasse Ich'. Auslegung von Malachias 1,2-5," *Bibel und Leben* 1 [1960]: 38). See the various historical reconstructions in Diana Vikander Edelman, ed., *You Shall Not Abhor an Edomite for He Is Your Brother: Edom and Seir in History and Tradition* [Archaeology and Biblical Studies, 3] (Atlanta: Scholars Press, 1995).

Bartlett rehearses the reasons why Edom came to be equated with Esau. He finally opts for the religious similarities between Edom and Israel; see "The Brother-hood of Edom," *JSOT* 4 (1977): 7. He lists the "brotherhood" texts as Gen. 25:19-34; 27:27-29, 39-40; 36:1, 8, 9, 19, 43; Num. 20:14-21; Deut. 2:4, 8; 23:7 (Heb. 23:8); Jer. 49:7-11; Amos 1:11; Obad. 10, 12.

31 Standard efforts to interpret this scene as a retrojection of later amicable diplo-matic relations between Edom and Israel into the personal lives of the respective eponymous ancestors unfortunately blunt the poignant theological emphasis of this profound narrative. Equally, the persistent efforts of interpreters to view this particular pericope and the whole Jacob-Esau story against a supposed socio-political background obscures the theological issues being addressed. For example, Frank Crüsemann argues that the reconciliation between the twins means that the divine word predicting ongoing national tension has not been fulfilled. But in the context of the ancestral stories in Genesis, the divine word means primarily that Esau/Edom will be subordinate to Jacob/Israel ("two nations are in your womb") with respect to God's promise to bless the world through this people (Gen. 12:1-3) and not with respect to the vagaries of ancient Near Eastern international politics. The divine will is achieved by Jacob's becoming the child of promise and not by a fatalistic, inexorably determined political fate of the countries Israel and Edom. See Crüsemann, "Dominion, Guilt, and Reconciliation: The Contribution of the Jacob Narrative in Genesis to Political Ethics," *Semeia* 66 (1994): 6.

33 On the issue of YHWH's choice of Jacob over Esau, see also Botterweck's conten-tion that the "love" (i.e., choice) of Jacob and "hatred" (i.e., rejection) of Esau was completely a function of YHWH's will ("Jakob habe Ich lieb," p. 35).

Notes to Chapter 2

37 On the relationship of Gen. 38 and its surrounding context, Walter Brueggemann's comment is typical: "This peculiar chapter [i.e. Genesis 38] stands alone, without connection to its context. It is isolated in every way and is most enigmatic" (see *Genesis*, Interpretation commentary series [Atlanta: John Knox Press, 1982], p. 307). For a list of scholars who also regard this chapter as extraneous to its con-text, see Steven D. Mathewson, "An Exegetical Study of Genesis 38," *Bibliotheca Sacra* 146 (1989): 373, fns. 2-5.

37 On the outsider motif, see Cowan's statement in "Genesis 38," p. 74: "The pair in-sider vs. outsider will be particularly meaningful in analyzing Genesis 38."

37 On the positioning of the Judah-Tamar story, see G. R. H. Wright, "The Posi-tioning of Genesis 38," *ZAW* 94 (1982): 523-529; Brevard S. Childs, *Introduction to the Old Testament as Scripture* (Philadelphia: Fortress, 1979), pp. 156-57. Of course,

those who see no connection between Genesis 37, 39–50 and Genesis 38 see the chapter as arbitrarily if not haphazardly placed.

37-38 On levirate marriage, see Millar Burrows, "The Ancient Oriental Background of Hebrew Levirate Marriage," *BASOR* 77 (1940): 2-15; see also "Levirate Marriage in Israel," *JBL* 59 (1940): 23-33; George W. Coats, "Widow's Rights: A Crux in the Structure of Genesis 38," *CBQ* XXXIV/4 (1972): 461-466. On the tribal history of Judah, see Susan Niditch, "The Wronged Woman Righted: An Analysis of Genesis 38," *HTR* 72 (1979): 143, fn. 4. See also von Rad's assertion: "The ancient reader . . . had no other possibility at all except that of connecting what is here related with historical tribal conditions of his time, i.e., of understanding it as aetiology, as previous history of internal Judean lines" (*Genesis* [OTL], trans. John Marks [Philadelphia: Westminster, 1961], p. 356). See also Nobuko Morimura, "Tamar and Judah — a Feminist Reading of Genesis 38," *The Japan Review* 59 (1993): 55-67; Cowan, "Genesis 38"; Johanna W. H. Bos, "Out of the Shadows: Genesis 38; Judges 4:17-22; Ruth 3," *Semeia* 42 (1988): 37-67.

38 On the linguistic links between Gen. 38 and the Joseph story, see the excellent bibliographies in Eva Salm, *Juda und Tamar: Eine exegetische Studie zu Gen 38* [Forschung zur Bibel] (Würzburg, Germany: Echter Verlag, 1996); Margaret Park Cowan, "Genesis 38: The Story of Judah and Tamar and Its Role in the Ancestral Narratives of Genesis" (unpublished Ph.D. diss., Vanderbilt University, 1990). J. P. Fokkelman regards Genesis 38 and other seemingly intrusive pericopes in Genesis as only "superficially digressive" but thematically integrated; see Fokkelman, "Genesis," in *The Literary Guide to the Bible,* ed. R. Alter and F. Kermode (Cambridge: Harvard University Press [Belknap], 1987), p. 40.

38-39 On Judah and the Canaanites: other uses of *yārad* are found in Gen. 37:35; 42:38; 44:29, 31. Cowan observes that "[i]n all these situations 'going down' places one in a precarious position, in alien territory." Likewise, Judah "goes down" to a foreign place. Cowan suggests — correctly in my view — that the repeated presence of the Adullamite "surrounds Judah with foreignness" (see Cowan, "Genesis 38," pp. 187-188). Genesis 34 is another pericope that depicts the problems of the family of promise marrying outsiders. Some scholars have linked the term *bat-šûaʿ* ("daughter of Shua") to Bat-Sheba, David's wife. On this reading, Genesis 38 is supposed to be a coded story relating to the Davidic monarchy (see Gary A. Rendsburg, "David and His Circle in Genesis XXXVIII," *VT* 36 [1986]: 438-446).

40-41 On Judah's presence in Chezib, Cowan comments that only one sentence appears to be "unmotivated in its context," namely, "And she was in Chezib when she bore him." In the first place, that is not what the Masoretic Text says. Granted, Judah's name has not occurred since v. 2; at the same time, there can hardly be any question that Judah is the "he" in Hebrew *wayyiqrāʾ* (v. 3). Given that, especially since

v. 4 contains only seven words (not counting the definite object indicator as a separate word), it is not much of a stretch to view Judah as the antecedent for the "he" in v. 5 as well. In the second place, why in such an economical text would one line suddenly appear "without motivation"? It seems to me that Cowan does not expend enough effort to find a suitable meaning for the text that is there before she either emends or dismisses it as irrelevant (see Cowan, "Genesis 38," pp. 99, 111). The NEB, Rashi, and Jerome translate Chezib as "she ceased to bear" (see Cowan, "Genesis 38," p. 111). Again, this assumes the LXX version. Several decades ago, Ben-Mordecai proposed that both pronouns in the sentence referred to Shelah. This would result in the following: "He (Shelah) was in Chezib when she bore him (Shelah)." In this rendering Chezib is taken to mean a "caul," the thin membrane that sometimes envelopes the head and face of the infant at birth. Ben-Mordecai is not deterred by either the fact that *kzb* never has the meaning "caul" in TANAK or that his translation makes the sentence utterly superfluous in the story (see C. A. Ben-Mordecai, "Chezib," *JBL* 58 [1939]: 283-286).

41 On Er's name, see F. van Dijk-Hemmes, "Tamar and the Limits of Patriarchy between Rape and Seduction" (2 Samuel 13 and Genesis 38)," in *Anti-Covenant: Counter-Reading Women's Lives in the Hebrew Bible*, ed. M. Bal (Sheffield: Almond Press, 1989), p. 147; Aaron Wildavsky, "Survival Must Not Be Gained Through Sin: The Moral of the Joseph Stories Prefigured Through Judah and Tamar," *JSOT* 62 (1994): 39, fn. 13.

42 On Onan and Tamar, see George W. Coats, "Widow's Rights: A Crux in the Structure of Genesis 38," *CBQ* XXXIV/4 (1972): 463. Driver takes the phrase *wᵉhāyāh 'im bā'* as frequentive; see Driver, *The Book of Genesis* (London: Methuen & Co., 1909 [1st published 1904]), p. 328. See Peter F. Lockwood, "Tamar's Place in the Joseph Cycle," *Lutheran Theological Journal* 26/1 (1992): 36. Other references to *zeraʿ* are found in Gen. 13:16; 15:5; 22:17; 26:4; 28:14; 32:12; 46:6, 7; 48:4, 11, 19.

42-43 On the issue of levirate dodgers, see Coats, "Widow's Rights," p. 462. Von Rad observes merely that Judah's firstborn died early without children, a fact that led the narrator to conclude that he displeased YHWH. As for Onan, YHWH let him die as well (*Genesis*, p. 353). Nobuko opines that the narrative "appears to be secular all the way through without any visible presence of God. It says nothing of God's action or speech . . ." (Morimura Nobuko, "Tamar and Judah," p. 63).

43 On God's providential hand in the Joseph story, see the statement by Lockwood: "The specific references to God in the Joseph cycle are minimal, but on reflection it becomes clear that he is the leading character throughout" ("Tamar's Place," p. 42). See also Charles T. Fritsch, "God Was With Him," *Interpretation* 9 (1955): 21-34.

44 Alter contrasts Judah's apparently short period of mourning for his wife with Jacob's mourning for his sons (Gen. 37:34-35; 42:36-38; 43:13-14; 44:30, 34). In the same vein, Judah is completely silent at the death of his two sons (see Robert Alter, *Art of Biblical Narrative* [New York: Basic Books, 1981], p. 7). Humphreys refers to Judah's reaction to his wife's death as a "minimal response"; see W. Lee Humphreys, *Joseph and His Family: A Literary Study* (Columbia, SC: University of South Carolina Press, 1988), p. 37.

44 About Tamar's location for her plan, Ira Robinson posits that Enaim is a *double entendre*, suggesting not only a place name but a posture indicating a sexual invitation (*"bᵉpetaḥ ʿênayīm* in Genesis 38:14," *JBL* 96 [1977]: 569. Technically, Tamar was apparently not to be either Onan's or Shelah's wife. Perhaps in this verse we are to understand the narration to mean that Tamar sees that she has not been given to Shelah *temporarily* as a wife (see Coats, "Widow's Rights," pp. 463, 465).

44 About the sheep-shearing time, see Mathewson, "Exegetical Study," p. 378. Astour remarks: "It is known that feasts of the pre-exilic period were accompanied by ritual fornication with the magic intention of securing rich crops and increase of herds" (M. C. Astour, "Tamar the Hierodule: An Essay in the Method of Vestigial Motifs," *JBL* 85 [1966]: 193).

46-47 On the change of the word for prostitute, Cowan takes the switch to indicate only Judah's misunderstanding of Tamar's identity ("Genesis 38," p. 137). Astour makes the audacious claim that the "central point" of Genesis 38 is the role of the temple harlot *(qᵉdēšāh)*. Somehow, he has deduced that in the "original story" Tamar was a hierodule, requiring a much different view of her childlessness. She was thus responsible for not getting pregnant — having to do with the role she was assuming. This interpretation seems entirely far-fetched and contrary to the plain meaning of the text (see Astour, "Tamar the Hierodule," pp. 185, 192).

48 On the question of narrative divisions, Cowan says that the four major sections of this story are introduced by references to time: "at that time" (Gen. 38:1); "after many days" (Gen. 38:12); "after three months" (Gen. 38:24); "at the time of her giving birth" (Gen. 38:28). See "Genesis 38," p. 166.

49 About Judah's swift move to judgment, Westermann says that in this situation an inquiry or legal process was required (see K. Westermann, *Genesis 37–50* [Minneapolis: Augsburg Publishing House, 1986 (Neukirchen-Vluyn: Neukirchener Verlag, 1982)], pp. 54-55). Von Rad suggests that, because Tamar was a dependent, no legal proceeding needed to take place.

49 On parallel appearances of "recognize," see Alter, *Art of Biblical Narrative*, p. 4; see also M. E. Andrew, "Moving from Death to Life: Verbs of Motion in the Story of Judah and Tamar in Gen. 38," *ZAW* 105/2 (1993): 266. Andrew observes that the use

of *nkr* in Genesis 37 is for the purpose of deception, in Genesis 38 for unmasking. See Cowan, "Genesis 38," pp. 190-91; Lockwood, "Tamar's Place," p. 35; Mathewson, "Exegetical Study," p. 386. On Judah's confession, see the excellent study of the history of interpretation of this phrase in a Jewish context by C. E. Hayes, "The Midrashic Career of the Confession of Judah (Genesis XXXVIII 26). Part I: The Extra-Canonical Texts, Targums and Other Versions," *VT* XLV/1 (1995): 62-81; Part II: The Rabbinic Midrashim," *VT* XLV/2 (1995): 174-187.

49-50 On the two potential versions of Judah's confession, see the enumeration of these two uses in the Old Testament in Hayes, "Midrashic Career, Part I," pp. 65-66. Nobuko points out that the feminine form of *ṣdq* is unique in that Tamar is the only woman in the Old Testament ever declared to be righteous ("Story of Tamar," p. 62).

51 On the birth of Tamar's twins, see Frank Zimmermann, "The Births of Perez and Zerah," *JBL* 64 (1945): 377-78. Zerah's descendants had their future taken away from them by divine judgment in the infamous Achan incident in Joshua 7 (see Josh. 7:1, 18, 24-26). Perez's relationship to David is expressed in the genealogy in Ruth 4:18-22. Finally, viewed from a Christian perspective, Tamar played a decisive role in getting the world blessed by YHWH not only through David but through the "son of David" (see Matt. 1:3; Luke 3:33).

Notes to Chapter 3

52 On "annihilating" the inhabitants of the land, the operative vocabulary is *grš* ("drive out" or "expel"), *yrš* ("dispossess"), *nkh* ("strike" or "smite"), *ḥrm* ("proscribe," "put to the ban," "annihilate"). Other phrases are sometimes used, such as "put to the sword." Many scholars have connected these and other similar terms as part of the vocabulary of "Holy War" ideology, and there is a voluminous bibliography on this subject. See, for example, Gerhard von Rad, *Der heilige Krieg im alten Israel* (Göttingen: Vandenhoeck & Ruprecht, 1962); R. Smend, *Jahwekrieg und Stämmebund* (Göttingen: Vandenhoeck and Ruprecht, 1963); Fritz Stoltz, *Jahwes und Israels Kriege: Kriegstheorien und Kriegserfahrungen im Glauben des alten Israel* (Zürich: Zwingli Verlag, 1972); G. H. Jones, "Holy War or YHWH War?" *Vetus Testamentum* 25 (1975): 642-58; M. Weippert, "'Heiliger Krieg' im Israel und Assyrien: Kritische Anmerkungen zu Gerhard von Rads Konzept des 'Heiligen Krieges im alten Israel,'" *Zeitschrift für die alttestamentliche Wissenschaft* 84 (1972): 460-93; P. Weimar, "Die Jahwekriegserzählungen in Exodus 14, Josua 10, Richter 4 und 1 Samuel 7," *Biblica* 57 (1976): 38-73. For a convenient listing of all the promises of the land in Torah, see David Clines, *The Theme of the Pentateuch* [JSOTSup 10]

(Sheffield, UK: JSOT, 1978), pp. 36-43. Clines ties the divine promise of the land closely to the promise of descendants and relationships.

52 Robert Cohn notes the reversal of the insiders/outsiders and outsiders/insiders relative to peoplehood and possession of the land; see Cohn, "Before Israel: The Canaanites as Other in Biblical Tradition," in *The Other in Jewish Thought: Constructions of Jewish Culture and Identity*, ed. Laurence J. Silberstein and Robert L. Cohn (New York & London: New York University Press, 1994), p. 77.

53 With the exception of the Girgashites, who appear only in Neh. 9:8 and the three full listings (Deut. 7:1; Josh. 3:10; 24:11), all the other nations are mentioned more or less regularly when the nations residing in the promised land are recited. All six nations (excepting the Girgashites): Ex. 3:8, 17; 23:23; 33:2; 34:11; Deut. 20:17; Josh. 9:1; 11:3; 12:8; Judg. 3:5. Five nations (excepting the Girgashites and Perizzites): Ex. 13:5. An abbreviated list of only three nations (excepting Amorites, Girgashites, Jebusites, Perizzites): Ex. 23:28. All but the Hivites, Girgashites, and Perizzites, with the addition of Amalekites, Anakites: Num. 13:28-29. All but the Hivites: Neh. 9:8. All but the Hivites and Girgashites, with the addition of the Ammonites, Moabites, Egyptians: Ezra 9:1. All but the Canaanites and Girgashites: 2 Chron. 8:7. Since the purpose of these lists has to do with contrasting Israel *religiously* (as opposed to ethnically), it seems not to matter that, strictly speaking, some of the peoples mentioned were never part of the indigenous population of the promised land (e.g., Ezra 9:1). To these references may be added Gen. 15:18-21, which lists the standard representatives (excepting the Hivites) and adds the Kenites, Kenizzites, Kadmonites, and Rephaim.

54 On the two spies' motives, Fewell and Gunn insist that they obviously wanted sex; and getting it from a woman who was Other and who would in any case soon be dead (assuming a successful assault on Jericho) gave them something of a moral free pass; see Danna Nolan Fewell and David M. Gunn, *Gender, Power, & Promise: The Subject of the Bible's First Story* (Nashville: Abingdon Press, 1993), p. 117. Hawk calls attention to the mention of Shittim in Josh. 2:1, which surely evokes the memories of the place where Israel "played the harlot" (*liznôt;* this is the verbal form of the noun *zônāh*, which indicates Rahab's profession) during the wilderness journey (Num. 25:1) (see L. Daniel Hawk, *Every Promise Fulfilled: Contesting Plots in Joshua* [Louisville: Westminster/John Knox, 1991], p. 61).

54-55 About puns on Rahab's name, see Tikva Frymer-Kensky, "Reading Rahab," in *Tehillah le-Moshe: Biblical and Judaic Studies in Honor of Moshe Greenberg*, ed. Mordechai Cogan, Barry L. Eichler, Jeffrey H. Tigay (Winona Lake, IN: Eisenbrauns, 1997), pp. 57, 66. Barstad also thinks Rahab was a nickname "harshly indicating the woman's métier" (see H. M. Barstad, "The Old Testament Feminine Personal Name *rahab*: An Onomastic Note," *Svensk Exegetisk Årsbok* 54 [1989]: 49).

Compare J. A. Montgomery, "Notes on the Mythological Epic Texts from Ras Shamra," *JAOS* 53 (1933): 121. Hawk also observes that Rahab's name, meaning "broad," has "ominous connotations" (see Hawk, *Every Promise Fulfilled*, p. 62). Judith McKinlay sees in Rahab's name an allusion to the land itself as a "broad" land. Ex. 3:8 refers to the promised land as "good and broad" *(ṭôbāh ûreḥābāh)*. There is nothing implausible about such a connection, in my view, though I think that, in the context of Joshua 2, the explicit sexual connotations are dominant (see McKinlay, "Rahab: A Hero/ine?" *Biblical Interpretation* 7/1 [1999]: 44-57).

55 On this verbal *double entendre,* I am indebted to an unpublished paper by Stanley Walters for the translation. McKinlay also notes the salacious character of the royal agents' accusation (see "Rahab: A Hero/ine?" p. 46). McKinlay also notices the lewd reference to "entering" Rahab and her house, respectively.

55-56 "Whoring after other gods," is found in, e.g., Ex. 34:15-16; Lev. 17:7; 20:5; Deut. 31:16; Judg. 2:17; 8:27, 33; Jer. 3:1; Ezek. 20:30; Hosea 2:7.
    The speeches of Joshua on idolatry in chapters 23-24, in my opinion, function as Joshua's "Deuteronomy." That is, just as Moses explicates, interprets, and articulates God's law for a new setting in the Book of Deuteronomy, Joshua, who is a sort of "second Moses," does the same for Israel after the conquest.

56 In my judgment, Hawk is quite correct when he observes that "Rahab represents the temptations of Canaan. . ." (see L. Daniel Hawk, "Strange Houseguests: Rahab, Lot, and the Dynamics of Deliverance," in *Reading Between Texts: Intertextuality and the Hebrew Bible,* ed. Danna Nolan Fewell (Louisville, KY: Westminster/John Knox, 1992), p. 91.

56 In my opinion, Wiseman completely misses the point of the narrative and ignores the explicit biblical text in his attempt to sanitize completely or at least soften Rahab's presentation as a *zônāh*. It is precisely her status as a Canaanite prostitute that makes her ultimate conversion such a radical statement. Refusing to allow the text its most transparent meaning, he suggests that *zônāh* is a bi-form of *zûn,* "to provide food or sustenance." This seems little more than moralistic eisegesis. See D. J. Wiseman, "Rahab of Jericho," *Tyndale Bulletin* 14 (1964): 8-11.

57 The point of Joshua's failure of nerve is emphasized by Robert Polzin, *Moses and the Deuteronomist* (New York: Seabury Press, 1980), p. 86. Frymer-Kensky likewise notes that the sending of the spies ended up being superfluous from a military perspective, for they gather no relevant military intelligence whatsoever (see "Reading Rahab," p. 57).

57 On the spies' covenant, Campbell argues that Joshua 2 is replete with covenant terminology; see K. M. Campbell, "Rahab's Covenant: A Short Note on Joshua ii 9-21," *Vetus Testamentum* 22 (1972): 243-44. Frymer-Kensky agrees that the spies' cov-

enant negotiations with Rahab are in direct violation of Deuteronomy 7:2 and 20:17. See also Lyle Eslinger, *Into the Hands of the Living God* (Sheffield, UK: Almond, 1989), pp. 24-54.

58 Concerning the humor of the Rahab situation, Yair Zakovitch notes other humorous elements in "Humor and Theology or the Successful Failure of Israelite Intelligence: A Literary-Folkloric Approach to Joshua 2," in *Text and Tradition: The Hebrew Bible and Folklore* (Atlanta, GA: Scholars Press, 1990), pp. 75-98.

58-61 About Rahab's recitation, though Langlamet concedes that Rahab's recitation was ". . . une sorte de credo," he nonetheless concludes that she was motivated by terror rather than faith; see F. Langlamet, "Josue, II, et les Traditions de l'Hexateuque," *Revue Biblique* 78 (1971): 344. Fewell and Gunn observe that Rahab sounds as though she has been reading the Book of Deuteronomy (see *Gender, Power, & Promise*, p. 118). Similarly, Frymer-Kensky ("Reading Rahab," pp. 62-63) argues that her speech contains all the essential elements of the classic Deuteronomic form of covenants. McKenzie describes Rahab as being "rather well read" in the Deuteronomic traditions; see John L. McKenzie, *The World of the Judges* (Englewood Cliffs, NJ: Prentice-Hall, 1966), p. 48. Even more emphatically, McKinlay wonders whether Rahab or a "rediviva Miriam" is speaking ("Rahab: A Hero/ine?" p. 47). Finally, Ottoson refers to Rahab as a "Deuteronomistic spokesperson"; see Magnus Ottoson, "Rahab and the Spies," in DUME-E2-DUB-BA-A: Studies in Honor of Åke W. Sjöberg [Occasional Publications of the Samuel Noah Kramer Fund, 11, Hermann Behrens, Darlene Loding, Martha T. Roth, eds.] (Philadelphia: The University Museum, 1989), p. 422.

59 On Rahab's "knowledge" that YHWH has given Israel the land, this "know" *(yāda'tî)* may be intended to be a sharp contrast to what she said to the king's operatives earlier: "I do not know" (Josh. 2:4). On this point see Hawk, *Every Promise Fulfilled*, pp. 65-66. Other non-Israelites have made religious confessions or their equivalent using the formula *yāda'tî kî* (Ex. 18:11; 1 Kgs. 17:24; 2 Kgs. 5:15). On this point, see Frymer-Kensky, "Reading Rahab," p. 62.

60 On Rahab's use of the word for "utterly annihilate," there is one other outsider who uses the term, but only in reference to conventional warfare (2 Kgs. 19:11; Isa. 37:11). This is almost the only time when the verb is not used in its specialized sense.

62 (See also p. 58.) It is conceivable that Rahab initially discloses the spies' whereabouts — the narrative is not forthcoming about how the king of Jericho learned that they were at Rahab's establishment — to get the ball rolling in the first place. Be that as it may, the arrangement she now makes with the spies precludes any further sharing of intelligence.

62 On the "scarlet thread," it goes without saying that this biblical allusion was not lost on Nathaniel Hawthorne when he wrote *The Scarlet Letter*. That Rahab lived in a "red rope district" has been perceived by J. P. Asmussen; see "Bemerkungen zur sakralen Prostitution im Alten Testament," *Studia Theologia* 11 (1958): 167-192. In a private communication, Larry Stager (via Stanley Walters) has affirmed this interpretation.

64 The disproportionate amount of textual space given to the conquest of Jericho underscores that the Book of Joshua should not be read primarily as a military record. The conquest of the whole land is outlined in chapters 2–11 (chap. 12 is a summary), yet fully five of those chapters (2–6) are dedicated to the taking of Jericho. Even chap. 7, properly speaking, keeps Jericho in view, since it deals with the sin that Achan committed during the conquest of that city. The point is that the narrative has been shaped for reasons other than providing a straightforward account of a military operation. L. Daniel Hawk has explicated features of the antipodal relationship between Rahab and Achan, and has also compared features of these two stories with the Gibeon story in Joshua 9 (see *Joshua* [Berit Olam: Studies in Hebrew Narrative & Poetry, David W. Cotter, ed.] [Collegeville, MN: The Liturgical Press, 2000], pp. 25-26, 29-30).

On the Ban, see Hawk, *Joshua*, p. 45. For the purification aspect of the Ban, see Joel S. Kaminsky, *Corporate Responsibility in the Hebrew Bible* [JSOTSup, 196] (Sheffield, UK: Sheffield University Press, 1995).

65 On Achan's pedigree: the only other character whose pedigree is given as fully occurs in Josh. 17:3 with Zelophehad. However, this is hardly incidental, for issues of allotment of land to his daughters (he had no sons) were involved. In the end, the deference accorded Zelophehad resulted in Manasseh, his great-great-grandfather and tribal ancestor, receiving ten portions for his allotment (17:3-6).

66 On the "melting of the people's hearts": Joshua 2:11 uses the same verb that is used in Josh. 7:5: *wayyimmas*. The same word is found in Josh. 5:1 to describe the reaction of the various kings at YHWH's drying up of the Jordan River. However, though a similar metaphor, another verb is used in Josh. 2:9: *nāmōgû*.

66 Joshua's complaint echoes similar complaints when Israel suffered reversals, even though their own behavior was the cause for God's abandoning them or putting them under judgment (Num. 14:2b-3, 13-16). See Hawk, *Joshua*, p. 115.

67 On Israelites with Canaanite behavior, Hawk aptly says, "Canaanized Israelites are not easily identified, but if they are not unmasked and eliminated, the entire community may disintegrate" *(Joshua*, p. 108).

68 On Achan's confession, the use of *'omnāh* ("indeed") is seen elsewhere only in Gen. 20:12, where it is also found in a confession. The "mantle from Shinar" is a

way of referring to this garment's great value, much as we might say "cashmere sweater" or "Corinthian leather." The word for "covet" *(ḥmd)* is the same as that found in the "ten words" (i.e., Ten Commandments), where coveting is forbidden (Ex. 20:17).

69 There may be more punning going on with Achan's name. Two of the root consonants in Achan's name are the same as two of the root consonants in Achor and "trouble." Hawk suggests further that Achan may be an anagram of *kn'*, the root from which Canaan derives (see Hawk, *Joshua*, p. 120). See also R. S. Hess, "Achan and Achor: Names and Wordplay in Joshua 7," *Hebrew Annual Review* 14 (1994): 89-98. So powerful was the negative message of the Valley of Achor that its transformation from a place bespeaking judgment and despair to a place of hope and transformation was accented by prophets proclaiming YHWH's restoration and forgiveness of Israel (Hosea 2:17 [Eng. 2:15]; Isa. 65:10).

70-71 On the reading of Joshua from the standpoint of ethnicity and militarism: the problem with that reading may be evidenced in the rise of other historical reconstructions. Some scholars saw the Book of Joshua as a myth of origins designed to glorify a mundane process whereby small groups of semi-nomads infiltrated and settled into a land that had been severely weakened by other invaders, the Sea Peoples. Others argued that the Book of Joshua was largely fictional, glossing over a complex process of internal and external sociopolitical pressures that led to the collapse of the interlocking network of city states and the rise of a new social amalgam called "Israel." See the helpful summary of the major theories in Norman Gottwald, *The Tribes of Yahweh* (Maryknoll, NY: Orbis, 1979), pp. 191-219.

Notes to Chapter 4

I have treated the Naaman story in an abbreviated form in *The Lectionary Commentary: Theological Exegesis for Sunday's Texts,* Vol. 1, Roger E. Van Harn, ed. (Grand Rapids; Cambridge: William B. Eerdmans Publishing Company, 2001), pp. 249-252.

The fact that the Naaman story is not considered compelling may partly explain why there is a relatively small bibliography available for 2 Kings 5. Of the seven stories I cover in this book, it clearly has not received the attention of the others, with the exception of the Tamar story in Genesis 38 (which was comparatively neglected because, first, it was not considered part of the Joseph story and, second, little of religious value was seen in it).

74-75 On Naaman's rank/position, Robert Cohn renders the term "field-marshal" (see Cohn, "Form and Perspective in 2 Kings V," *Vetus Testamentum* XXXIII/2 (1983):

173. It does not appear that "great man" is a technical military or political term, though Naaman's being described in this way is important later in the story. I have translated $n^e\bar{s}\hat{u}$ $p\bar{a}n\hat{i}m$ as "highly praised"; literally, it means "lifted up of face." For other nuances of the latter phrase, see M. I. Gruber, "The Many Faces of Hebrew $n\acute{s}$ $pnym$ 'lift up the face,'" ZAW 95 (1983): 252-60.

76 Cogan and Tadmor state without reservation that true leprosy does not appear in the Bible, i.e., the Hebrew Bible. See M. Cogan and H. Tadmor, II $Kings$ [AB, 11] (New York: Doubleday, 1988), p. 63. See also E. V. Hulse, "The Nature of Biblical 'Leprosy' and the Use of Alternate Medical Terms in Modern Translations of the Bible," $Palestine$ $Exploration$ $Quarterly$ 107 (1975): 87-105. There is an extensive bibliography in John E. Hartley, $Leviticus$ [AB, 11] (New York: Doubleday, 1988), pp. 170-71.

76 On what Israelites or Arameans knew: as a literary strategy, it is necessary to distinguish between what the implied narrator knew and what characters confined to the "story-world" knew. Since the narrator was obviously an Israelite, in that sense Israel — or at least some Israelites — knew of YHWH's activities with nations other than Israel. But in the constructed narrative, it cannot be assumed that characters always know what the narrator knows.

76-77 Cohn's translation of "mighty man" is "valorous hero" (see "Form and Perspective," p. 173).

77-78 On impurity and the temple, see Hartley, $Leviticus,$ p. 184; see also Jacob Milgrom, $Leviticus$ $1–16$ [AB, 3] (New York: Doubleday, 1991), p. 817. Hobbs, mistakenly in my judgment, discounts this view of Naaman's illness even though he acknowledges a similarity of vocabulary between 2 Kings 5 and Leviticus 13–14; see T. R. Hobbs, 2 $Kings$ [WBC, 13] (Waco, TX: Word Books, 1985), pp. 63-64. On the contrary, Provan believes Naaman's disease suggests not only ritual uncleanness — thus evoking Leviticus 13–14 — but perhaps also divine judgment; see Iain W. Provan, 1 and 2 $Kings$ [NIBC] (Peabody, MA: Hendrickson, 1995), p. 194.

78 On the question of the "little girl," Solomon refers to himself as a "young lad" $(na\acute{}ar$ $q\bar{a}t\hat{o}n)$ in 1 Kgs. 3:7. In this context the phrase seems to mean something like "young and inexperienced," especially since it is further explained with the statement, "I do not know how to go out or come in."

79 On the question of timing, Cohn remarks that the girl's words "travel like lightning" (see "Form and Perspective," p. 174).

79-80 On royal power, see Gerhard von Rad, God at $Work$ in $Israel,$ trans. John H. Marks, (Nashville: Abingdon, 1980), p. 49.

80-81 Concerning royal letters: for an analysis of thepattern of delivered messages, including letters, see Ann M. Vater, "Narrative Patterns for the Story of Commissioned Communication in the Old Testament," *JBL* 99 (1980): 365-382.

81 On washing in the Jordan, the operative terms in this verse are *rḥṣ* ("wash"), *šûb* ("restore/return"), and *ṭhr* ("be clean"). These words are found in Leviticus 13–14 (*rḥṣ*: Lev. 14:8-9; *šûb*: Lev. 13:16; 14:39, 43; *ṭhr* [in various nominal and verbal forms]: Lev. 13:6, 13, 17, 23, 28, 34, 37, 39, 40, 41, 58, 59; 14:4, 7, 8, 9, 11, 14, 17, 18, 19, 20, 25, 28, 29, 31, 53, 57). Milgrom points out that the words meaning "pure" (*ṭhr*) and "impure" (*ṭm'*) in Leviticus 13–14 underscore the importance of the religious ideas involved. This material is not about medicine but about religious ritual and religious concepts (see Milgrom, *Leviticus*, p. 817).

82 On Naaman's view of how Elisha should come out and "stand": the word "stand" (*'md*) appears often in this little story: vv. 9, 11, 15, 16, 25. It is not clear what nuance Naaman had in mind when he wanted Elisha to "stand." Also, it is likely that the hand-waving Naaman expected was a grand gesture indicating the solemnity of the occasion rather than a ritualistic waving over the spot of the disease, though the latter is possible. The word for "heal" used here is the same as that used by the little girl and the king in his letter: *'sp*.

82 On the helpfulness of Naaman's servants, see Robert L. Cohn, *2 Kings* [Berit Olam: Studies in Hebrew Narrative and Poetry], David W. Cotter, ed. (Collegeville, MN: The Liturgical Press, 2000), p. 38.

83 On terms for the prophet: "Man of God" (*'îš hā'ĕlōhîm*) is one of several technical terms for prophet (used also in vv. 8, 14, 15, 20). The most common term is *nābî'* (used in this chapter in vv. 3, 8, 13). Other terms found elsewhere in the Bible are *ḥōzeh* and *rô'eh*, both of which mean "seer."

84 On Naaman's self-designation as "your servant," see Terence E. Fretheim, *First and Second Kings* (Louisville: Westminster John Knox Press, 1999), p. 153.

84 On gifts or fees for services rendered, compare 1 Sam. 9:7ff.; 1 Kgs. 14:3; 2 Kgs. 8:7ff. See the treatment in D. P. O'Brien, "'Is this the time to accept . . . ?' (2 Kings V 26b): Simply Moralizing (LXX) or an Ominous Foreboding of Yahweh's Rejection of Israel (MT)," *Vetus Testamentum* XLVI/4 (1996): 448-49.

85-86 On the sense of sacred space, note Fretheim's comment: "This [request for dirt] is not a lapse into syncretism, but a recognition that the life of faith must be lived out in ambiguous situations and away from the community of faith" (see *First and Second Kings*, p. 153). Hobbs thinks this scene combines elements of monotheism and universalism with the notion of the localization of YHWH in Israel (see *2 Kings*, p. 66). See the juxtaposition of the ideas that God cannot be contained in any space or even on the whole earth with the concept of the temple as sacred space in 1 Kgs. 8:27-30.

85-86 On Naaman's altar of soil: if stones were used for the altar, this was permissible as long as they were unhewn (see Ex. 20:25).

87 On Naaman's "turning around," see, for example, 1 Kgs. 8:33, 47-48; Isa. 6:10; 10:21-22; Jer. 3:7, 10, 12, 14, 22; 4:1; 5:3; Hosea 3:5; 5:4; 6:1; 7:10; 11:5; 14:2-3 [Eng. vv. 1-2]; Ps. 51:15 [Eng. v. 13].
Bāśār as the whole body: Ex. 30:32; Lev. 6:3 [Eng. v. 10]; 14:9; 15:13, 16; 16:4, 24, 26, 28; 17:16; 19:28; 21:5; 22:6; Num. 8:7; 19:7-8; 1 Kgs. 21:27; Eccl. 2:3; 4:5; 5:5; 11:10; 12:12. *Bāśār* in relationship to *nepeš*, "soul," in the sense of the whole person: Isa. 10:18 (here it is ambiguous whether *bāśār* plus *nepeš* means one's total being or the "physical" along with the "spiritual"); Job 14:22; Ps. 63:2 [Eng. v. 1]. *Bāśār* as humanity over against deity: Gen. 6:3; Ps. 56:5 [Eng. v. 4]; Ps. 78:39. *Bāśār* as living beings: Gen. 6:17, 19; 7:21; 9:11, 15, 16, 17; Lev. 17:14; Num. 18:15; Job 34:15; Ps. 136:25. *Bāśār* as humanity in general: Gen. 6:12, 13; Num. 16:22; 27:16; Deut. 5:23 [Eng. v. 26]; Isa. 40:5, 6; 49:26 [2nd instance]; 66:16, 23, 24; Jer. 12:12; 25:31; 32:27; 45:5; Ezek. 21:4, 9, 10; Joel 3:1; Zech 2:17 [Eng. v. 13]; Job 12:10; Ps. 65:3 [Eng. v. 2]; 145:21.

87 On "victory" and "salvation," see Psalms 51:16 [Eng. 14]; 119:41, 81; 2 Chron. 6:41.

89 On Elisha's "boy": the term is *naʿar*, often used to designate not simply a person of a certain age but an aide. Of course, in our story the Israelite girl who appeared in the first scene was a *naʿărāh qᵉṭannāh*, a "little girl." But in that instance, the emphasis seemed to be on something other than her work status, though that nuance may have been present as well. An example of *naʿar* as servant may be seen in 1 Sam. 9:3, 5, 7, 8, 10. Elisha's aide who delivered the message to Naaman was called a *malʾāk*, "messenger," rather than *naʿar* (2 Kgs. 5:10).

89 On Gehazi's thought process: the term *ʾāmar* usually means "say," but may mean "think" as well. The latter is especially likely when there is no one around to hear what is supposedly being said, as is the situation here.

90 On Gehazi's remaining an Israelite, Cohn notes that "the ignoble Israelite Gehazi serves as a foil to the God-fearing foreigner Naaman" ("Form and Perspective," p. 180).

90 About Naaman's urging Gehazi to take more than he asked for: in v. 16, when Naaman urges Elisha to accept the present, the verb *wayyipṣar* is used, whereas in v. 23, when Naaman urges Gehazi, the verb *wayyiprāṣ* is used. While the roots are different, the two words convey more or less similar meanings. Interestingly, the three root consonants of the two words are the same, though the last two consonants have a different order *(pṣr; prṣ)*. Of course, when Elisha is "urged," he still re-

sists, but when Gehazi is "urged," he readily accepts the gracious offer that goes beyond his request.

91 On Elisha's rhetorical question of Gehazi, see O'Brien's argument that Elisha's list of gifts taken, which Naaman does not offer and Gehazi does not in fact take, is suggestive of a rationale that transcends and is much more extensive than either simple greed or moralism (see O'Brien, "'Is this the time . . . ,'" pp. 448-457, especially p. 454).

92-93 About Gehazi's future: there is, of course, the possibility that what has happened to Naaman can also happen to Gehazi in the interval, i.e., that he be cleansed through repentance, confession, and washing. That would mean that Elisha's "for ever" is not to be taken absolutely, for which there are other examples in the Bible. For instance, God told David through the prophet Nathan that his kingship would be established "for ever" (*'ad 'ôlām;* 2 Sam. 7:13, 16), even though later the kingship was made contingent on obedience by David himself (1 Kgs. 2:1-4); subsequently, David's kingdom was destroyed (2 Kgs. 22-25). The author of Psalm 89 takes literally that David's covenant will be in effect "for ever," thus leading to an irreconcilable theological problem when David's kingship fails. The author then accuses YHWH of breaking the promise (vv. 39-52 [Eng. 38-51]).

Notes to Chapter 5

94 That Jonah is a strange story is a longstanding viewpoint on the book (see E. J. Bickerman, *Four Strange Books of the Bible: Jonah, Daniel, Koheleth, Esther* [New York: Schocken Books, 1967]).

95-96 The command formula in and of itself has the effect of casting Jonah "precisely as a prophet," despite the lack of the usual nomenclature (see John C. Holbert, "'Deliverance Belongs to Yahweh!': Satire in the Book of Jonah," *JSOT* 21 [1981]: 63). Elijah was sent by God into foreign territory, but in that case it was to anoint Hazael king of Aram (1 Kings 19:15). In addition, God sent Moses (back) to Egypt to order the king to let the Hebrew slaves go, but this was for a variety of reasons, a different set of circumstances than what obtains in Jonah's call. James Ackerman considers Jonah's summons a considerable expansion of the prophetic vocation (see Ackerman, "Jonah," in *The Literary Guide to the Bible,* Robert Alter and Frank Kermode, eds. [Cambridge: Harvard University Press (Belknap Press), 1987], p. 235).

96 On Nineveh, the "great city": in Jeremiah 22:8 the phrase "great city" is applied to Jerusalem. Trible takes the phrase as suggestive of the "gravity of Nineveh" (see Phyllis Trible, *Rhetorical Criticism: Context, Method, and the Book of Jonah* [Minne-

apolis: Fortress Press, 1994], p. 126). There are a number of "greats" in this book: great city (1:2; 3:2, 3; 4:11); great wind (1:4); great storm (1:4, 12); great fear (1:10, 16); great fish (2:1); great anger (4:1); great joy (4:6). Payne notes that Nineveh ". . . stood as the epitome of everything that was cruelly hostile to Israel and Judah" (see David F. Payne, "Jonah from the Perspective of Its Audience," *JSOT* 13 [1979]: 7).

Assyria is used in a number of different ways in the prophetic corpus. On occasion, its pagan status notwithstanding, the country is used as an instrument of YHWH's judgment against Israel (e.g., Isa. 7:18; 10:5). At other times, Israel is criticized by prophets for seeking Assyria as an ally against another enemy (e.g., Hos. 7:11; 12:2). Yet again, in spite of God's using Assyria as a means of punishing a disobedient Israel, the foreign country itself will also eventually come under divine judgment (Isa. 10:24-25; 14:25; Zeph. 2:13). In Zephaniah 2:14-15, Assyria *and* Nineveh are slated for destruction. Equally, Assyria's conversion to YHWH is also part of prophetic prediction (see Is. 19:25). Arguing that a Hellenistic context rather than either a Near Eastern or biblical one is appropriate for understanding Jonah, Bolin strongly questions the assumption that Nineveh in the Book of Jonah represents the quintessentially Gentile world, not only distinct from but inimical to Israel (see Thomas M. Bolin, "'Should I Not Also Pity Nineveh?' Divine Freedom in the Book of Jonah," *JSOT* 67 [1995]: 109). Bolin seems not to consider that while he may be right in terms of the Book of Jonah's original composition and circulation, the canonical context of the work does in fact affect the way it now functions and is to be read, which is the case for a great deal of the biblical material.

97 On Jonah's "oracle of judgment," see Sasson's comments on the phrase "to cry against" *(qārā' 'al)* in Jack M. Sasson, *Jonah* (New York: Doubleday, 1990), p. 87. Note that Jonah does not preface his oracle with the customary "Thus says YHWH" (Jonah 3:4).

97 About Jonah's flight: God has said *qûm,* "Arise." At first, it looks as though Jonah meant to obey, for "he arose" *(wayyāqom).* But the second verb changes everything, for Jonah arises only to "flee," rather than "go," as God initially commanded.

98 On Tarshish's distance, Ackerman suggests that Nineveh and Tarshish are positioned at opposite poles from each other (see "Jonah," p. 235). Sasson suggests that Tarshish "seems always to lie just beyond the geographic knowledge of those who try to pinpoint its location." That is, Tarshish is evocative of the greatest possible distance away from Israel or Nineveh rather than an exact geographical site (see Sasson, *Jonah,* p. 79). Von Rad says that Tarshish represents the "outer limits of the ancient world" (see Gerhard von Rad, "The Prophet Jonah," in *God at Work in Israel,* John H. Marks, trans. [Nashville: Abingdon, 1980], p. 59).

99 Attributing human emotions and thought processes to an inanimate object is called *prosopopoeia* (see Trible, *Rhetorical Criticism,* p. 132).

99 Because Jonah is the only passenger ever spoken about in the story, Sasson believes that Jonah was not on a passenger ship but on a charter, that is, he had hired the whole ship to take him to Tarshish. If that is a correct assumption, only Jonah and the crew were threatened by the storm (see Sasson, *Jonah*, p. 83).

100 On Jonah's "going down" into the hold: there are several times where "going down" *(yārad)* is used, perhaps in contrast to YHWH's command to arise *(qûm):* 1:², 5; 2:7 (see Holbert, "Deliverance," p. 64).

101 Person sees the casting of lots as an explicitly pagan practice proscribed by Israelite sources. However, Israelites were simply warned about divination, which is not necessarily the same as casting lots. See, e.g., Josh. 7; see Raymond F. Person, Jr., *In Conversation with Jonah: Conversation Analysis, Literary Criticism, and the Book of Jonah* [JSOTSup, 220] (Sheffield, UK: Sheffield Academic Press, 1996), pp. 56, 86.

101 On Jonah's theological orthodoxy, Good points to the irony involved in the juxtaposition of Jonah's exquisite theology and shabby actions: "Jonah's theology is unexceptionable, but, like so much theology, it seems to make no difference to his action" (see Edwin M. Good, *Irony in the Old Testament* [Sheffield, UK: The Almond Press, 1981], p. 45).

103, 105 On the sailors' noble behavior, see Sasson, *Jonah*, p. 142 and fn. 20. On their fear:
104-5 Trible notes that the sailors fear "double jeopardy": "They perish if Jonah stays on board; they perish if they throw an innocent man overboard" (see *Rhetorical Criticism*, p. 148).

107 On the "great fish," von Rad cites an eighteenth-century professor who attempted to explain the implausibility of a man being swallowed by a fish and surviving. The professor suggested that after Jonah was tossed overboard, a ship happened by and rescued Jonah. As you might have guessed, the name of that ship was *The Great Fish* (see von Rad, "The Prophet Jonah," p. 58).

108-9 On Jonah's prayer: there has been a long-standing scholarly consensus that this prayer was a later addition to the prose elements of the story. In a time when Scripture scholars were primarily concerned with the history of the formation of any particular piece of biblical literature, this assessment had the effect of truncating the story of Jonah. It was perfectly acceptable to interpret the book without considering the interpolated psalm as an integral part of the account. In more recent decades, scholars have argued that the history of a book's development is an important datum, but not necessarily decisive for its *literary* interpretation. The fact is that some redactor or redactors put the material into the form in which we now find it, presumably believing that it makes sense in its present arrangement. See Hans Walter Wolff, *Obadiah and Jonah*, trans. Margaret Kohl [originally published as *Obadja und Jona* (Neukirchen-Vluyn: Neukirchener Verlag, 1977)] (Minneapolis: Augsburg Publishing House, 1986), pp. 128-129; compare the treatment in Trible, *Rhetorical Criticism,* pp. 160ff.

109 On Jonah's prayer's distorted piety, see Trible, *Rhetorical Criticism,* p. 172.

110 On Nineveh's size: YHWH did refer to it in the second instance as "the great city" (Jonah 3:2), but the narrator explicates further by saying that Nineveh was "a great city to God" (Jonah 3:3), immediately after which comes the detail about its size. Whether its considerable size is all the narrator had in mind with this designation is difficult to determine.

110 On Jonah's oracle's "unstable properties," see Trible, *Rhetorical Criticism,* p. 180. The Hebrew verb *nehpāket* has a negative connotation in Gen. 19:21, 25, 29; Deut. 29:22; Jer. 20:16; Lam. 4:6; it has a positive connotation in Deut. 23:5; Jer. 31:13; Ps. 66:6. Trible argues that Jonah's audience "controlled" the meaning of the words. Not only did Nineveh choose to construe what Jonah said in positive terms, but they acted in accordance with such a stance (see *Rhetorical Criticism,* p. 190).

111 On Nineveh's royal decree, Good suggests that the theology of the Ninevites is "sophisticated" (see Good, *Irony,* p. 50).

112 On the distribution and importance of the expression "who knows," see James L. Crenshaw, "The expression *mî yôda'* in the Hebrew Bible," *VT* XXXVI/3 (1986): 274-288.

112-13 For a comparison of the sentiments expressed in Jonah's prayer with similar ones elsewhere in the Bible, especially Joel, see Thomas B. Dozeman, "Inner-Biblical Interpretation of Yahweh's Gracious and Compassionate Character," *JBL* 108/2 (1989): 207-223.

   The Phyllis Trible quote is from *Rhetorical Criticism,* p. 190.

Notes to Chapter 6

117 The Book of Ruth as an "island of tranquility" is from Katherine Doob Sakenfeld, *Ruth* (Louisville: John Knox Press, 1999), p. 1.

117 Auerbach's famous assertion is from Eric Auerbach, *Mimesis: The Representation of Reality in Western Literature,* trans. Willard R. Trask (Princeton: Princeton University Press, 1953), p. 12.

117-18 On the translation of "judges" and judges as instruments of YHWH's sovereignty, see Norman K. Gottwald, *The Tribes of Yahweh* (Maryknoll, N.Y.: Orbis, 1979), p. 52. Despite the fact that some of these judges were morally reprobate, God was still able to use them for divine purposes (cf. Judg. 13-16).

120n. On Bethlehem as the "house of bread," see the same point made for another section of the story by Greg A. King, "Between Text and Sermon: Ruth 2:1-13," *Interpretation 52/2* (1998): 182.

120 On the story of Lot and his daughters, see Frank Anthony Spina, "Lot," in *The Anchor Bible Dictionary*, Vol. IV, David Noel Freedman, ed. (New York: Doubleday, 1992), pp. 372-374. As we shall see, the incident that led to the birth of Moab also led to the birth of Ammon. So both these countries had the same depraved origins, though only Moab is in play in the Ruth story.

121 See the treatment of the Balaam story by Dennis T. Olson, *Numbers* (Louisville: John Knox Press, 1996), pp. 140-151. For a socio-historical interpretation of the incident related in Numbers 25, see George E. Mendenhall, *The Tenth Generation* (Baltimore and London: The Johns Hopkins University Press, 1973), pp. 105-121. When Moab oppressed Israel for eighteen years, Moab was joined by its "sibling" Ammon. The Amelekites also were part of the oppressor group. Still, one must not lose sight of the fact that YHWH was instrumental in strengthening Moab and the others against Israel (Judges 3:12). So Moab still functioned as a bitter enemy of Israel.

121 On Elimelech's family opting for life, see Phyllis Trible, *God and the Rhetoric of Sexuality* [Overtures to Biblical Theology], (Philadelphia: Fortress, 1978), p. 167. Much biblical legislation has to do with providing for widows and orphans, thus emphasizing the vulnerability of both (see Otto J. Baab, "Widow," *Interpreter's Dictionary of the Bible*, 4:842-43).

122 The intimation that Ruth was barren all this time has the effect of placing her in the line of other famous biblical women who were initially unable to conceive: Sarah, Rachel, Hannah (see Sakenfeld, *Ruth*, p. 20).

122 On the Israelites having relations with Moabite women, the language is quite brazen: "They began to *whore around* with Moabite women" (Numbers 25:1).

123-24 On Ruth and Orpah returning to their mothers' homes: it is more common in the Bible for the phrase "father's house" to be used: Gen. 38:11; Lev. 22:13; Num. 30:17; Deut. 22:21; Judg. 19:2-3. However, "mother's house" does appear in Gen. 24:28. See the comment by E. F. Campbell, Jr., *Ruth* [AB, 7] (Garden City, N.Y.: Doubleday and Company, 1975), pp. 64-65. Michael S. Moore argues that there is a "blessing-of-foreigners trajectory" in the Book of Ruth (see Moore, "Ruth the Moabite and the Blessing of Foreigners," *Catholic Biblical Quarterly* 60/2 [1998]: 203-217).

125 On Ruth's declaration to Naomi: Trible argues that Ruth's break with Moab and insistence on following Naomi is an "Abram type" move in that she has disavowed the solidarity of family, abandoned national identity, and renounced religious af-

filiation. The one difference is that Abram did this under the impetus of a divine call, whereas Ruth did it on her own (see Trible, *God and the Rhetoric of Sexuality*, p. 173).

126 For a discussion of the name Mara, see Campbell, *Ruth*, pp. 52-53.

126 On Ruth's foreign identity, King points out that the narrator "delights" in going out of his way to remind us of Ruth's Moabite status; some references are obviously superfluous: Ruth 1:4, 22; 2:2, 6, 21; 4:5, 10 (see "Between Text and Sermon," p. 184).

128 On the "providential accident," see Trible, *God and the Rhetoric of Sexuality*, p. 176.

130 In Ruth 1:8, Naomi has asked that YHWH treat the women with *ḥesed* (graciously or kindly), just as they had treated the deceased before they died and her up until now. Likewise, in Ruth 2:20, she construes Boaz's kindness as a function of YHWH's *ḥesed*. This term is one of the most common to express the covenant relationship between God and Israel, a relationship based on divine grace. See Katharine Doob Sakenfeld, *Faithfulness in Action: Loyalty in Biblical Perspective* [Overtures to Biblical Theology] (Philadelphia: Fortress Press, 1985).

131 On Ruth's preparations for Boaz, Van Wolde notes that both Ruth and Tamar take part in "seduction scenes" that involve clothing, washing, make-up, etc. That is, they make themselves attractive, but not recognizable. At the same time, all we are told about Tamar is that she changed from widow's clothing into a veiled outfit; Ruth does not actually disguise herself (see Ellen Van Wolde, "Texts in Dialogue with Texts: Intertextuality in the Ruth and Tamar Narratives," *Biblical Interpretation* V/1 [1997]: 12). This section is replete with *double-entendres* and sexual innuendoes. See Tod Linafelt, *Ruth* [Berit Olam], David W. Cotter, ed. (Collegeville, MN: Liturgical Press, 1999), pp. 48-49.

131 On Ruth's identifying Boaz as a close relative, the term is *gō'ēl*, which is conventionally translated "redeemer." In this context it refers to the obligation and right that certain relatives have in some situations to exercise economic and social perogratives. See Donald A. Leggett, *The Levirate and Goel Institutions in the Old Testament, With Special Attention to the Book of Ruth* (Cherry Hill, N.J., 1974).

133 On "Mr. So-and-so," see the discussion and interpretive history of this enigmatic non-name in Jack M. Sasson, *Ruth* (Baltimore: Johns Hopkins University Press, 1979), pp. 105-107. On Boaz's trump card, see Sasson, *Ruth*, p. 115. On Boaz's offer to his relative, see the detailed discussion in Sasson, *Ruth*, pp. 120-136.

Notes to Chapter 7

137 On the relationship between "Christ" and "messiah," see Wayne A. Meeks, "Galilee and Judea in the Fourth Gospel," *Journal of Biblical Literature* 85 (1966): 159. On the genealogy of Jesus, see Raymond Brown, "Rachab in Matt 1:5 Probably Is Rahab of Jericho," *Biblica* 63 (1982): 79-80; Jerome Quinn, "Is Rachab in Matt 1:5 Rahab of Jericho?" *Biblica* 62 (1981): 225-28; F. Schnider and W. Stenger, "Die Frauen im Stammbaum Jesu nach Mattäus: Strukturale Beobachtungen zu Mt 1,1-17," *Biblische Zeitschrift* 23 (1979): 186-196.

138 I have dealt with the Jonah episode in Chapter 5 of the present study. The visit of the Queen of Sheba ("queen of the South" in Matthew's Gospel) is recounted in 1 Kings 10:1-13; 2 Chronicles 9:1-12. When Jesus speaks of his ministry being reserved for Israelites, he uses the very same phrase that is found in Matthew 10:5-6: "the lost sheep of the house of Israel."

140 On the Synoptic question, see James M. Robinson, Paul Hoffmann, and John S. Kloppenborg, *The Critical Edition of Q* (Minneapolis: Fortress Press; Leuven: Peeters Publishers, 2000). On the issue of geographical locations and names being more than places to be found on a map, see, for example, Wayne Meeks, "Galilee and Judea in the Fourth Gospel," *Journal of Biblical Literature* 85 (1966): 159-69. On the Acts narrative, see the brief but helpful treatment in James M. Robinson, "Acts," in *The Literary Guide to the Bible*, ed. Robert Alter and Frank Kermode (Cambridge: Harvard University Press [Belknap], 1987), pp. 467-478, esp. pp. 472-73.

142 In addition to the "woman at the well" story's compelling drama and brilliant rhetorical appeal, it arguably functions at a literary level very much on a par with Old Testament stories; see Joseph Cahill, "Narrative Art in John IV," *Religious Studies Bulletin* 2 (1982): 41. On the issue of "this fold" and "other sheep," see Raymond Brown, *The Gospel According to John I-XII* (Garden City, N.Y.: Doubleday, 1966), pp. 190, 387.

142-44 On the issue of the Jews and anti-Judaism (see R. Alan Culpepper, "Anti-Judaism in the Fourth Gospel as a Theological Problem for Christian Interpreters," in *Anti-Judaism and the Fourth Gospel*, ed. R. Bieringer, D. Pollefeyt, F. Vandecasteele-Vanneuville (Louisville, London, Leiden: Westminster John Knox, 2001), p. 72; Martinus C. de Boer, "The Depiction of 'the Jews' in John's Gospel: Matters of Behavior and Identity," in *Anti-Judaism and the Fourth Gospel*, p. 144 (and the other essays in that volume). See also Urban C. von Wahlde, "The Johannine 'Jews': A Critical Survey," *New Testament Studies* 28 (1982): 33-60; see also James D. G. Dunn, *The Partings of the Ways between Christianity and Judaism* (London: SCM, 1991).

The way "the Jews" are depicted in the Gospel of John has led many scholars (and laity) to conclude that John is anti-Semitic. Others, however, have argued that this position fails to see the Gospel in either its historical or literary context. For example, the prophets' use of scatological rhetoric against those they see either as apostate (from within their own religion) or as pagan (outside of their religion) is a well-known prophetic ploy. For example, Amos refers to immoral *Israelite* women as "cows of Bashan" (4:1). Of course, the prophetic calumniation of foreign nations is too well known to require citation (e.g., Nahum). Johnson has shown that the Gospel of John uses rhetoric fully consistent with the strong language of intramural religious debate; see Luke T. Johnson, "The New Testament's Anti-Jewish Slander and the Conventions of Ancient Polemic," *Journal of Biblical Literature* 108/3 (1989): 419-41; compare Jon Levenson, "Is There a Counterpart in the Hebrew Bible to New Testament Antisemitism?" *Journal of Ecumenical Studies* 22/2 (1985): 242-60.

143-44 On the demonizing vocabulary of the first century, see Richard B. Hays, *The Moral Vision of the New Testament* (San Francisco: Harper, 1996), pp. 407-443.

144-45 On how geographical movement in the Gospel narratives may signify more than mere geography, Meeks observes that John 4:43, 45, 46, 47, 54 all repeat that Jesus had traveled from Judea to Galilee ("Galilee and Judea," p. 163); Wilhelm Wrede has made the same point in *Das Messiasgeheimnis in den Evangelien*, p. 182 (cited in Meeks, p. 168). See also Hendrikus Boers, *Neither on This Mountain nor in Jerusalem: A Study of John 4* [Society of Biblical Literature Monograph Series, 35] (Atlanta: Scholars Press, 1988), p. 153; Colleen M. Conway, *Men and Women in the Fourth Gospel: Gender and Johannine Characterization* [Society of Biblical Literature Dissertation Series, 167] (Atlanta: Society of Biblical Literature, 1999), p. 105.

145-46 On Jesus, Jews, and Samaritans, see J. Bowman, "Samaritan Studies," *Bulletin of the John Rylands Library* 40 (1957-58): 298-329; G. W. Buchanan, "The Samaritan Origin of the Fourth Gospel," *Theological Studies* 36 (1975): 688-99; R. J. Coggins, *Samaritans and Jews: The Origins of Samaritanism Reconsidered* (Oxford: Blackwell, 1975); O. Cullmann, "Samaria and the Origins of the Christian Mission," in *The Early Church* (London: SCM, 1956), pp. 185-92; John Macdonald, *The Theology of the Samaritans* (Philadelphia: Westminster, 1964); James D. Purvis, "The Samaritans and Judaism," in *Early Judaism and Its Modern Interpreters*, ed. Robert Kraft and George W. E. Nickelsburg (Atlanta: Scholars Press, 1986), pp. 81-98; Charles H. H. Scobie, "The Origin and Development of Samaritan Christianity," *New Testament Studies* 19 (1972-73): 390-414.

148 There is no reference in the Old Testament to Jacob's well or to Jacob's giving a plot of ground to Joseph. This is an extrabiblical tradition.

Some scholars have suggested that Jesus' encounter with the woman at the well is a "type scene," a narrative form with certain required elements. In the Old Testament, wells are where wives are found by important narrative characters. For example, in Genesis 24:11ff., Abraham's servant meets Rebekah at a well, the very woman whom he takes back to Canaan to marry Isaac. Likewise, Jacob is smitten with Rachel at a well (Genesis 29:1-12). Finally, Moses meets Zipporah at a well and later marries her (Exodus 2:15-22). Robert Alter has discussed the well type-scene in detail in *The Art of Biblical Narrative* (New York: Basic Books, 1981), p. 52. Though most of these scenes are betrothal scenes, the story in John 4 seems in that sense a variation on the type (see Cahill, "Narrative Art," p. 45; he also cites Walter Rend, *Die Typischen Scenen bei Homer* [1933]). Lyle Eslinger is one scholar who insists that the type-scene in John 4 is no less romantic or erotic in flavor than other such type-scenes; see "The Wooing of the Woman at the Well: Jesus, the Reader and Reader-Response Criticism," *Journal of Literature and Theology* 1 (September, 1987): 167-183.

147 In the second reference identifying the woman, she is not "from Samaria," but is a "Samaritan woman" *(gynē ek tēs samareias; gynaikos samaritidos ousēs).*

147 On the question of Jews "having no dealings with Samaritans," Daube argues that that Greek term is to be understood in a cultic context, meaning that Jews and Samaritans would avoid at all costs using one another's vessels or other objects, since touching them would render one ritually unclean; see David Daube, "Jesus and the Samaritan Woman: The Meaning of συγχράομαι," *Journal of Biblical Literature* 69 (1950): 137-47. Painter (in *The Quest for the Messiah,* p. 99) points out that since the disciples had gone into the village to buy food, Jews had at least *some* dealings with Samaritans (cited by Larry Paul Jones, *The Symbol of Water in the Gospel of John* [JSNTSup 145] [Sheffield: Sheffield Academic Press, 1997], p 98). Sandra Schneiders takes the term as indicative of the fact that Jews should neither be talking to a woman in public nor suggesting the sharing of utensils; see Schneiders, *The Revelatory Text: Interpreting the New Testament as Sacred Scripture,* 2nd ed. (Collegeville, Minnesota: Liturgical Press, 1999), p. 189.

149 On the importance of the symbolism of water in John's Gospel, see Jones, *The Symbol of Water.* This is one of the most extensive dialogues involving Jesus and someone else in the whole gospel tradition. Jones notes that Jesus' thirst arouses the woman's thirst (*The Symbol of Water,* p. 99).

It is perhaps not accidental that Nicodemus is named whereas the Samaritan woman is not. Interestingly, several unnamed characters in the Fourth Gospel encounter Jesus and eventually express faith in him: Jesus' mother (2:1-5; 19:25-27 [she is never named in John's Gospel]); the Samaritan woman (4:1-42); the royal official (4:46-53); the lame man (5:2-16); the adulterous woman (7:53–8:11); the blind man (9:1-41); even the "beloved disciple" is never named; see David R. Beck, "The Narrative Function of Anonymity in Fourth Gospel Characterization," *Semeia* 63 (1993): 145. See Schneiders' remark about the contrast between

Nicodemus' and the woman's response to Jesus: "As he comes to Jesus at night and disappears into the shadows, confused by Jesus' self-revelation, she encounters Jesus at high noon, accepts his self-revelation, and brings others to him by her testimony" (*The Revelatory Text*, p. 187).

150 On the woman's "sordid" life: Eslinger types her as coquettish and loose, in effect, a woman who is "asking for it." Duke calls her a "five-time loser currently committed to an illicit affair," in short, a "tramp." See also Conway, *Men and Women in the Fourth Gospel*, p. 108; compare Eslinger, "The Wooing of the Woman at the Well." Jones sees the woman as "possibly of questionable integrity" (see *The Symbol of Water*, p. 90). On Jesus' mild criticism of her, see Conway, *Men and Women in the Fourth Gospel*, p. 117; Schneiders, *The Revelatory Text*, p. 188.

150-51 For previous instances of Jesus' miraculous knowledge, see John 1:42, 47-49. There are other places in the Gospel of John where people identify Jesus as a prophet following something he says or does: John 6:14; 7:40; 9:17 (note also the occasion when it is argued that Jesus could not be a prophet given his Galilean provenance [John 7:52]). Schneiders argues that Jesus' reference to the woman's many husbands and the one who now is "not your husband" is symbolic of the idolatry that Samaritanism represented from the Jewish point of view. Therefore, what Jesus says to her is "a classic prophetic denunciation of false worship." This is quite conceivable, though it does not alter the main point that Jesus is in the process of making a prophetic declaration; indeed, it confirms it (see Schneiders, *The Revelatory Text*, pp. 190-191).

From a Jewish point of view, Samaritanism is conventionally traced to the events on which 2 Kings 17:24-41 is based. However, recent scholars have concluded that Samaritanism is, on the one hand, much more variegated and complex than previously believed and, on the other, a religion whose origins cannot be explained by a single incident (see Purvis, "The Samaritans and Judaism").

151-52 On the subject of worship, Cahill calls attention to the inordinate emphasis on worship in the dialogue between the woman and Jesus. He concludes that the woman's "unholy marital alliances" are intended to symbolize false worship. This metaphor evokes the Old Testament's equating of bogus worship with adultery (see "Narrative Art," p. 44).

152-53 On the question of the expected messiah, Raymond Brown notes that the Samaritans did not expect a messiah in the sense of an anointed king of the Davidic house, which was the standard belief of the Jews. Rather, the Samaritans were looking for a latter-day prophetic figure who would be able to enhance and confirm divine revelation. Thus, even though in this story the woman uses the standard Jewish designation "messiah," she fits that nomenclature into a more Samaritan understanding (see Brown, *The Gospel According to John I–XII*, p. 172).

153 On Jesus' declaration, it is well known that in John's Gospel there are a number of "I am" sayings attributed to Jesus, virtually all of which speak to his "high Christological" position: John 6:20, 35, 41, 48, 51; 7:34, 36; 8:12, 18, 24, 28, 58; 9:9; 10:7, 9, 11, 14; 11:25; 12:26; 13:19; 14:3; 15:1, 5; 17:24; 18:5, 6, 8. Thus, it is quite possible to see the "I am" in this conversation as part of this Johannine pattern (see Brown, *The Gospel According to John I–XII*, pp. 172-73, 533-38).

153-54 Jones makes much of the contrast between the woman scurrying off to her village and the disciples standing around mute with their hands full of just-purchased food: "The disciples stand motionless at the well with their hands filled with food bought from the town but their mouths shut. The woman of Samaria leaves the well in a hurry, empty-handed but filled with a message to proclaim to the townspeople." Jones concludes that living water has already begun to "well up" in her (see *The Symbol of Water*, p. 106).

154-59 Schneiders argues that the entire story of the woman at the well is symbolic of Jesus' whole public ministry among the Samaritan community as well as the influence of Samaritan converts within the community reflected by the Fourth Gospel (see *The Revelatory Text*, p. 186). Conway suggests that the words, "Come, see . . ." echo similar imperatives in John 1:39, 46. Thus her "words resonate with the language of witness and discipleship that have already been established in the Gospel" (see *Men and Women in the Fourth Gospel*, p. 123). Boers points out the wonderful irony that Jesus initially asks the woman to bring him a single man ("Go, call your husband"), which the woman cannot do (he is not her husband), but in the end she delivers to Jesus a whole village (see *Neither on This Mountain*, p. 192).

Index of Names and Places

Index of Subjects

Index of Hebrew and Greek Terms and Phrases

HEBREW TERMS AND PHRASES

GREEK TERMS AND PHRASES

Index of Scripture References